IMAGES
of America

AROUND BAKERSVILLE

On the Cover: Seen here is the partially completed Cloudland Hotel as it rises above Roan Mountain, among the highest mountains east of the Rocky Mountain range. Leaving the problems of summer heat, some folks stayed the entire season. While there, guests and workers recall seeing circular rainbows and hearing eerie sounds. (Appalachia Archives, ETSU, Murrell Collection.)

IMAGES
of America

AROUND BAKERSVILLE

Bruce Koran and Sandy Grisham

ARCADIA
PUBLISHING

ISBN 978-0-7385-8764-6

Published by Arcadia Publishing
Charleston, South Carolina

Printed in the United States of America

Library of Congress Control Number: 2011920750

For all general information, please contact Arcadia Publishing:
Telephone 843-853-2070
Fax 843-853-0044
E-mail sales@arcadiapublishing.com
For customer service and orders:
Toll-Free 1-888-313-2665

Visit us on the Internet at www.arcadiapublishing.com

This book is warmly dedicated to the people of the small villages around Bakersville, who have so diligently kept the integrity of their places.

CONTENTS

ACKNOWLEDGMENTS

This work rests on the broad shoulders of the many people who so graciously opened their homes and their memories to us and helped these two outsiders to learn about their new home area. In no particular order, they are: Helen McKinney and the folks who met for "history gathering" in Bandana; Frank and Faye Griffith; L.G. Sheets; Pam Johnson; Jack Dellinger; Ray Dellinger; Ronnie and Libby McKinney; Leila Wilson; George and Robbie Morgan; Barbara Middleton; Eddie Sharpe; Beth Davis; Anne and Phil Castro, and her mom, Marie Greene Wilson; Mark McKinney; David Biddix; Chris Hollifield; Daniel Barron; Emma Lee Sparks; Inez McRae; Star Bennett; Paulette McMahan Davis; Wade Campbell; Brenda Willis; Thelma Hughes Cumbie; Wayne Ledford; Gail and Scott Griffith; Barbara Hollifield; Wayne Ayers; Debra Barnett; Iva Laws; Joyce Boon; John Burn; Maxie Gouge Buchanan; James Byrd; Joyce Beauchamp; Mildred Masters; Shelby Street; Rhonda Gouge; Linda Duncan; the Appalachia Archive staff at ETSU; Everett and Sena Mae Gouge; Bud McKinney; Alvin Livingston; Carolyn Townsend; Bob Hensley; Phil Thomas Jr.; Louise Ferguson, and Gary Gouge.

A special thank you to Mary Vogel for the amazing restoration that she provided for many of the original Jim Jones photographs.

Thanks also to the Arcadia Publishing staff, especially Lindsay Carter, Michael Sigalas, Laura Saylor, and Suzanne Almgren.

Our list would not be complete without acknowledging our spouses: Frances Koran and Vaughn Grisham. They waited meals, postponed tasks, and patiently listened as we eagerly shared the discoveries we made while whisking ourselves into your hills and hollers. Without their help, support, and active assistance this book would not be a reality.

We have attempted to present a clear picture of the places around Bakersville, but as in all human endeavors, there may be mistakes. The authors accept any and all responsibilities for those errors.

INTRODUCTION

Though the earlier Arcadia book, Images of America: *Mitchell County*, provides a detailed history for all of Mitchell County, this book specifically focuses upon the smaller communities in the county's upper or northern part: the villages of Bakersville, Buladean, Brummetts Creek, Cane Creek, Clarissa, Harrell Hill, Huntdale, Ledger, Loafers Glory, Glen Ayre, Hawk, Pigeon Roost, Poplar, Red Hill, Tipton Hill, McKinney Cove, Young Cove, and Toecane. This narrowed focus will allow the authors to spend more time on these villages and their stories.

Speculators who received land in 1778 sold those properties to the earliest European settlers of the area—people whose names are lost to history. David Baker, a Patriot, bought 100 acres (advertised as 5¢ per acre in 1790) and brought his family from Morganton to a new log-cabin home. Reputed to be the first white family to actually live in the area, the Bakers' home was near the Baker Spring, where the Young Hotel later stood. Before it became Bakersville in the 1840s, the area was called "Baker's Plantation" or "Baker's Place." Upon selection as the site of the county seat, the village was renamed Davis for the president of the Confederacy. By 1868, the original name of Bakersville was restored by the Republican-controlled North Carolina General Assembly.

The Charleston, Cincinnati and Chicago Railroad (later the Clinchfield Railroad) planned to build a railroad from Ironton, Ohio, to Charleston, South Carolina, to transport coal through the area. In the initial phases in 1888, the road was to extend through Erwin, Tennessee, to Marion, North Carolina, and through Bakersville. However, by the time the rails were laid, other communities had contributed land and Bakersville had not. A local legend states that the county seat's citizens thought the railroad noise would scare their cows; others thought that this railroad would not be a commercial success. Local stops in the early days of the 20th century included Poplar, Huntdale, Toecane, and others—but not Bakersville.

After the Civil War, many Northerners, drawn by the extensive forests, came South and went into the timber business. Because they denuded the tree-covered mountains in the area, erosion was rampant and contributed to the frequent floods. With the heavy rains of 1901, the flood in May came to be called "the May Freshet" and devastated Bakersville. It covered several blocks of the commercial area and separated one part of town from the other.

As with most of the rural United States, the Great Depression and World War II brought social changes to the area around Bakersville. The farmers who had left the area, migrating to the cities and factories, felt the economic disaster first. Those who had remained on the land were likely to be able to feed their families, and many children of the Depression have said they were poor but did not know it.

The national tragedy of Pearl Harbor drew many Mitchell Countians into the ranks of the military; their girlfriends followed them and became their wives. With war's end, few returned to their family homes. They settled in the cities, using the GI Bill to further their education, and found their employment in the larger organizations that mushroomed out of the postwar affluence.

Some of the engineers who helped put a man on the moon were born in upper Mitchell County. Doctors, lawyers, educators, and business leaders learned their ABCs in the county's small, rural schools. Those same school populations plummeted in the 1950s, 1960s, and 1970s; churches found that older members made up the vast majority of their congregations, and stores closed their doors for lack of business. These decades saw the area's mica mining and manufacturing reach a peak before outsourcing and mechanization reduced the number of factories. Locals found themselves in what might be best described as ghost towns. Newly paved roads allowed residents to pass by the crossroads where the small country stores stood. Soon, those stores were empty and boarded up. Automobiles replaced railroads, and passenger trains vanished. Depots were abandoned and virtually disappeared.

People living in such rural areas were often both the judge and jury. For starters, there is the infamous Charlie and Frankie Silver case in which one Christmas, a wife reputedly murdered her husband and buried his butchered body in several holes in the ground around their home. K.B. and S.R. Whitson have also written interestingly of the murder of Kit Byrd of Red Hill and the subsequent lives of the Whitson Brothers, who are said to have committed the act. A teacher just cashing his check was found drowned in a stream near Buladean, and theories abound as to the cause. Glen Ayre saw the murder of Anderson Burleson in 1907, and Till Robinson was murdered in Bandana. When possible, Bakersville, as the county seat, held trials and investigations, and a magistrate would often meet on Saturdays in Tipton Hill to administer the long arm of the law to those who had engaged in minor infractions.

The earliest settlers created schools in the area. Those first schools were financed by subscription or by churches. Classes were held a few weeks each year either in summer or early fall. During the 1800s, most schools were built and operated by church denominations. Church-run schools continued into the early 20th century, and included the establishment by the Presbyterian Church of a high school in Buladean and the building of a two-story high school in Tipton Hill, financed by public donations and aid from the Methodist church. One exception was the Bowman Academy, which was founded by J.C. Bowman in the 1870s.

The tradition of religious worship was very strong, and churches were organized as soon as possible. Settlers lived in an isolated area where travel was often difficult. As a result, the local community—often an area of only three or four miles across—became the center of social and spiritual activity, with the local church as the hub.

Rev. Stephen Morgan founded Roan Mountain Baptist Church in 1813. As settlement spread throughout Mitchell County, other congregations organized. Presbyterian, Methodists, Baptists, Church of the Brethren, Freewill Baptists, and others formed congregations and built churches.

The importance of the churches as a center of life in an isolated area cannot be overemphasized. At their best, these church congregations were a reflection of the community itself, acting as friends, neighbors, teachers, social workers, and spiritual mentors. The church, the pastor, and the congregation, indeed, formed the heart and soul of the community.

While the primary function of churches was religious activity, many churches took on projects that benefited their congregation in ways that transcended or at least enhanced religious worship. During the 1800s and early 1900s, public education was not available throughout much of the area, and church schools took up the challenge. There were many excellent church-sponsored schools that sprang up all around Mitchell County. Most were small one- or two-room schoolhouses, such as Ledger School, which was taught by Rev. John Gouge. The Presbyterian High School in Buladean and the Mitchell Collegiate Institute are two examples of secondary schools that achieved high academic standards.

Local churches often allowed church buildings to be used for nonreligious purposes. Many churches doubled as polling places during elections, and churches like Bear Creek Baptist allowed their building to be used as a courtroom.

Though religious observance still remained an important component of life for many Mitchell County residents, the times began to change. The era of the community church started to disappear as the physical isolation that once existed began to vanish and church congregations were no longer restricted to a limited area. As the small communities became, largely, names on a map or signs along the road, the churches continued to flourish, but their role as the persona of a specific community has been greatly diminished.

Music was an important part of mountain family life. Appalachian Mountain music is a direct descendant of the musical tradition of the Scotch-Irish settlers that crossed the Atlantic. This book's pages are full of families who played instruments such as fiddles, guitars, homemade banjos, and dulcimers. Many ballads and folk songs from this area have been collected and become well known across the country. Early country music was greatly enhanced by many wonderful musicians from the area. Among these players and singers were the Carolina Ramblers, made up of the Ledford family and Buffalo Nichols (from Glen Ayre) and Fiddlin' Red Wilson (from Ledger). The tradition passed down by these talented musicians continues to this day and is still practiced in living rooms and on stages throughout the area.

In addition to the usual business of commerce, the crossroads stores were, with churches, the social centers of the villages. When bad weather kept the men from the fields, they gathered around the potbellied stoves in local country stores to debate politics—deep divides still exist between the Republicans and the Democrats—which often brought on heated discussions. Other subjects included the prices of crops, gossip, and jokes. When the women came in, it was to buy the goods needed for the family: clothing, fabric for sewing clothes, shoes, flour, sugar, and more.

Just after the end of the Civil War, Union general John Thomas Wilder ventured into the area to mine ore in the Cranberry and Buladean areas. He recognized the natural beauty at the top of Roan Mountain, bought 46,000 acres atop it, and built Cloudland Hotel there. His initial inn had 20 rooms, but the later hotel had 268 rooms for travelers. By 1885, railroads and wagons brought well-off folks from the cities of the East to the cool rhododendron gardens. Advertised as a place to be healthy from hay fever and other coastal-area ailments, it remained in business for 25 years. The hotel also provided employment for folks from Buladean and Glen Ayre. Women from Buladean cooked and walked miles up and down the mountain to work there or to deliver goods that the hotel needed.

During Prohibition, white lightning makers honed their skills to make money, though not quite legally. The Federal revenuers often tried to locate the stills, but once they found one and shut it down, another went up. Mitchell County had its share of these creative "blenders," and running from the government men on these mountain roads, according to local legend, helped give birth to NASCAR. These challenging roads made an exciting chase as brewers fled to avoid arrest and to sell their products. To ignore the importance of the industry is to miss some of the wonderful culture of the mountains.

For most of the residents of northern Mitchell County, agriculture was essential for subsistence. Almost every family farmed, but most of the crops were destined for the family table, not for market.

Unlike their cousins in the flatland, mountain farmers faced special challenges. The land was not especially suited for agriculture. Even after it was cleared, the ground was rocky, the soil was mostly poor, and plowing on hillsides could be especially difficult.

Corn, the main crop, was ground into meal and grits by local mills. It was not a cash crop but was kept for the use of the family. Likewise, farmers planted potatoes and various other vegetables for family consumption.

There were, however, ways for farmers to supplement their income. Many of them planted fruit orchards, and the surplus harvest could be sold for needed cash. Others tended commercial beehives and sold the honey. Milk could also be sold to dairies and provide a steady source of income. Many farmers cut timber or worked part-time in one of the area mines to raise additional cash.

Tobacco was grown successfully in the area, but for many farmers it was not an option. Tobacco growing is very labor intensive, and after 1933, tobacco farming became embroiled in government regulations and quotas. Since tobacco could only be grown on land that had received a government quota, many farmers were excluded.

Mining operations have been carried out in the area long before the arrival of permanent

European settlers. There appears to be solid evidence that Native Americans and Spaniards took quantities of mica from several mines in northern Mitchell County. There is also evidence that Native American miners delivered feldspar to the British from the Sink Hole Mine in 1744

Commercial mica mining began in the mid-19th century. Mica was mined extensively throughout the county with more than 100 known mines. It is estimated that the bulk of the 400,000 tons of mica mined in North Carolina from 1862 to 1882 came from Mitchell. By the 1960s, however, the demand for mica had fallen, and almost all mica mining has ceased.

Local feldspar has been mined for centuries. As the value of feldspar increased, mining of it began to grow. Many farmers turned to mining feldspar on a part-time basis, as a ready source of cash. Some local farmers eventually turned to mining as a full-time occupation. By 1940, feldspar mining had been taken over by large mining corporations and the small mining operations had been displaced. Large-scale feldspar mining continues in Mitchell County to this day.

One

LEDGER

The area that is now Mitchell County began to see a number of white settlers in the late 1700s. By 1830, the growing number of residents led to the establishment of Bear Creek Church by Rev. Stephen Morgan. The name Bear Creek is thought to refer to the large number of black bears that inhabited the area. By 1849, the church had 51 members. Owing to the relative isolation of the area, Bear Creek Baptist (and other area churches) became a center for community activity and fellowship.

Dr. Charles Hallet Wing, a chemistry professor from Boston, moved to the area of Bear Creek in 1887. It is said the name Ledger came from Wing's attempt to establish a post office in the community. Apparently, he kept a ledger to document the population growth of the community, trying to convince the government that a post office was needed. Wing's initiative was successful and the US Postal Service named the new post office Ledger.

Wing is best known for his establishment of the Good Will School or Wing Academy and the Good Will Free Library that boasted more than 27,000 volumes. Both the school and library were free to the public. Wing donated or personally solicited the entire collection of the library. Eventually, Wing expanded the scope of the school to include manual training, domestic science, and practical farming techniques for adults. It is said that Wing paid these adults 50¢ per day to attend classes.

The Bear Creek area was largely agricultural, but logging was active in the area, and the nearby Chestnut Flat Mine was a large producer of feldspar. However, owing to its location in central Mitchell County and to improved roads, it was possible, by the mid-1900s, for residents to obtain jobs in other parts of Mitchell and surrounding counties. Regrettably, many of these jobs have since traveled overseas.

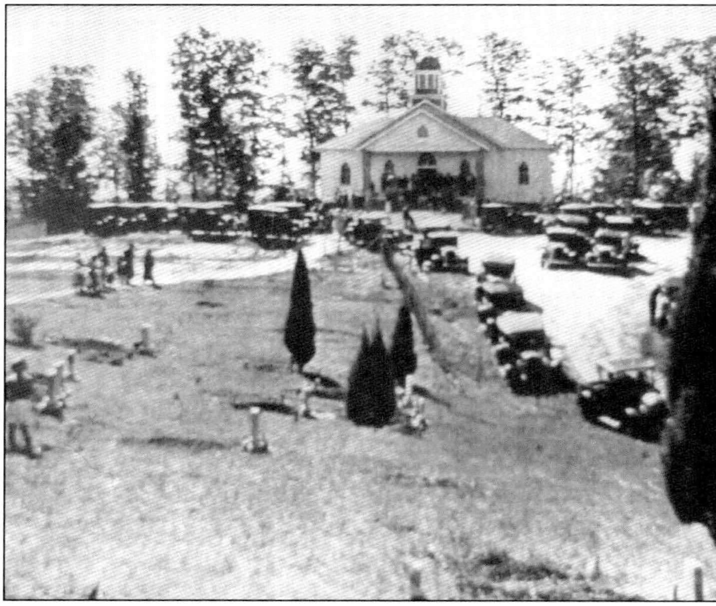

This photograph of Bear Creek Baptist Church dates from the early 1930s. Since 1830, there have been four buildings that housed Bear Creek Baptist Church. The first building—little more than a log hut with a hole in the roof for smoke—served many uses, including a courtroom and meeting hall. The second church was built in 1891 and was replaced by the building pictured at left in 1926. The fourth church building was erected in 1959. (Bear Creek Baptist Church.)

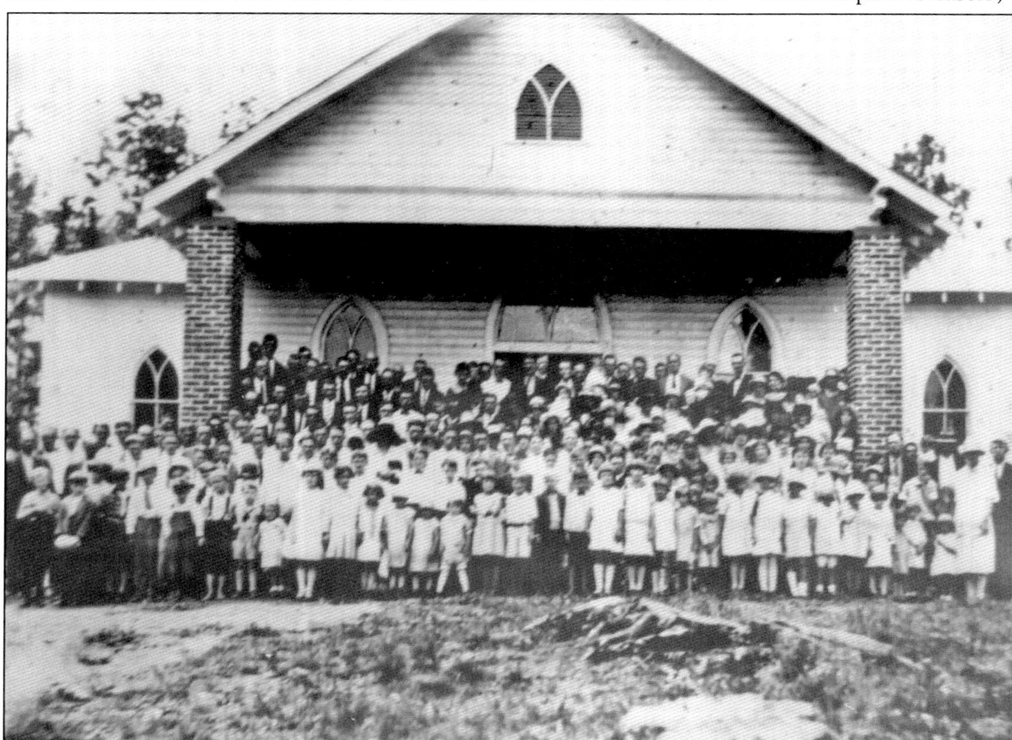

One of the church activities common throughout Mitchell County (and much of the country) was the shape-note singing school. Shape-note or sacred-harp singing was very popular because it typically employed four or seven shapes attached to notes to represent the pitch of the notes on the major and minor scales. It was easy to learn, and singing schools such as this were always well attended. (Bear Creek Baptist Church.)

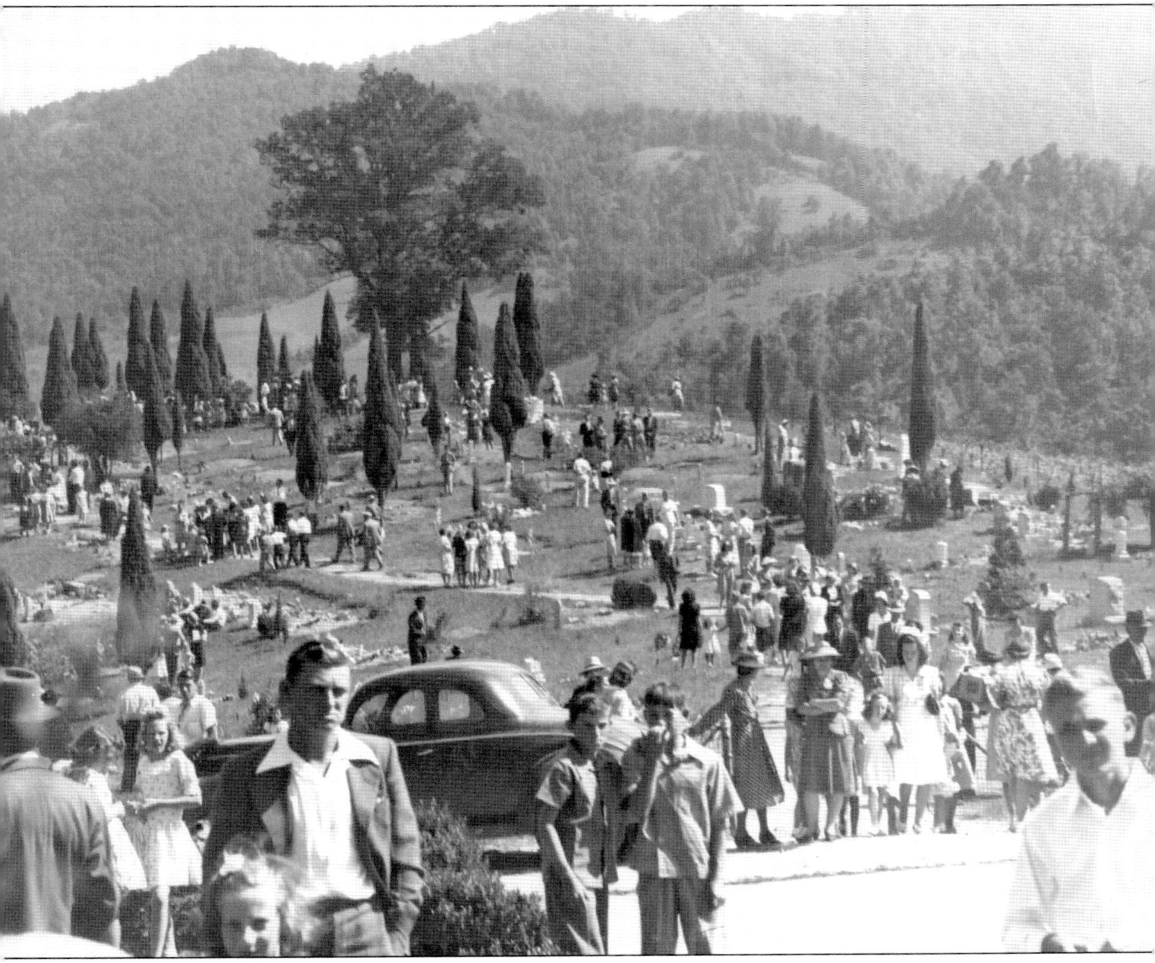

Decoration Day is a tradition celebrated annually in cemeteries throughout the region. Every cemetery sets aside its own particular day for the event. Friends and relatives, living near and far, gather to place flowers on graves and spend time with loved ones. Decoration Day at Bear Creek Cemetery is the fourth Sunday in June. This 1937 photograph shows the festivities at the cemetery. Decoration Day was the original name for the Memorial Day holiday that is traditionally celebrated on May 30. The Southern Decoration Day seems to have originated in Virginia and the Carolinas, probably as a customary family observance at family cemeteries. It then evolved into a community observance as family cemeteries evolved into community cemeteries. Today it is practiced from the Southern and Central Appalachians westward and southwestward to northeast Texas and eastern Oklahoma. (Linda Duncan.)

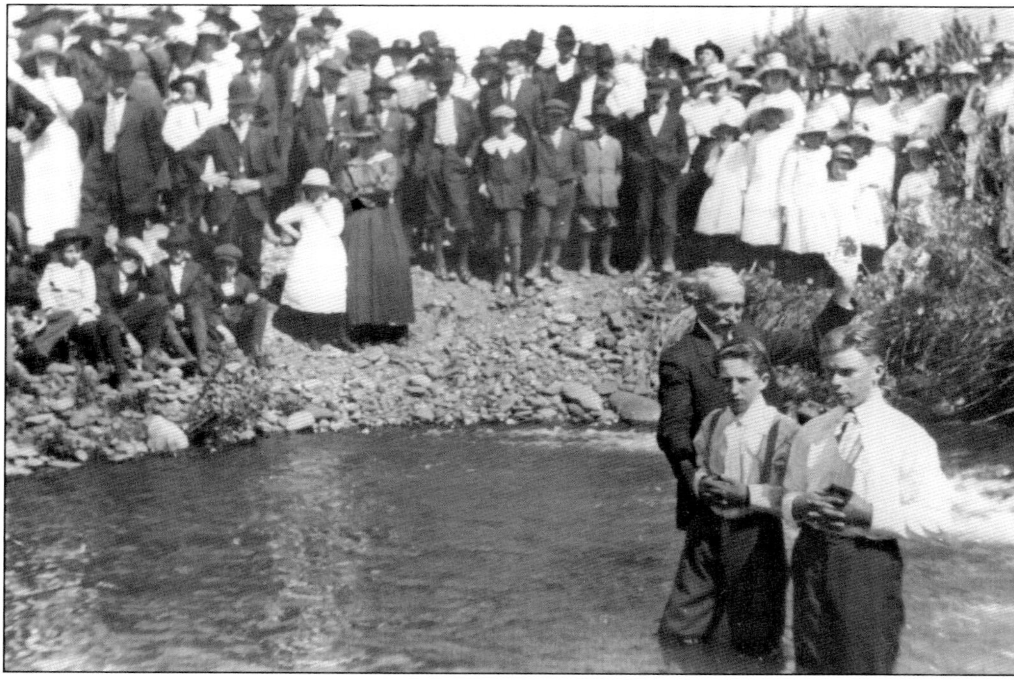

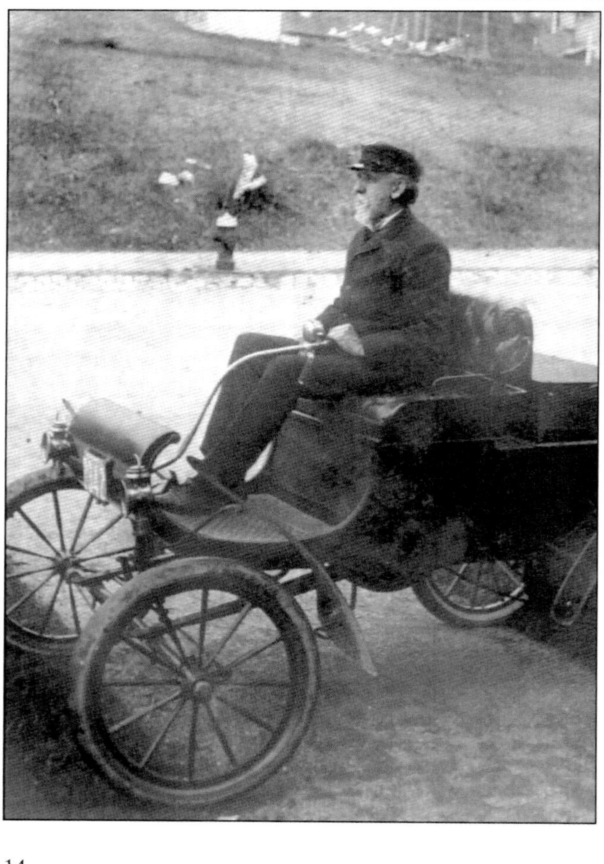

Rev. Stephen Greene was pastor at Bear Creek Baptist in the late 1800s and again from 1903–1907. This photograph, said to be taken around 1905, shows Rev. Greene standing in a creek as two young men prepare to be baptized. (Bear Creek Baptist Church.)

This is the only known photograph of Dr. Charles Hallet Wing, thought to be taken in Boston. Born in 1836, Wing was a professor at Cornell University and the Massachusetts Institute of Technology. He moved to the Bear Creek area after retirement in 1884 and devoted considerable energy to the establishment of the Good Will Free School. He built a schoolhouse and provided teachers and equipment for manual training. The entire cost of the school—including building construction, teachers' salaries, and equipment—was donated by Wing. (Longleaf Media.)

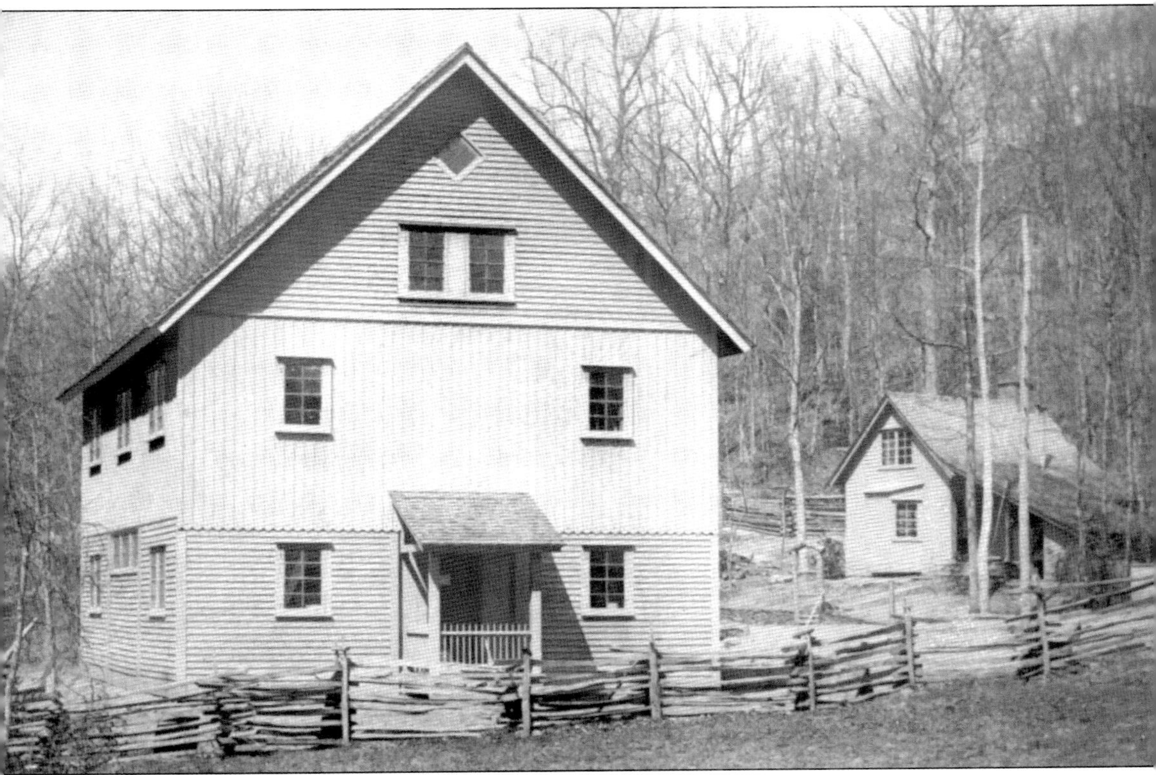

The Good Will Free Library was the first free public library in North Carolina. The library and schools stemmed from Professor Charles Hallet Wing's deep desire to bring advanced education to the mountains. Wing's collection of books was built from his own collection as well as the donations he solicited. The library rules were simple: anyone could borrow a book at absolutely no cost. During the almost 30 years that the library existed, few—if any—books went unaccounted for. The school and library were eventually absorbed into the Mitchell County public school system after Wing became ill and returned to Boston. This photograph of the library dates to 1915, the year of Wing's death. (North Carolina Collection, UNC Library at Chapel Hill.)

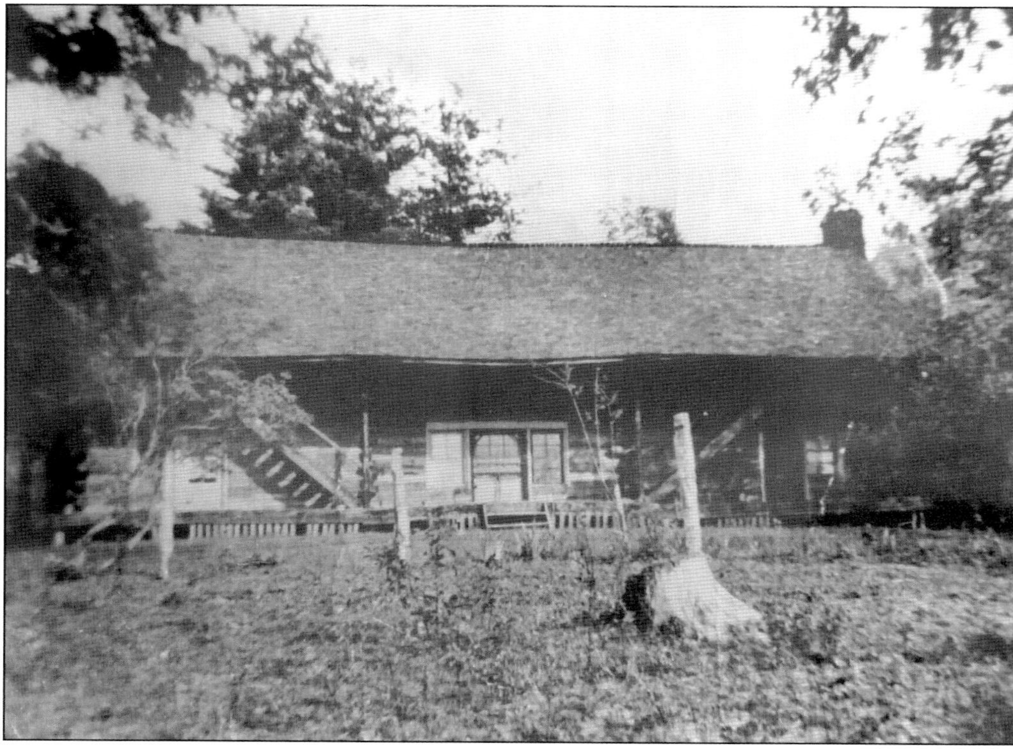

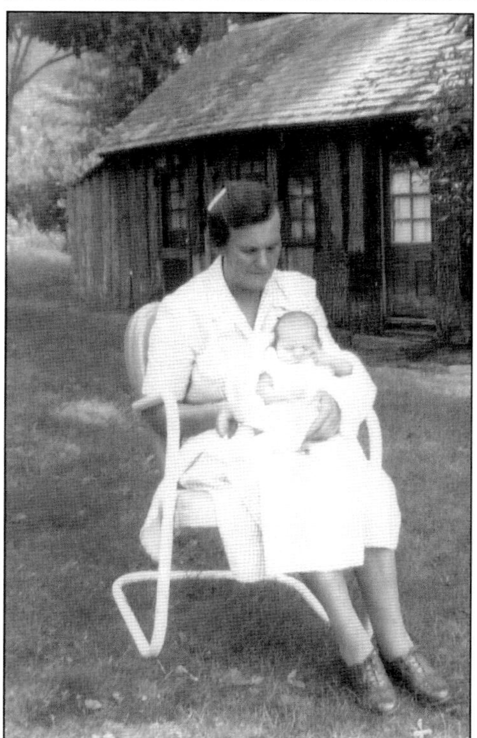

The c. 1945 photograph above shows the house built by Prof. Charles Hallet Wing after he moved to Bear Creek in 1884. Wing spared no expense to bring modern amenities to his residence, where he installed electric lights and purchased a gasoline generator and storage batteries to supply the electricity. This was the first-known use of electric power in Mitchell County. The photograph at left shows the separate kitchen that adjoined Wing's residence. Unlike the residence, the kitchen sported running water and a bathtub. The photograph at left was taken years after Wing moved back to Boston. In the foreground is Minnie Gouge and her granddaughter Rhonda Gouge. (Both, Everett and Sena Mae Gouge.)

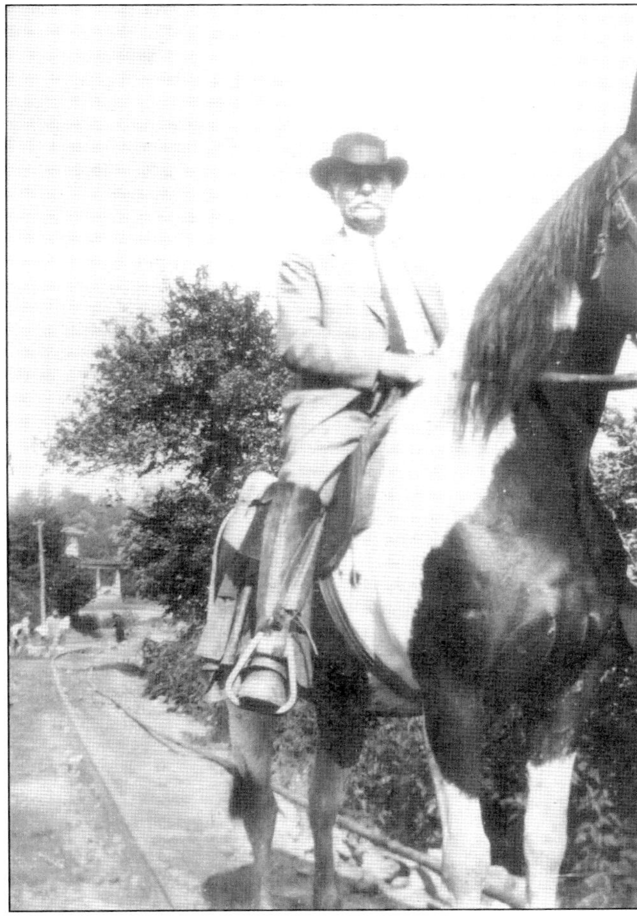

Dr. Charles E. Smith was the epitome of the country doctor. During the early 20th century, Smith could be seen riding his horse or driving his buggy in most parts of the county. He was the first doctor to ride to the small schoolhouses and check the children's tonsils. He would often see patients who lived more than 15 miles away from his house in Ledger. (Mitchell Historical Society.)

This photograph of the Ledger School dates to 1937. The school and adjoining gymnasium were essentially a primary and middle school for students in the Bear Creek area. High school classes were held at Bowman High School in Bakersville. (Longleaf Media.)

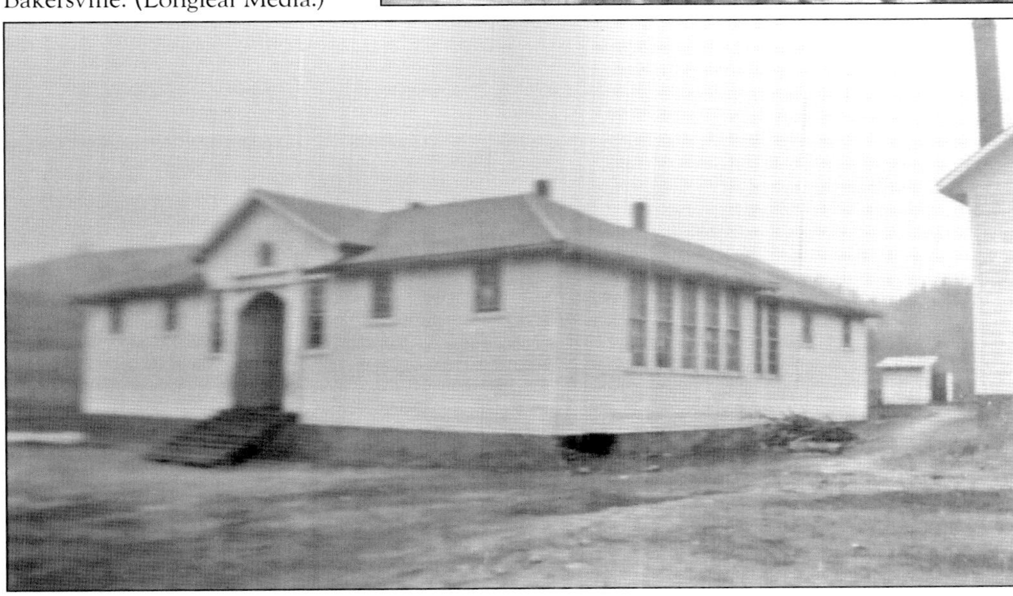

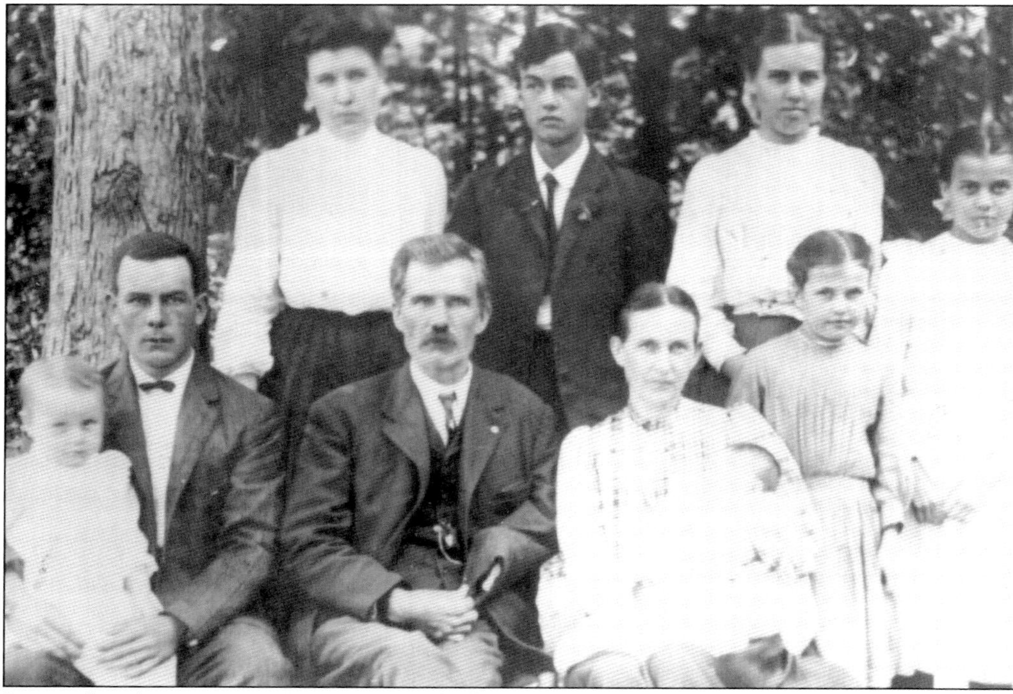

Pictured in the center are D.W. "Doc" and Ella McNeal Greene. Surrounding the couple are Doc and Ella's children. Clarence (far left) died in his teens, but all of the others—other than Will (holding Clarence)—became educators. Doc later became the first superintendent of schools for Mitchell County. All of the Greene family attended Prof. Charles Hallet Wing's school, a testament to the legacy of the professor. (Ann Castro.)

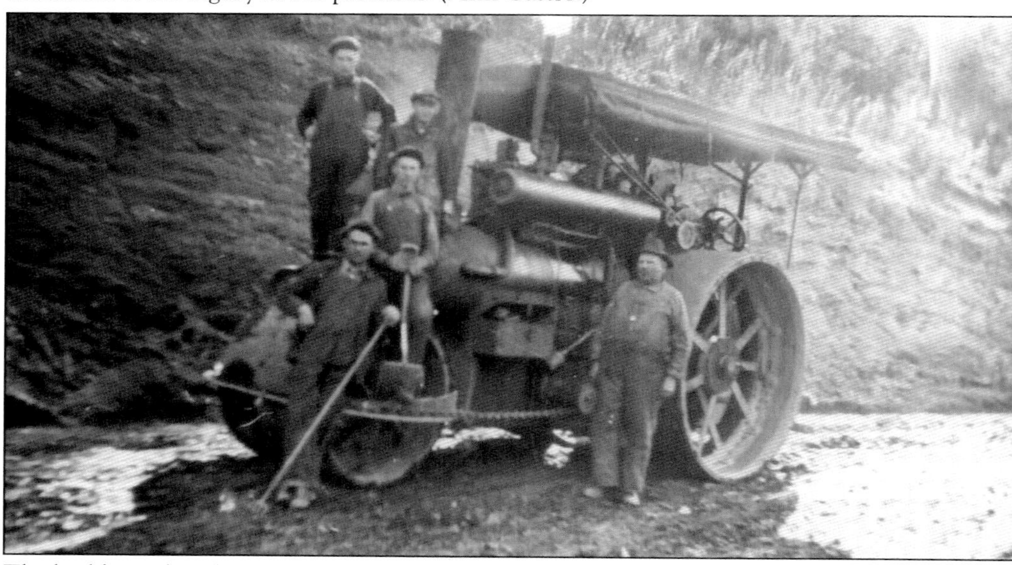

The building of roads in the area was critical to lifting the isolation imposed by the mountainous terrain. This photograph, from the 1930s, shows a road crew at work somewhere near Ledger. Pictured are Dock Morris, Lawrence Conley, Maurice Jarrett, Paul Ellis, and Emmett Ellis. (Bear Creek Baptist Church.)

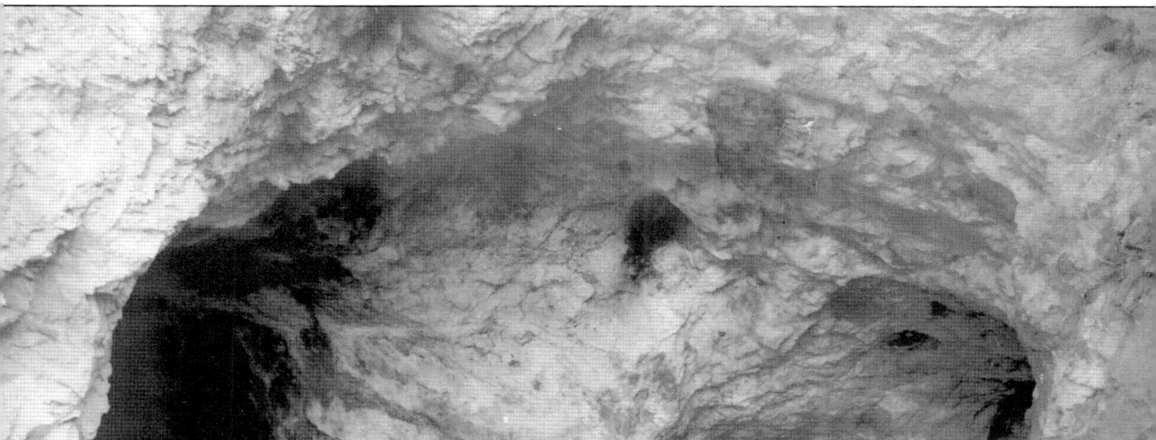

The Chestnut Flat Mine was a major producer of feldspar. Local feldspar has been mined for centuries. Originally used for ceramics and as a cleaning powder, feldspar was often discarded as waste by the miners of mica. As the value of feldspar increased, feldspar mining began to grow. Many farmers turned to mining feldspar on a part-time basis, as a ready source of cash. Some local farmers eventually turned to mining as a full-time occupation. Most of the early feldspar mines were small operations, but the Large Chestnut Flat Mine opened in 1913. By 1940, Feldspar mining had been taken over by the large mining corporations; the small mining operations had been displaced. Large-scale feldspar mining continues in Mitchell County to this day. The above photograph was taken in the early 1930s and shows the entrance to the mine. (Linda Duncan.)

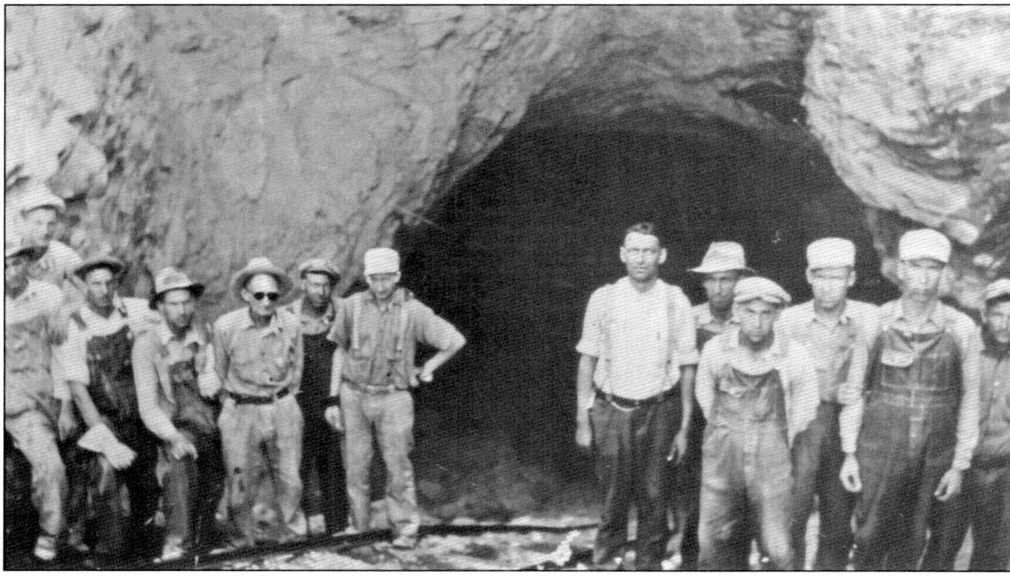

This photograph from the 1930s shows a group of miners as they pose in front of the Chestnut Flat Mine. From left to right, they are Carroll Buchanan, Fred Duncan, Emmitt Duncan, Paul Duncan, Mardie Sparks, George Davis, Carroll Sparks, Bob Duncan, Raymond Pittman, Dale Harris, Paul Stewart, Avery Stewart, and Flink Smith. (Linda Duncan.)

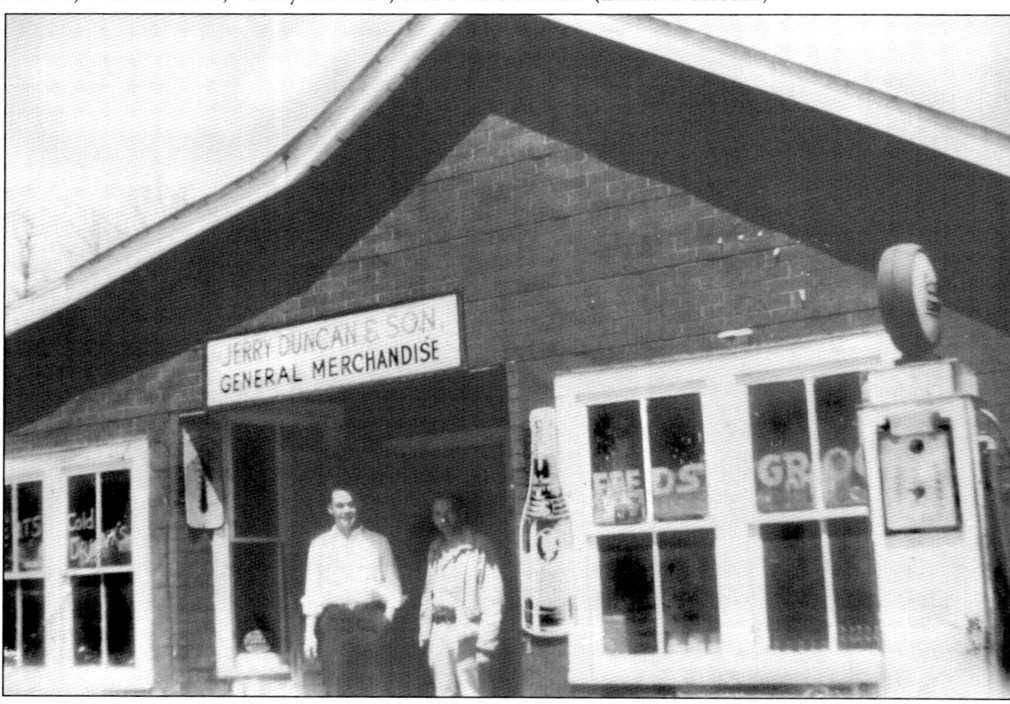

Jerry Duncan and his son Jack owned a store down the road from Ledger at Pine Branch. While the store was not in Ledger proper, the Duncans lived in the area. This photograph shows a typical general store from the 1950s that sold groceries, gasoline, and other general merchandise. (Bear Creek Baptist Church.)

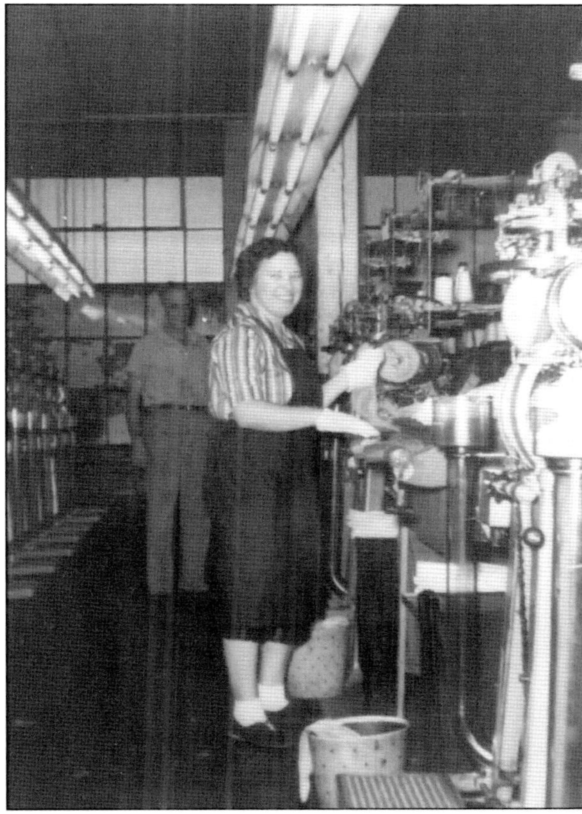

Area residents often had to travel many miles if they wanted jobs unrelated to agriculture or mining. The lack of local industry has, in fact, led to many young people leaving the mountains in search of better opportunities. In the 1950s, the Hosiery Mill in Spruce Pine became a source of employment for many people across Mitchell County. Pictured at right is a 1959 photograph of Ledger resident Mildred Duncan. Pictured below is Cleopus Bartlett (left). This photograph was also taken at the Hosiery Mill in the late 1950s. (Bear Creek Baptist Church.)

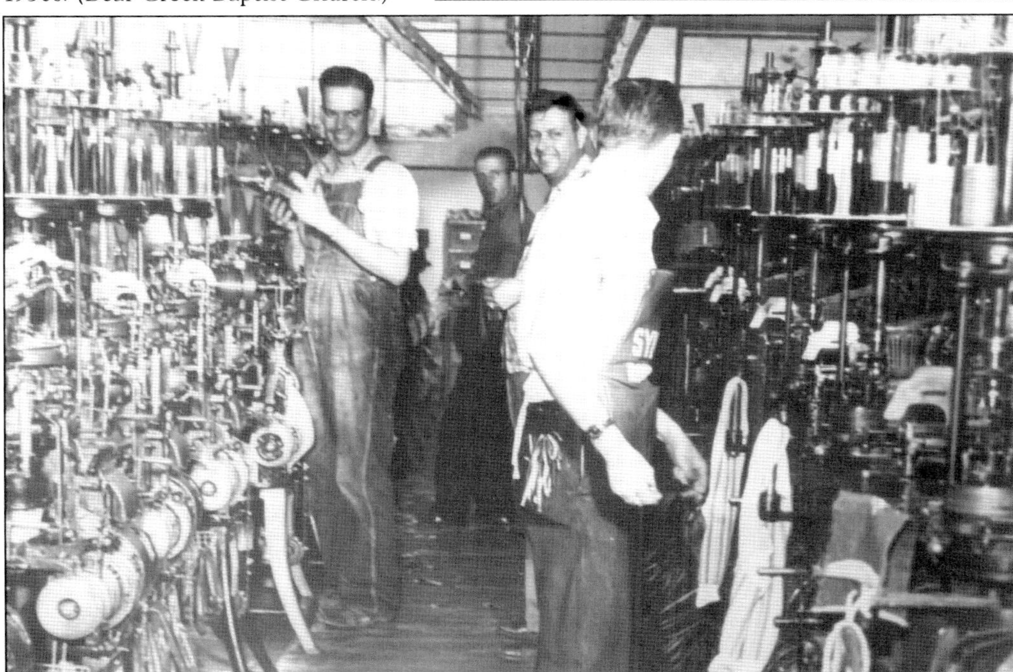

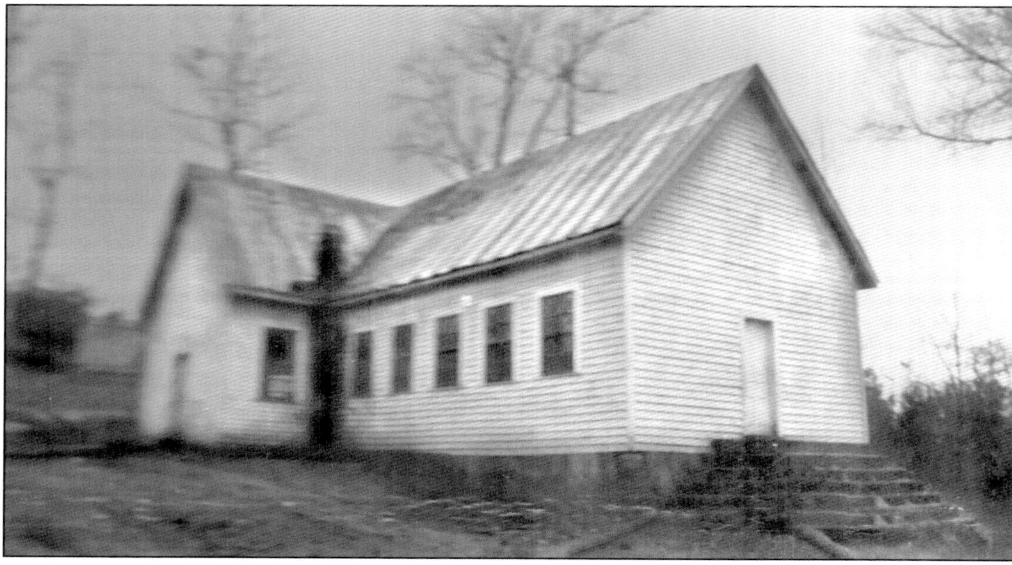

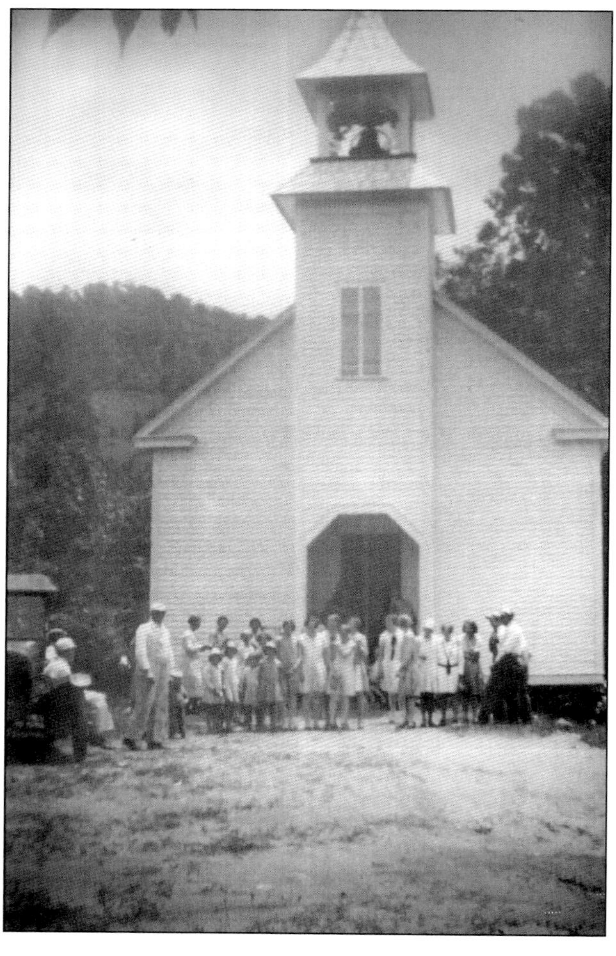

This two-room primary school served students in the area south of Ledger near Lily Branch Creek. The school operated from the early 1900s until the mid-1930s, when all students were sent to the larger school at Ledger. As was common in these small schools, Lily Branch School had no indoor plumping and was heated by two potbellied stoves. (Mark McKinney.)

Also located near Lily Branch Creek, named for the wild lilies that grew along the banks, Lily Branch Church was organized in 1859. This 1920s photograph shows the second building, erected in 1870. It caught fire and burned down in 1939. The present church was built in 1948. (Mark McKinney.)

Two

Bandana and Kona

The two villages of Bandana and Kona, located fewer than five miles from each other, are often linked because of their proximity. Kona was purportedly named for the abbreviations of minerals such as kaolin. Bandana had three versions of how it got its name: first, 20 years before it was recognized as Bandana, a politician came through town wearing a red bandana. Second, it was said that one of the railroad men marked the site for a train station by tying his bandana to a laurel bush to mark it. A third story is that it got its name from the bandana that was tied to a pole if folks wanted the train to stop to pick up mail or passengers.

Nearby, Native Americans used the Sink Hole Mine for at least 300 years prior to modern mining. In the mid-1800s, outsiders invested in developing mines and local people began to look for mica spots in surrounding land. It quickly became a "get rich quick" proposition. Greed led to the lawlessness that occurred on occasion.

Like many of the mountain towns, Bandana and Kona had their share of crimes. The Frankie and Charlie Silver case is by far the most prominent. Charlie came home drunk late on Christmas Eve, 1831, and Frankie killed him with an ax, cut him into many pieces, and buried him in several spots. In 1833, she became the first woman from the region executed by the State of North Carolina. Most of the violence in the area centered on jealousy (two men fighting over a woman), property infringement, infidelity, or domestic violence.

As with other towns in the region, Bandana and Kona used to be bustling places. There were stores and other businesses. In Kona, the depot brought many people to ride the train to the outer world. Now, there are no stores, no schools, and even fewer families. Fields have been reclaimed by forest, and people from outside come here to summer. A lone church is visible from the road, attesting to the peace and tranquility of this place.

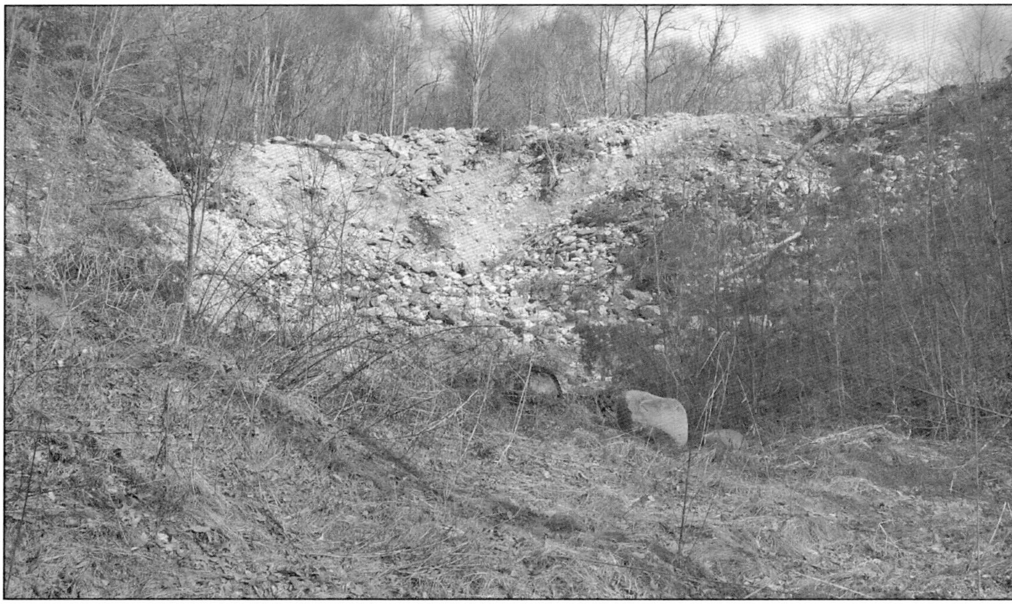

The Sink Hole Mine provided a living for many residents of Bandana and Kona from the late 19th to the mid-20th centuries. The main tunnel of the mine extended over 900 feet, crossing under State Highway 104 near the Silver Chapel church, and was dotted with numerous shafts as deep as 350 feet. Using the crudest tools, miners shaped circular steps to descend into the shafts creating many levels and large "rooms" in each level. (Bruce Koran and Sandy Grisham.)

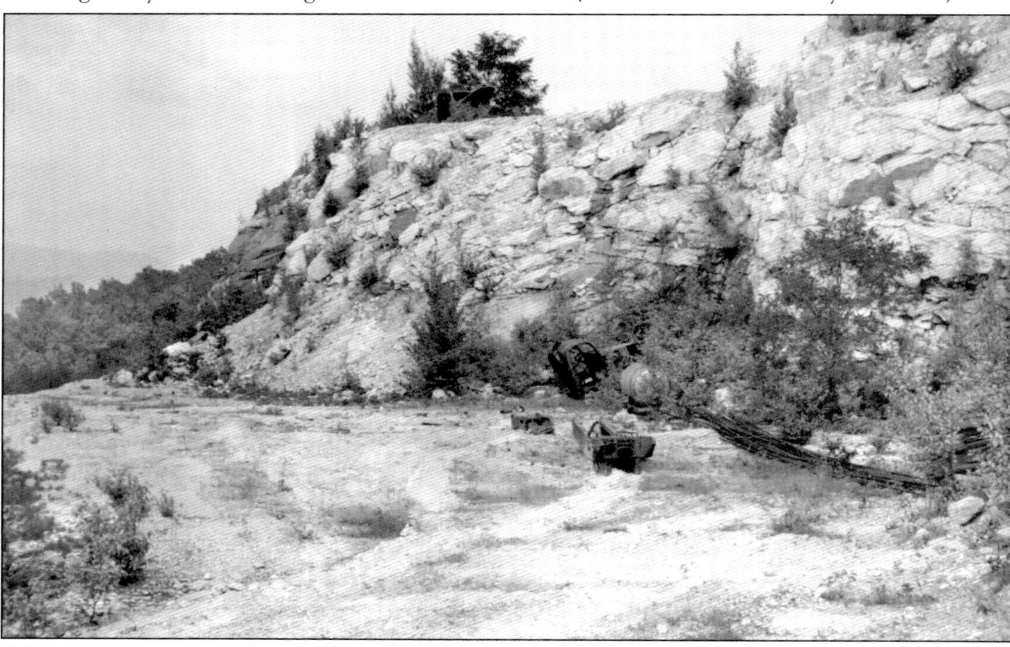

Feldspar was mined in all areas of Mitchell County. Historians are not certain where this photograph was taken, but the scene is typical of the small-scale, often part-time, mining operations of the early 1930s. By the end of the decade, these mines began to give way to large-scale mining operators. (George Morgan.)

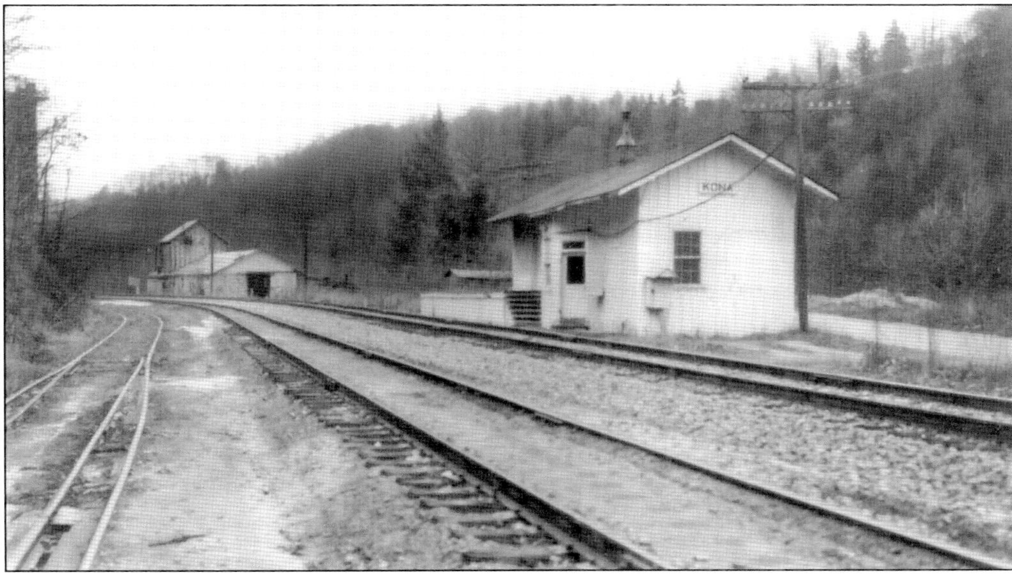

Kona was a small depot, but it provided a way to connect with the outside world. The Yancey (Black Mountain) Railway joined the main line here, and mail from New York and New Orleans was exchanged at this location. Station to station fares were 10¢, or 20¢ to ride from Roses Branch to Spruce Pine. (Mark McKinney.)

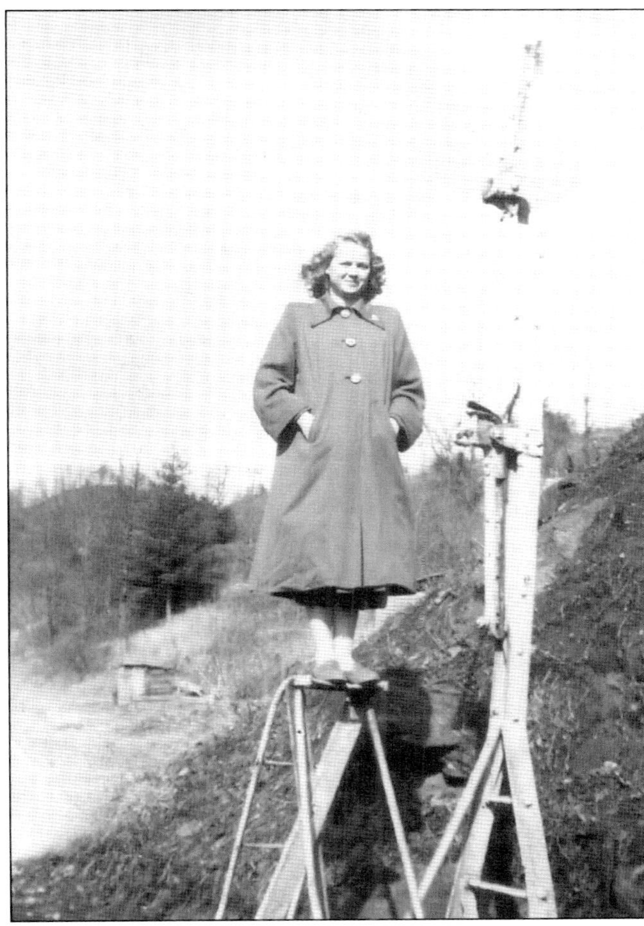

Perched on a ladder high enough to reach the Bandana mail drop, Mae Burleson is a self-styled "Miss Bandana" in this 1940s photograph. Passing trains would use the pole to drop off and pick up mail destined for delivery by Marshall Putman. This was the signal for the trainmen to either grab the mailbag off the pole or stop. (Helen McKinney.)

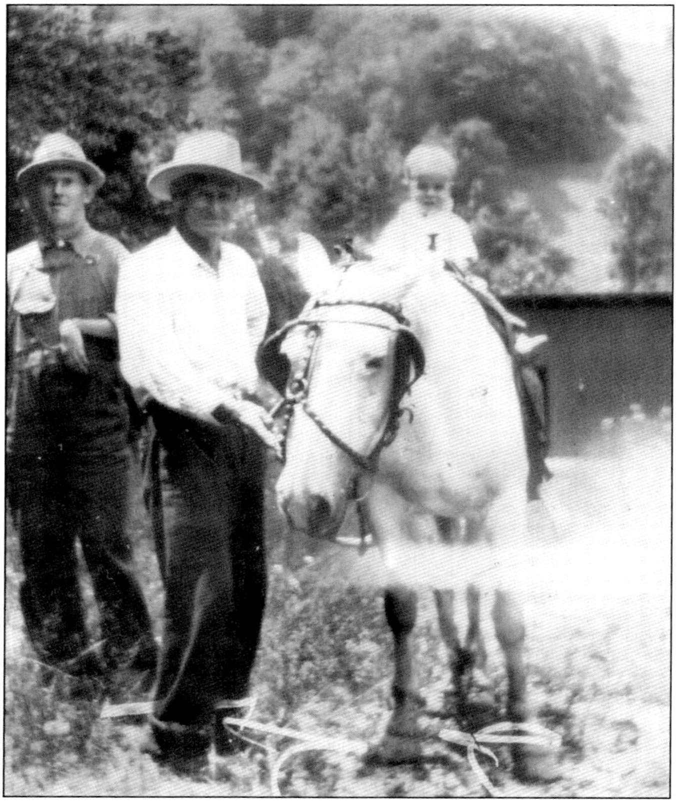

Pictured is Marshall Putman (1863–1953) with the white horse that often was tied up at the depot while he waited for the mail or dropped some off for the train. Initially, he took mail from Tennessee to the Cloudland Hotel before he moved to Bandana. (Helen McKinney.)

This old country store (Dave's Store) was torn down recently, an ignominious end to a place that was one of the central gathering places in Bandana. As with all these country stores, owners provided customers with just about everything they needed to survive. In addition, store owners often put goods on account or traded goods for vegetables and meats. (Helen McKinney.)

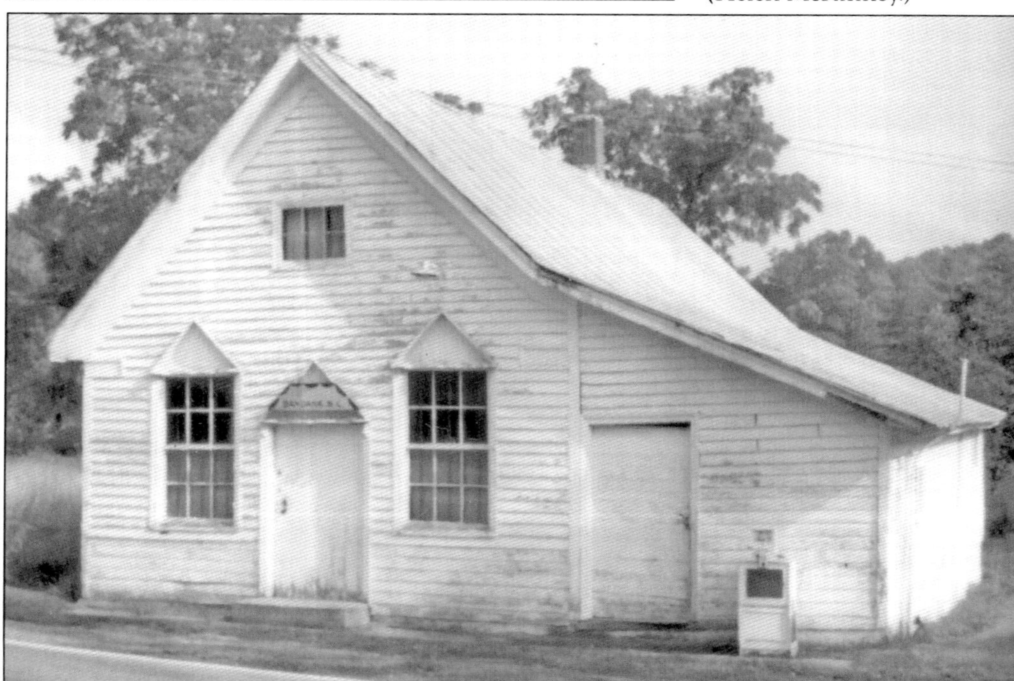

Pictured here is the first-grade class in Bandana in 1946. The teacher is Lola Gouge (Helen McKinney's mother). Gouge went to Ohio for two years of college to become a teacher. Bandana School initially had six grades, with two classes per grade, until students above grade three were bussed to Bakersville. After that, Bandana taught just the first three grades. (Helen McKinney.)

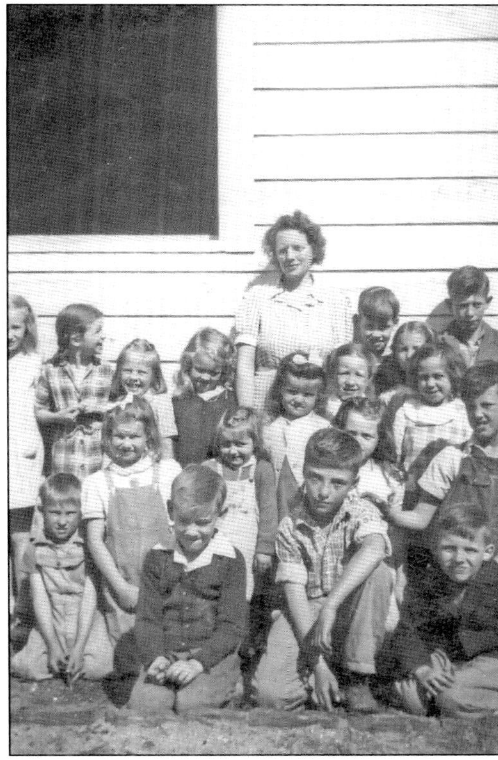

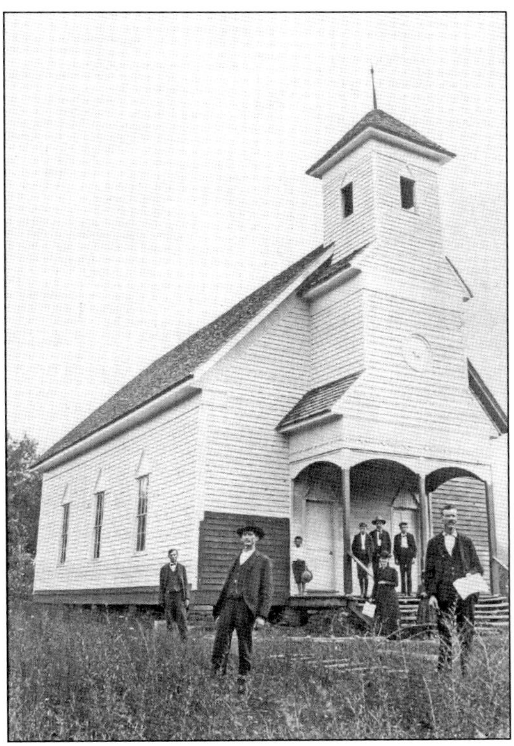

Pictured here in 1900, the wood-frame Bandana Silver Chapel is a good example of the church architecture of its time and place, with its steeple and porch attached to the front of the structure. Churches were central to the lives of the families in Bandana and Kona. (Helen McKinney.)

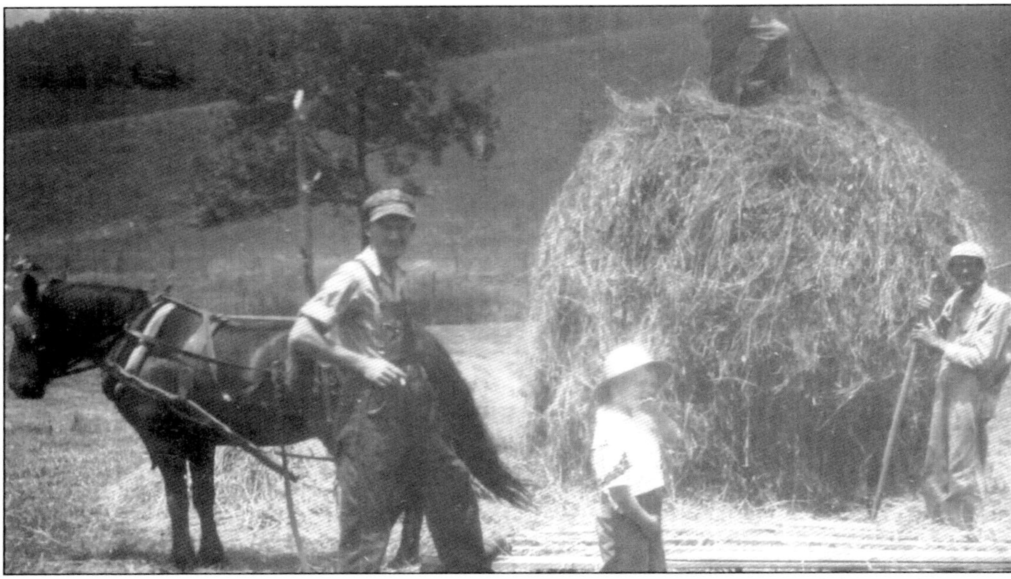

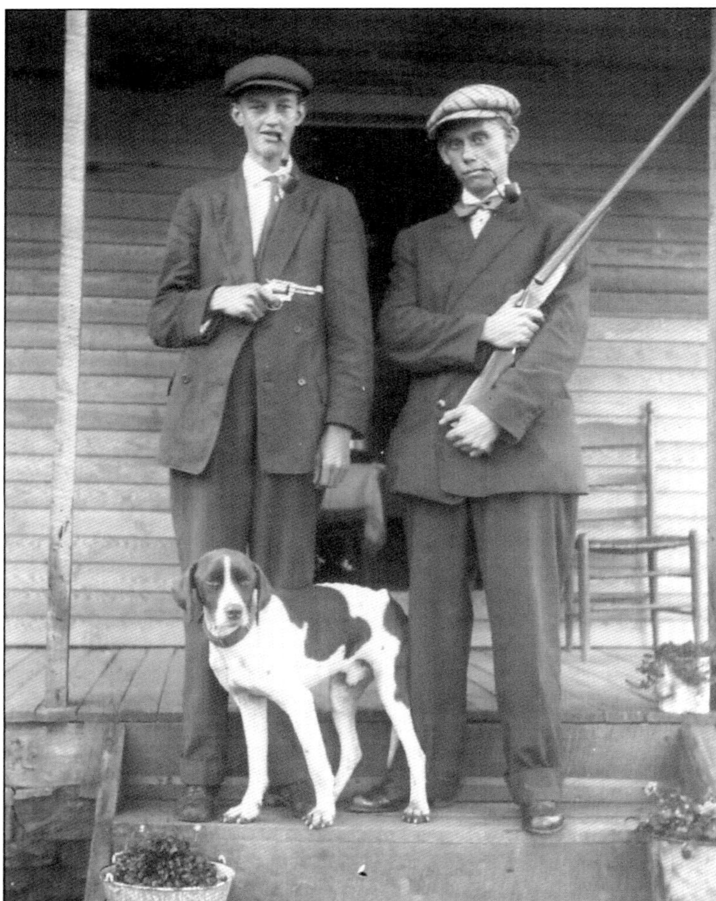

From left to right, Phil Thomas Sr., Phil Thomas Jr., and Walter Hensley are photographed as they rake hay into large stacks for winter feed. Note the sled-like conveyance, most likely used to bring hay from the other fields to put on the top of the stack. (Helen McKinney.)

Ready to go hunting, Walter Hensley (left) and Bob Ellis are armed with a pistol, long rifle, and good hunting dog. Using firearms was a skill taught early in life. Children, especially boys, were pressed to hunt food and were taught how to use guns to protect themselves and their families. (Mark McKinney.)

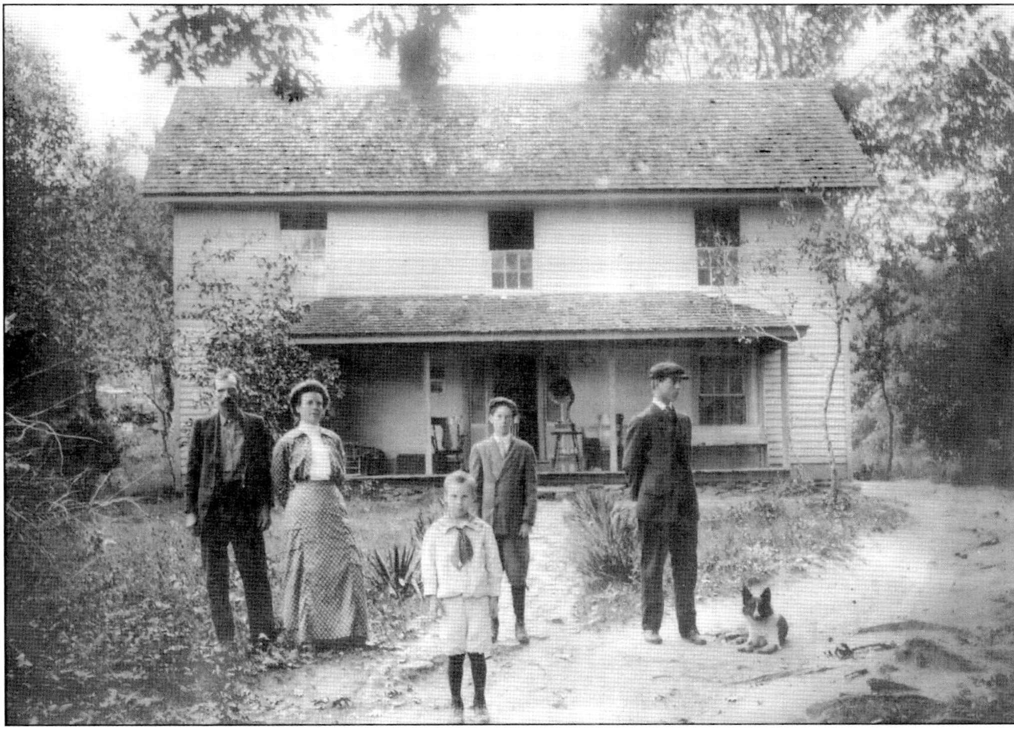

A quick look at "Pink" Chandler's home shows that his family could be counted as belonging to one of the better economic levels in Bandana. As in most places, there were clearly class distinctions in Bandana: the upper classes often considered the poor to be "dirty and barefooted," while the lower classes considered the (relatively) wealthy to be "snooty." (Mark McKinney.)

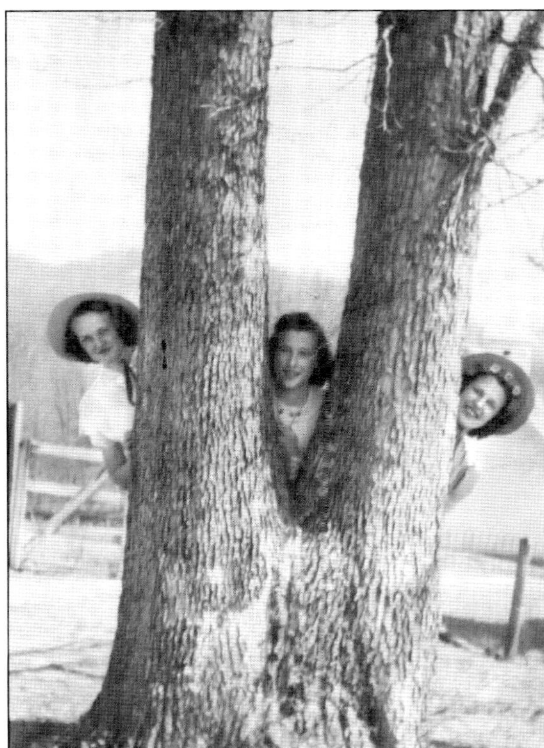

Dressed in their Sunday best, from left to right, Evelyn Hensley, Hattie Putman, and Wilma Putman arrange themselves behind a large tree in this photograph, which probably dates to the late 1930s. Behind the three friends stands Silver Chapel church. (Phil Thomas Jr.)

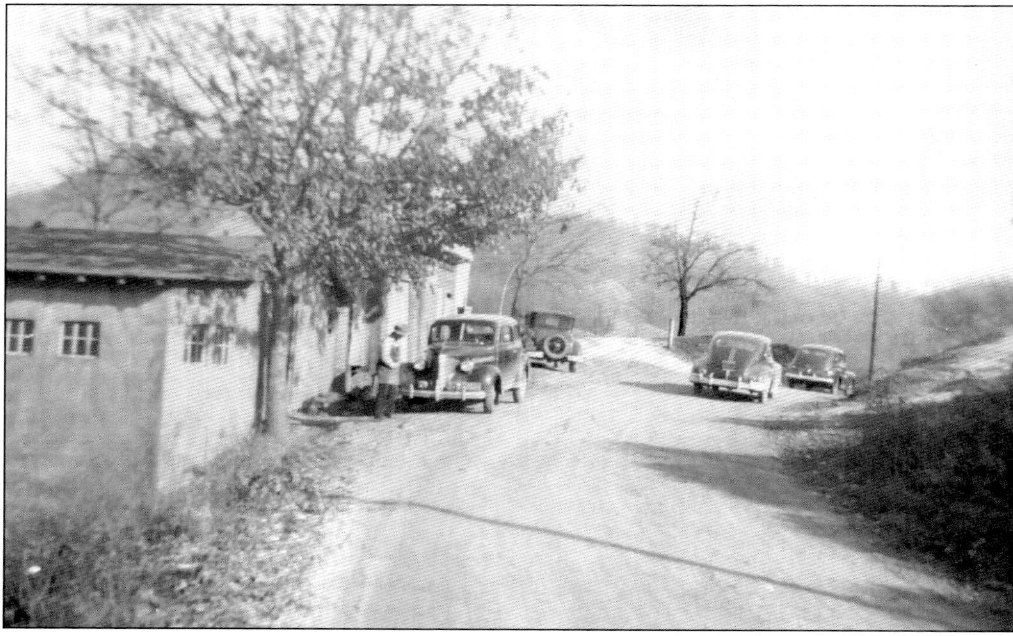

Near Silver Chapel, this mica house was one of four in Bandana. Mica was brought to the houses in toe sacks weighing 50 to 75 pounds. The men did the sheeting, and the women did the trimming. After working in the mines, one resident decided to dig in the backyard of his home and found a sheet of mica that, when sold, nearly paid for his 1937 Plymouth. (Alvin Livingston.)

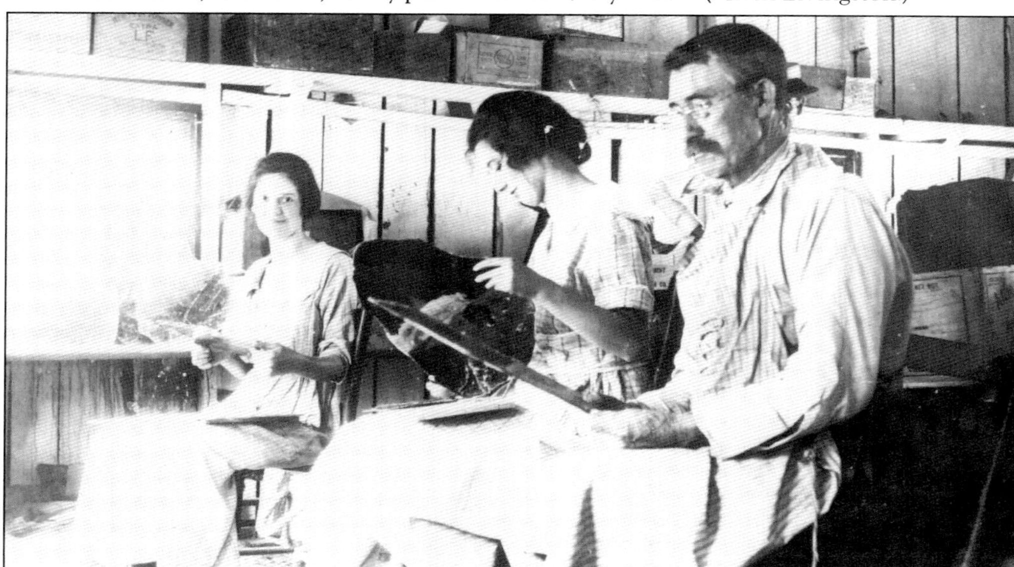

This photograph from the early 1930s shows a typical mica house, this one located near Penland. The best grade of mica was ruby, from the Sink Hole Mine, and the next grade was clear, as from the Phillips Mine. Each mine's mica had to be kept separate. Mica houses were active until World War II when Sen. Harry Truman passed legislation that centralized mica distribution and all the local sheeting and trimming was to be done in Spruce Pine. (North Carolina Collection, UNC Library at Chapel Hill.)

Looking like quite the 19th-century rural couple, Hiram and Sarah Silver Hensley symbolize all that living in the mountains meant. Look closely at their hands, strong and gnarled from the hard work needed to scrape a living from the rugged soil. The Silver name carries with it the reference to Frankie's murder of her husband, Charlie Silver. (Helen McKinney.)

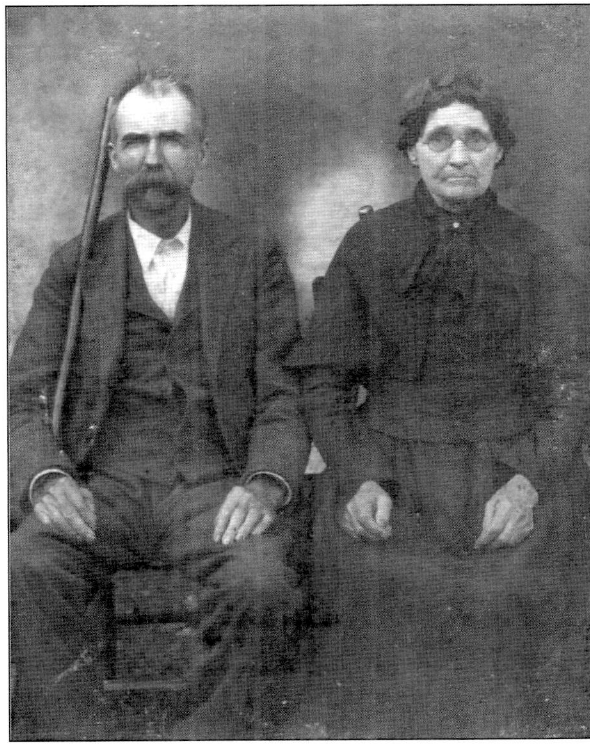

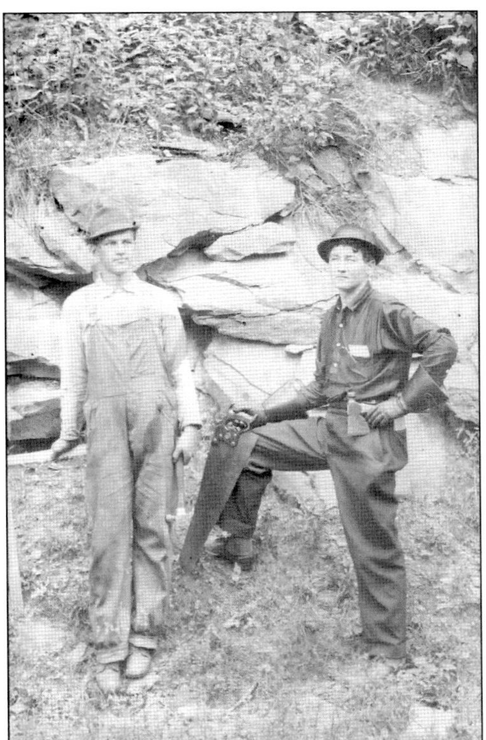

Armed with an axe, saw, and square, C.H. Hensley (left) and Grover Gouge appear to be setting out to get some wood to use for basic carpentry. (Phil Thomas Jr.)

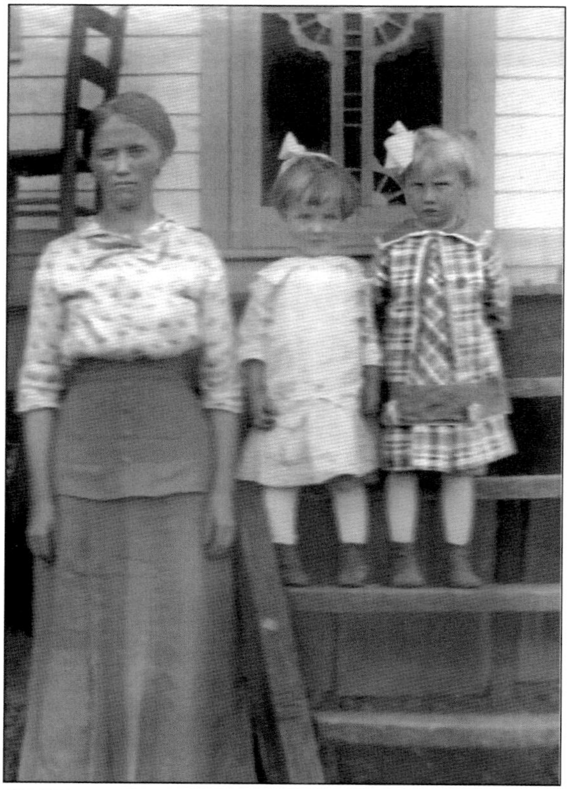

Geneva Robinson is pictured here with her two daughters, Irena and Madge. Like many children of this period, Irena died young, after falling off a "foot log" (a flattened log used for walking over branches of larger creeks). In general, infant and child mortalities were common in the mountains, due to illnesses and accidents. (Mark McKinney.)

Posing prettily for the camera, the entire Dexter Burleson family sits on the porch of their home in Bandana. Like many others, the Burlesons were a farm family when this picture was taken around 1915. Seen here from left to right are (first row) Dexter, Ruby, and Emma Pauline; (second row) Cecil, Jennie, and Nellis. Note that the baby has a large bow in her hair, and Nellis, Cecil, and Dexter have ties on. (Mark McKinney.)

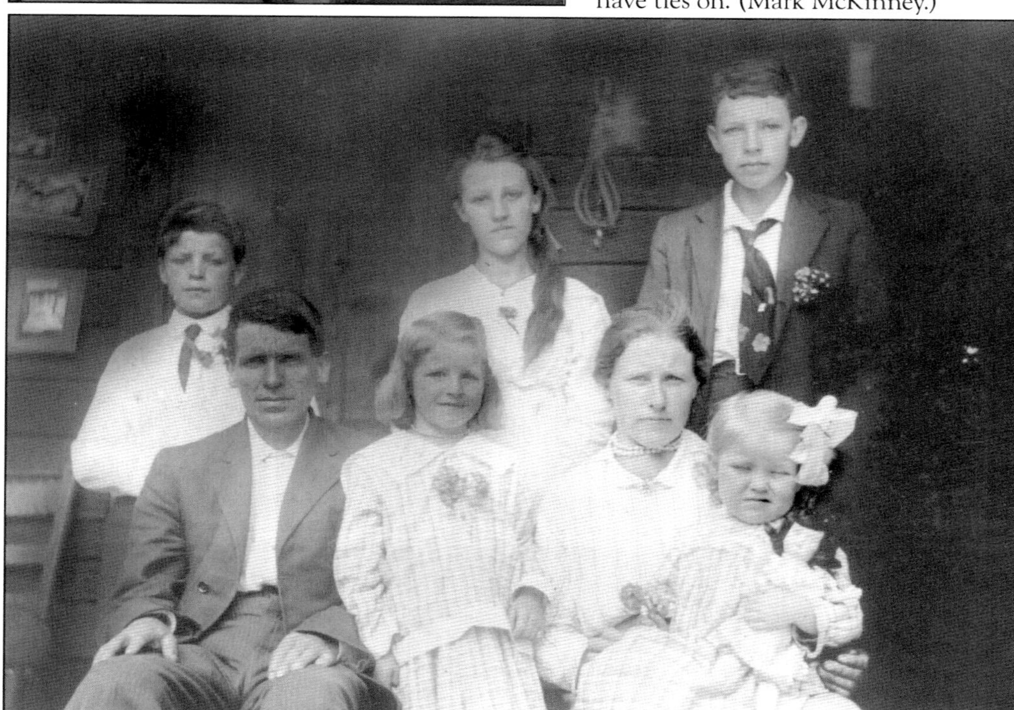

Three

Cane Creek, Clarissa, Green Cove, Hawk, Mckinney Cove, Young Cove

Europeans originally settled the area surrounding Cane Creek in the late 1700s, and Daniel Boone is reputed to have been a frequent visitor to the area. Early settlers found evidence of Native American activity in the area. While there were never large permanent Native American settlements in the area, Native American artifacts can still be found. What is now Cane Creek Road was a section of a larger trail connecting the Piedmont area of North Carolina with Tennessee. As more settlers began to arrive, the surrounding areas began to be settled as well. Communities now known as McKinney Cove, Young Cove, Green Cove, Hawk, and others began to grow. By 1813, Roan Mountain Baptist Church was established on Cane Creek in present-day Clarissa. Eventually, churches and schools were established near these settlements.

The area was not naturally suited for agriculture. Fields had to be cleared from heavily wooded hillsides, and farming on steep hills could be challenging at best. Timber was, in fact, a source of income, and the discovery of numerous sources of mica led to wealth for some and employment for others. Thomas Greene opened the Cloudland Mine in Greene Cove in 1870, and the mining company owned by John G. Heap and E.B. Clapp began to operate the Clarissa Mine and the Hawk Mine. By 1896, these mines had produced more than $350,000 worth of mica.

Society in the Cane Creek area revolved around the church. In addition to Roan Mountain Baptist Church, the early churches included Cane Creek Baptist and McKinney Cove Baptist Church. Schools were established in the Cane Creek area. The largest was Roan Mountain School near Clarissa. Until the early 1930s, Roan Mountain School offered classes from grade school through high school. By 1938, the only public school still open on Cane Creek was Hawk School.

Even though the Cane Creek area was close to Bakersville, there were a number of general stores throughout the area. During the 1930s, the Hawk community had at least two stores and a post office. Sadly, better roads have caused these stores to disappear from the scene.

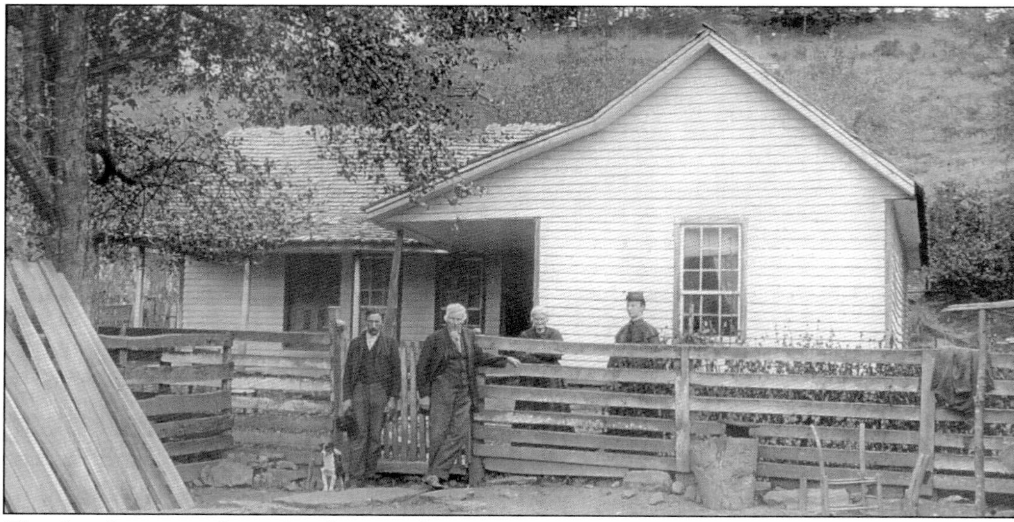

This farmhouse on Cane Creek near Clarissa belonged to Mose Young, second from the left. At far left is his son-in-law Reuben Wilson. Behind the fence, next to Mose, is his wife, Elizabeth Young, and next to her is Reuben's wife, Emma Young Wilson. This house was destroyed in the flood of 1901. (Emily Sparks.)

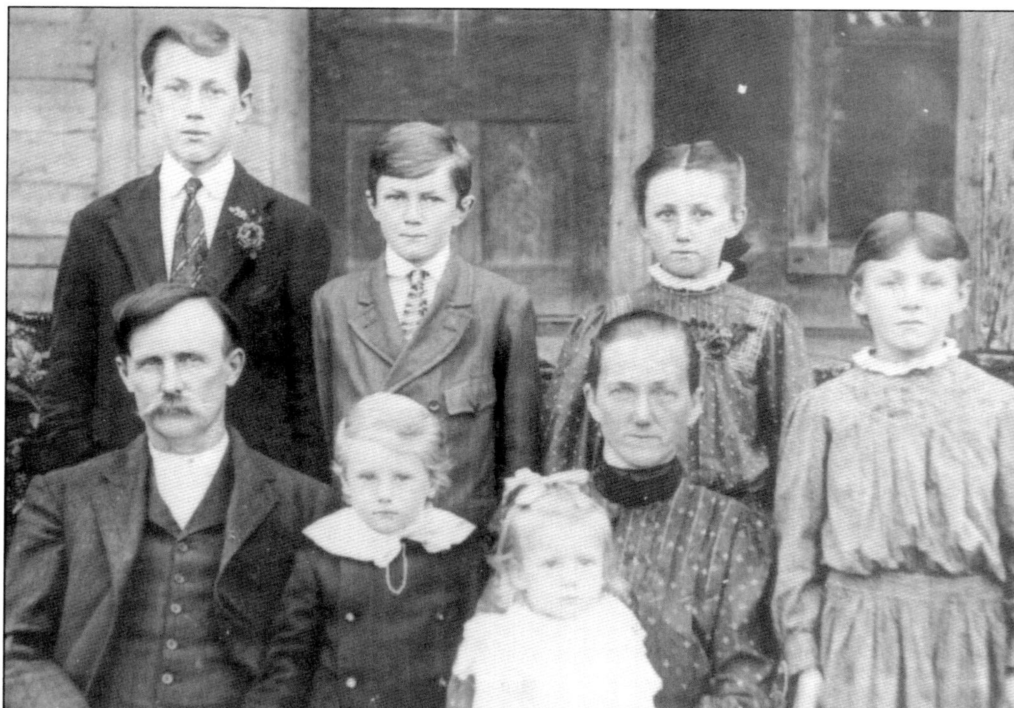

This c. 1906 photograph shows the McKinney family that lived near the head of Young Cove. Shown are Mose McKinney, his wife, Martha Blevins McKinney, and their children. Mose descended from the McKinneys that lived near Altapass, who had planted apple orchards in that area. He established apple and pear orchards in Young Cove and made his living through the sale of produce using the transportation facilities available at Toecane. (Paulette McMahan Davis.)

George McKinney lived at the head of Young Cove. Besides farming, he had several dairy cows and sold milk to Biltmore Dairy in Asheville. This 1954 photograph shows McKinney hauling milk to the road in his homemade cart. (Paulette McMahan Davis.)

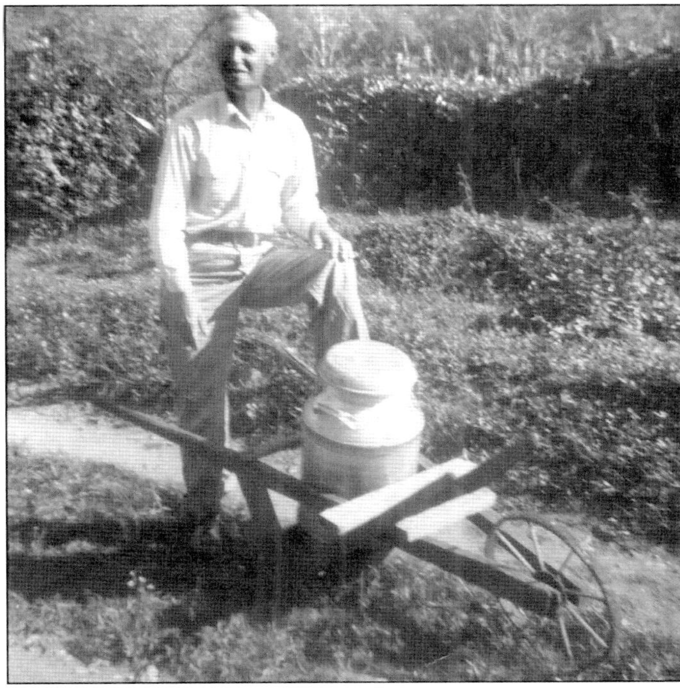

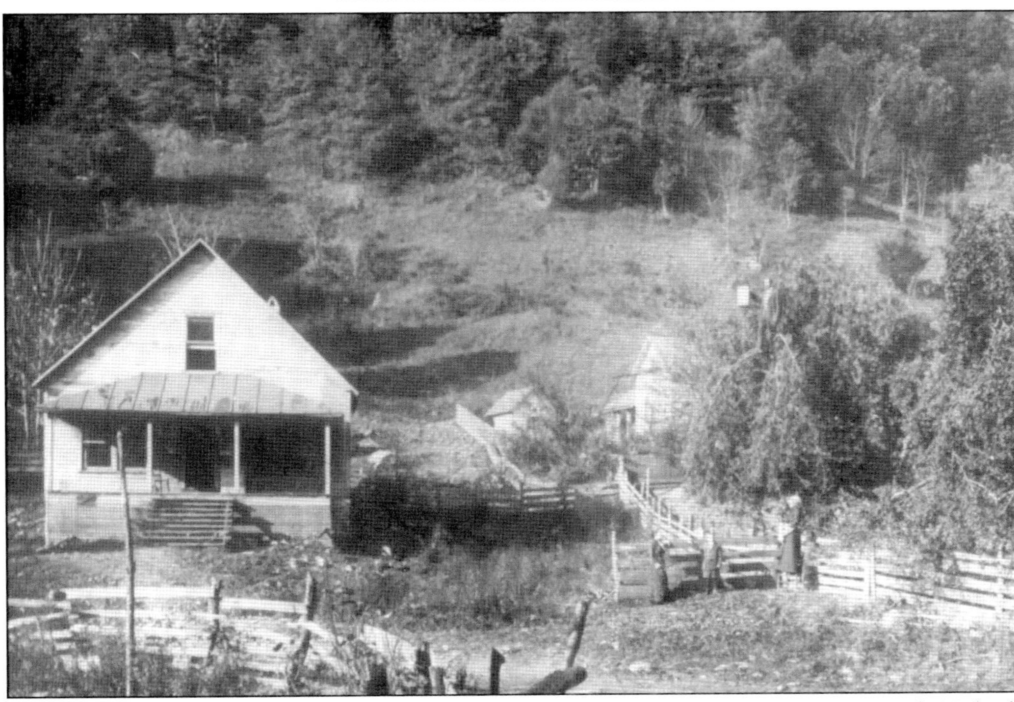

This photograph from the early 1930s shows a farmhouse that was located on Cane Creek. Nobody knows the exact location of the house or the name of the family that lived there. The father is standing at the top of a persimmon tree, picking fruit. His wife is on a small ladder and appears to be doing the same. Their children are standing on the side, watching. (Ann Castro.)

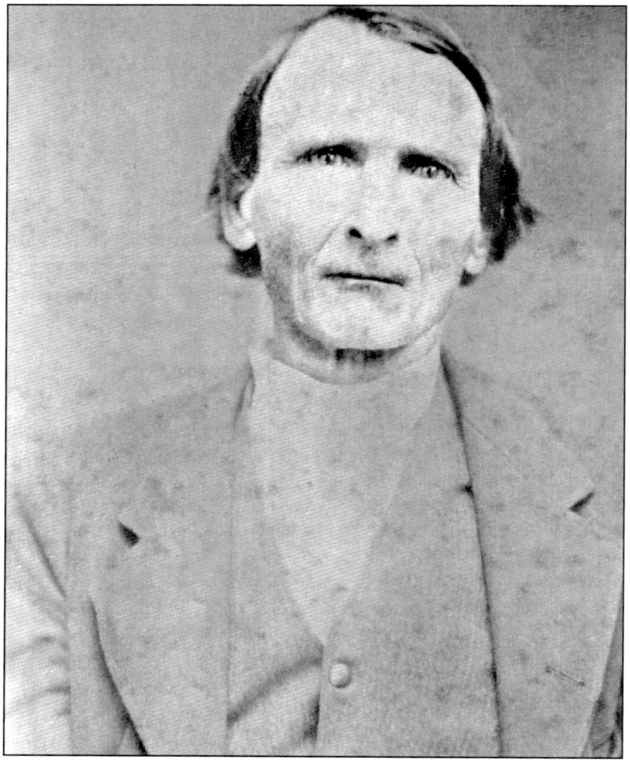

This photograph from 1870 depicts Josiah L. Green, the son of Shadrack Green. The elder Green, the namesake of Green Cove, arrived in the area in the late 1700s. Josiah owned a large tact of land and was considered a prominent member of the community. (Ray Dellinger.)

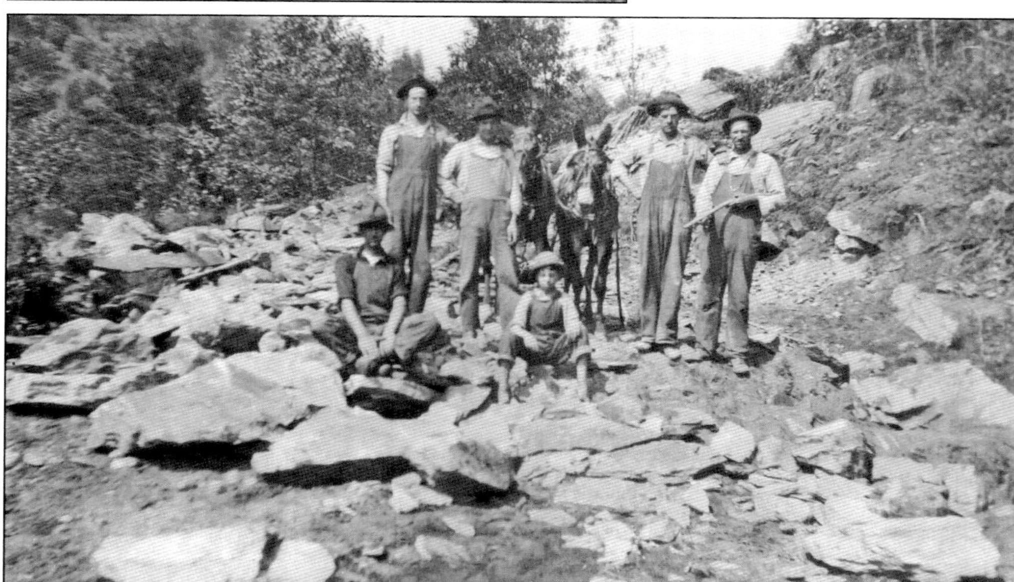

This photograph shows Bruce Morgan (second from the left, next to the mule) and friends at the site of the Hawk Mine. Although there is evidence the mica was mined locally, well before the arrival of white men, the Hawk Mine began large-scale mica mining in 1870. It produced sheets of high-quality mica. This mine was one of three large mines in the Cane Creek area. (George Morgan.)

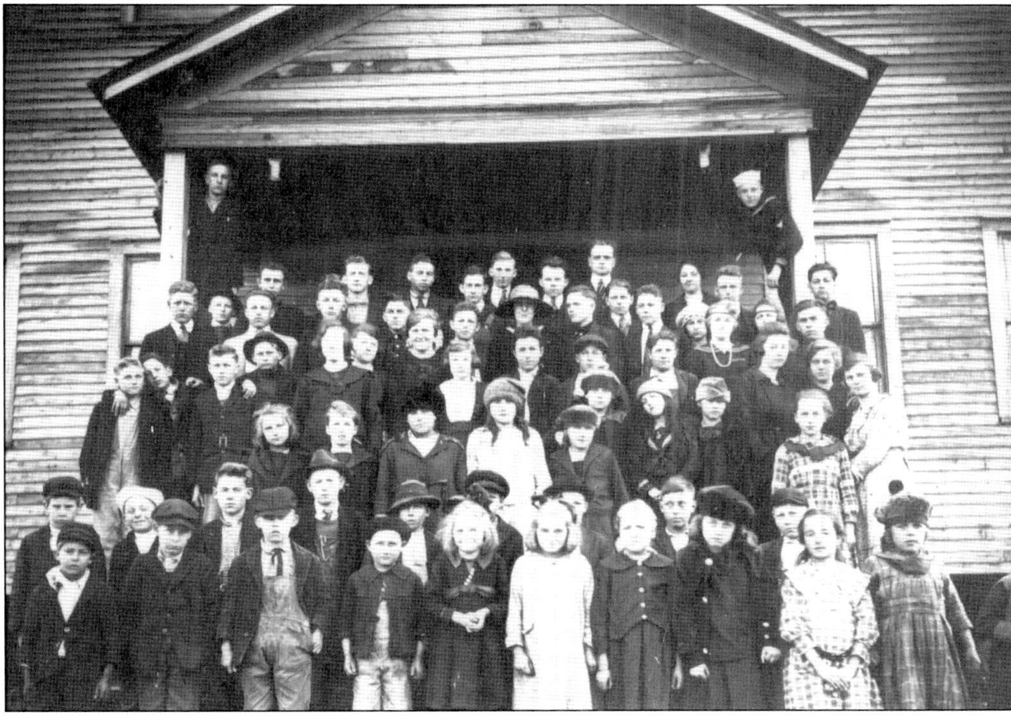

The above photograph is from 1920 and shows the entire student body of Roan Mountain School. As can be seen, this two-story schoolhouse accommodated students of all ages. Eventually, all high school students traveled to Bakersville, and when the school was closed around 1932, all Clarissa students attended classes there, too. After 1933, Roan Mountain School was used as a National Recovery Act work center. Below is a photograph of Hawk School as it appeared in 1920. The school building remained essentially unchanged until it closed in the 1940s. The Hawk School taught children through fifth grade; afterwards, students attended high school at Roan Mountain School (and, in later years, at Bakersville). (Above, Maxie Gouge Buchanan; below, Jack Dellinger.)

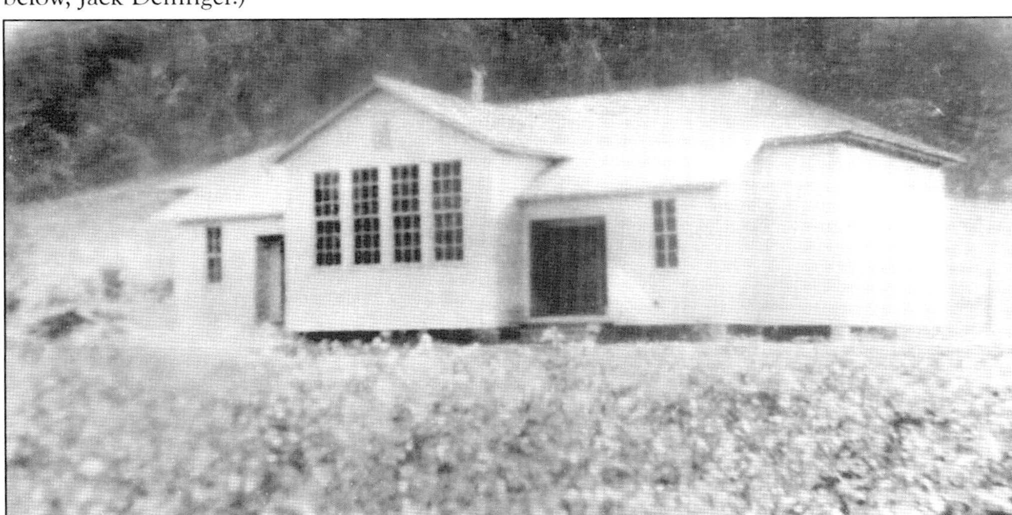

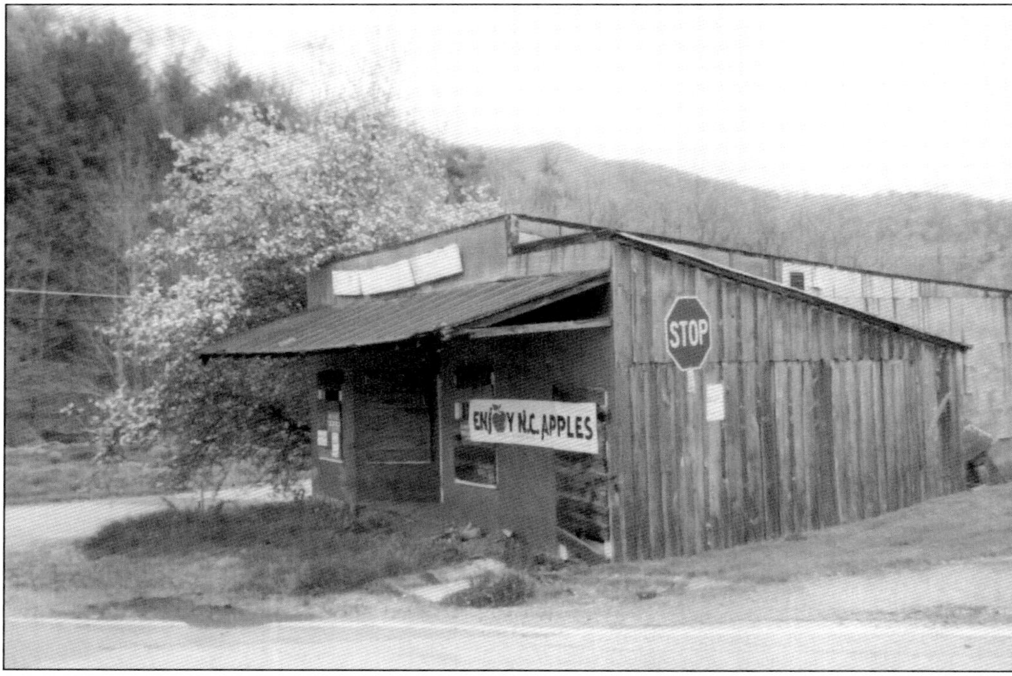

The Clarissa General Store was built in 1939 by Burgess Burleson and was located on Greene Cove Road in Clarissa near the post office. Just down the road, Hawk Supply and Clarence Edward's store served the Hawk community. These merchants were able to supply almost all the needs of the farmers and their families that dotted the area. (Ray Dellinger.)

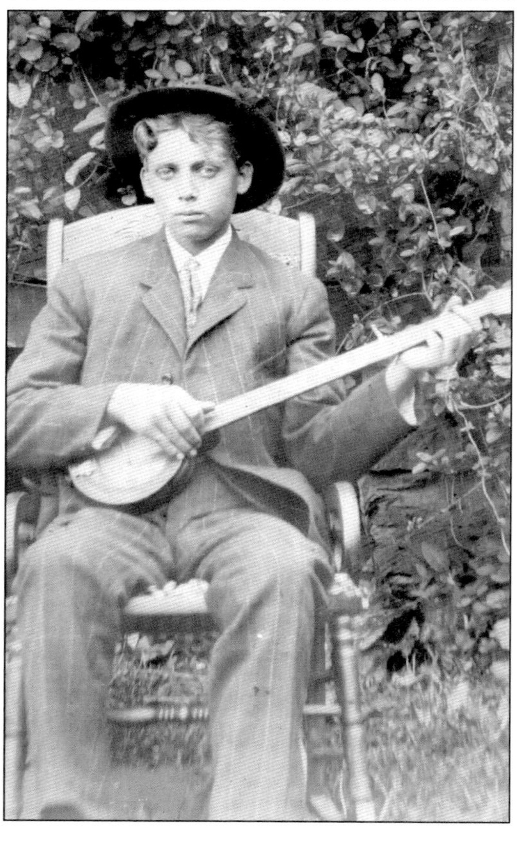

Zeb Buchanan lived in Clarissa. He is pictured around 1915 playing a homemade fretless banjo. Buchanan lived in the area most of his life. He was not known as a musician but was active as a blacksmith, farmer, and miner. At one point, he transported the US mail from Asheville to Bakersville. (Emily Sparks.)

This charming photograph of Mark Morgan was taken in 1934. Morgan and his family lived near Cane Creek. The family was preparing to travel on a vacation to the Atlantic coast when he jumped on the hood of the family truck. (George Morgan.)

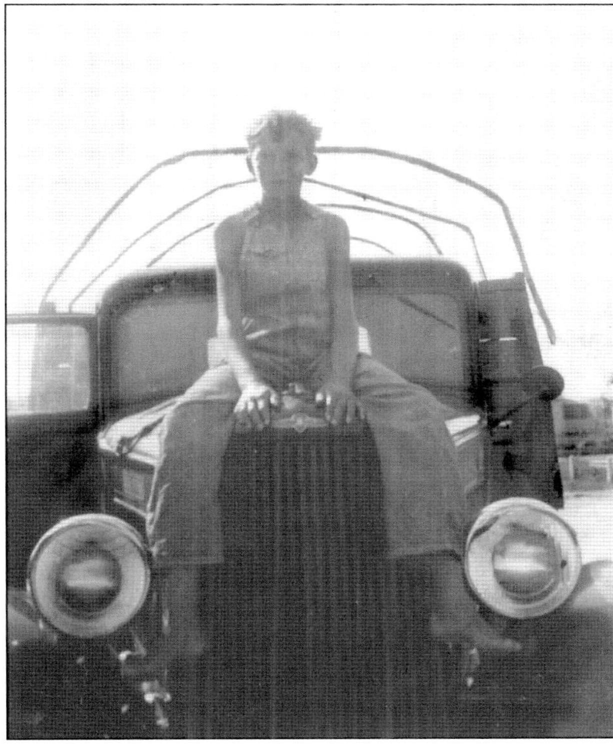

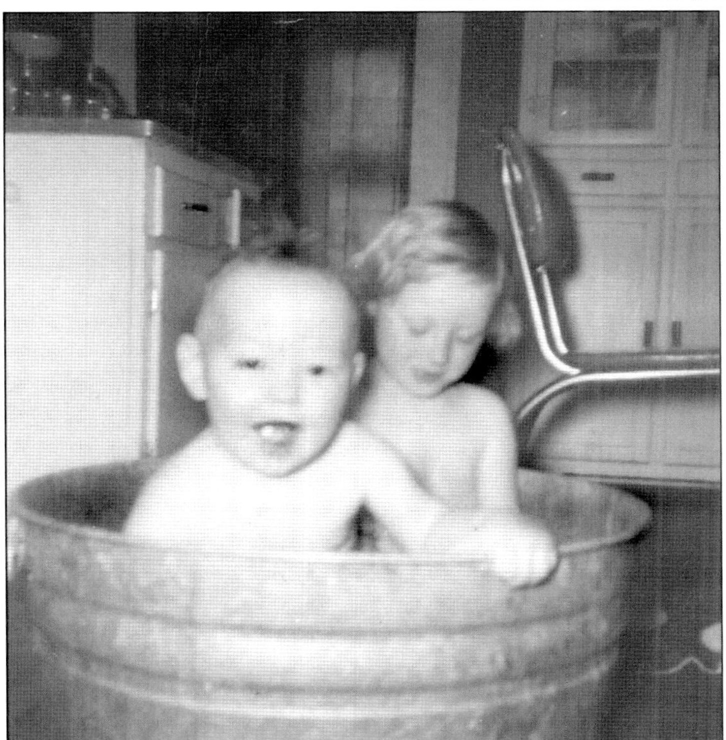

For many folks, Saturday night was bathing night. Pictured are Paulette and Jerry McMahan in 1957 at their home on Priors Creek. Their mother would bring buckets of water from the spring and heat the water on the wood stove. In the days before widespread indoor plumbing, this was a common practice. (Paulette McMahan Davis.)

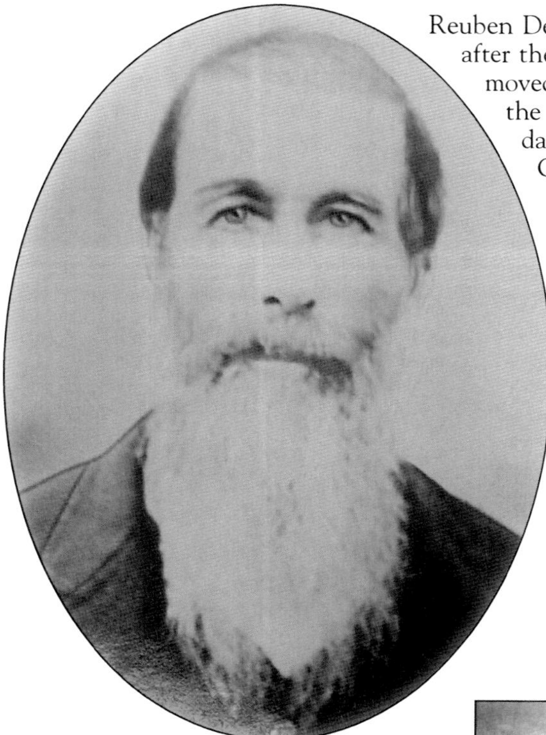

Reuben Dellinger established Dellinger Mill in 1867, after the death of his first wife, Mary Jane, Reuben moved his mill across Cane Creek Mountain, from the community of Three Mile Creek in present-day Avery County to a new location on Cane Creek near Hawk. The mill that Reuben established continues to operate today. Still owned by the Dellinger family, the miller is now Reuben's great-grandson, Jack Dellinger. (Jack Dellinger.)

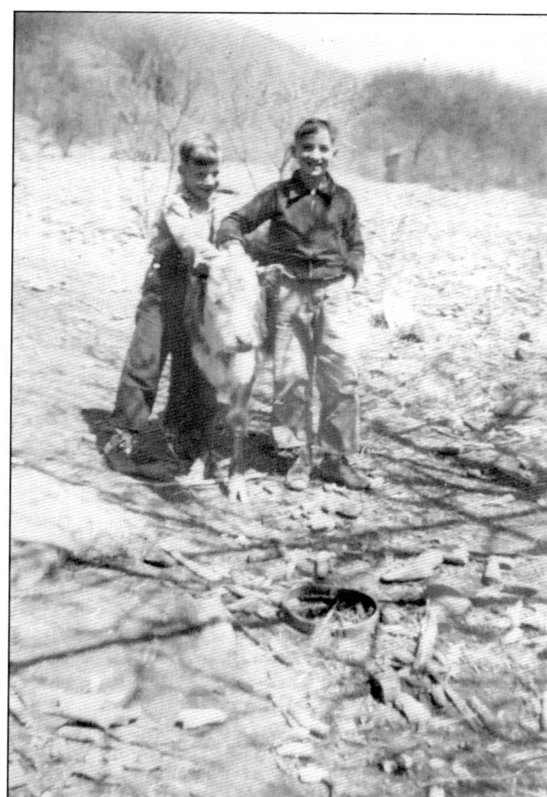

Pictured in 1939 are bothers Jack (right) and Wayne Dellinger and their calf Briggam. The boys are standing on cleared ground on their father's property. While the boys had time to pose with their calf, there was always lots of work to do when helping to farm the hilly, rocky fields. (Jack Dellinger.)

The Dellinger family operated a gristmill and a water-powered sawmill, but they also farmed and grew apples. This photograph from around 1940 shows the farmhouse, mill, and apple house. The mill was a center of activity in the area and it ground corn for farmers in Clarissa, Green Cove, and both forks of Cane Creek. The fee for this service, "the Miller's Toll," was one-tenth of a bushel of shelled corn. (Jack Dellinger.)

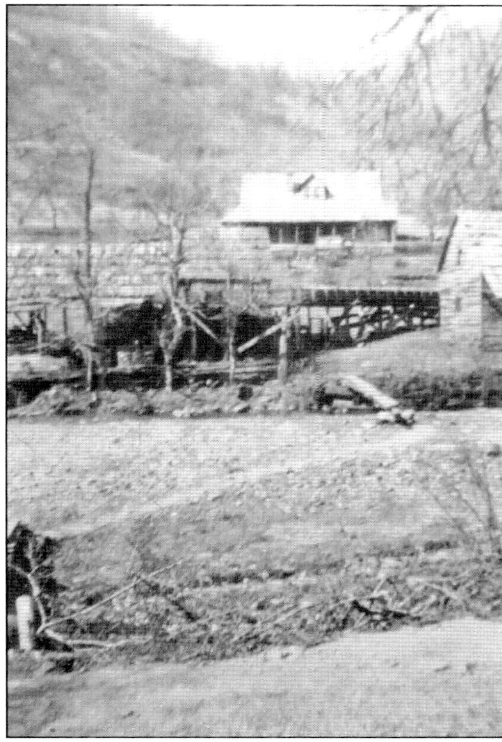

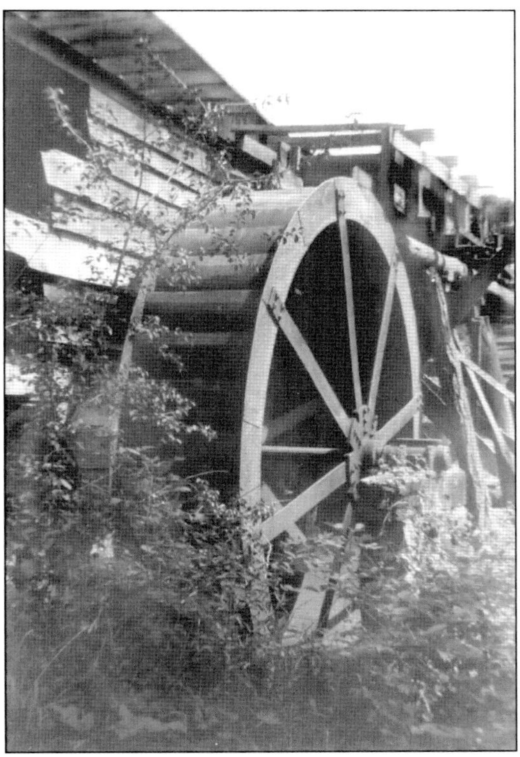

This is a close view of the Dellinger waterwheel from 1952. One of the first steel waterwheels, it was manufactured by the Fitz Waterwheel Company of Hanover, Pennsylvania, sometime in the 1850s. When Reuben Dellinger moved the mill to Hawk, he was able to disassemble the wheel (made up of eight sections, each weighing 500 pounds) and haul the sections by wagon over Cane Creek Mountain to its present location. (Jack Dellinger.)

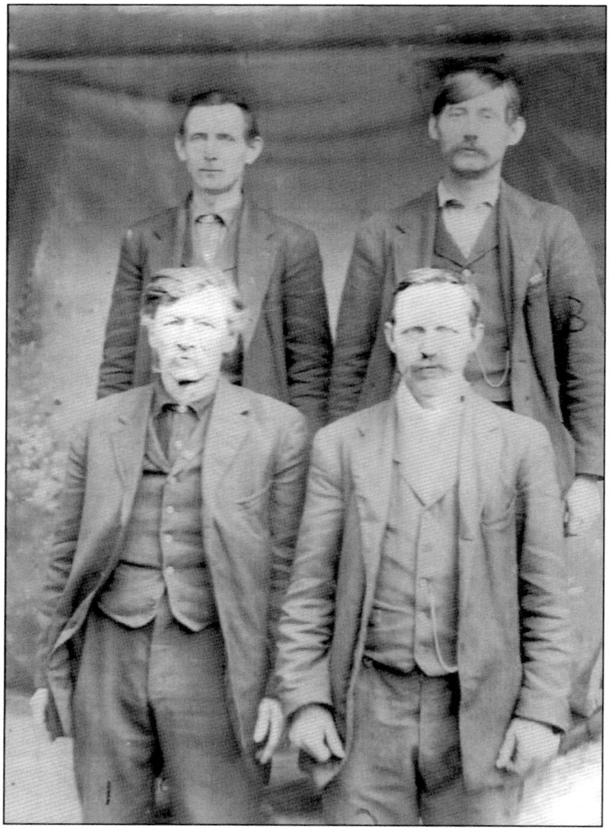

Pictured at left, from the late 1920s, are four gentlemen of Hawk. At the bottom left is Dave Dellinger, the second of the Dellinger millers. On his right is Art Pitman. At the top left is Frank Staton, and at the top right is Gus Snyder. Pitman, Staton, and Snyder farmed and cut timber. All were members of the Cane Creek Baptist Church. (Jack Dellinger.)

This sawmill was probably located near Cane Creek and has been identified by some researchers as Dave Dellinger's sawmill. He did have a sawmill, but it was attached to the waterwheel that ran the Dellinger gristmill. The photograph dates to 1900, but the real owner of the sawmill pictured here remains a mystery. (George Morgan.)

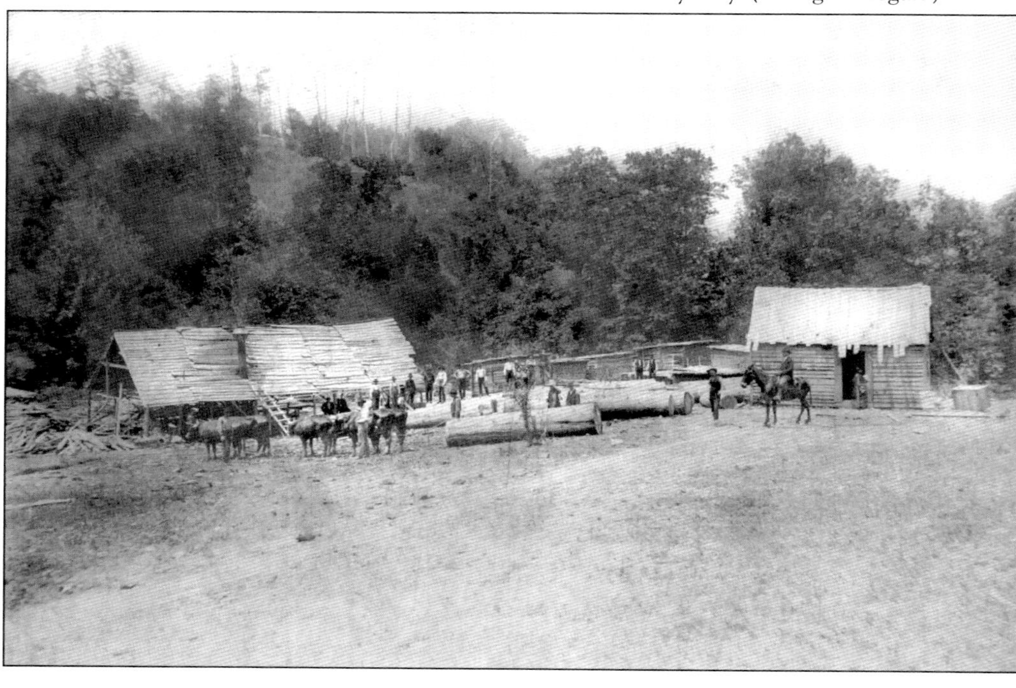

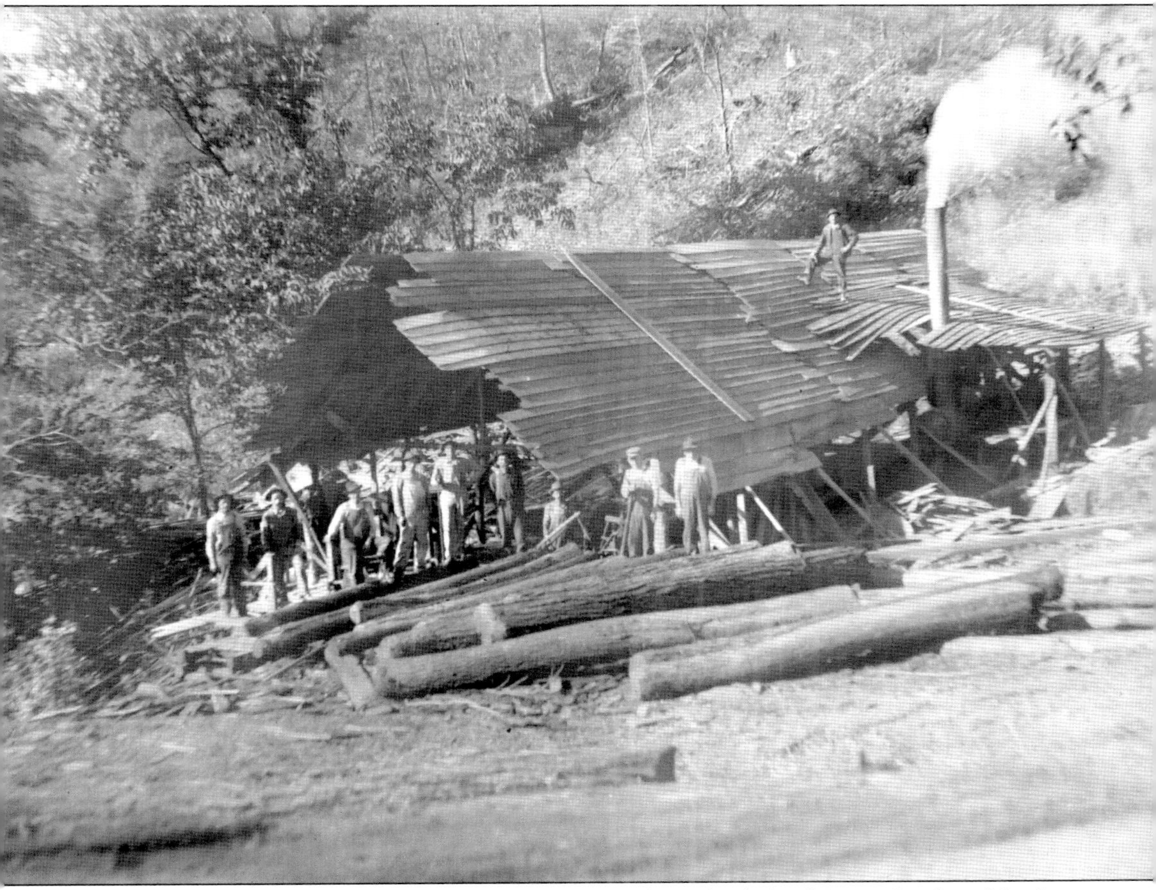

Sherman Burleson owned a steam-powered sawmill on the right fork of Cane Creek in Hawk. This exceptional photograph from the 1930s was taken by Paul Buchanan, "Picture Paul." During his career, Buchanan, a Hawk resident, shot hundreds of wonderful photographs of the people of Mitchell and surrounding counties. Paul would travel all over the area with his camera. Typically, he did not pose his subjects, but was content to let them strike whatever pose seemed to please them. The result is a body of photographs that tell the genuine story of the people and the places where they lived. (Longleaf Media.)

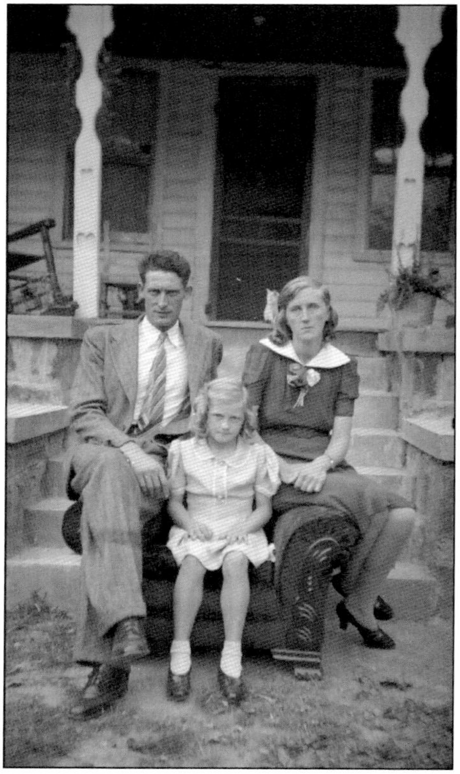

Another of Paul Buchanan's photographs shows the family of Brack Buchanan, his wife, Madith Stamey Buchanan, and daughter Bobbie Jean. Dressed in their best clothes, the family is seated in front of their house in Clarissa sometime in the late 1930s. The house still stands, and Bobbie Jean lives in Marion, North Carolina. (Longleaf Media.)

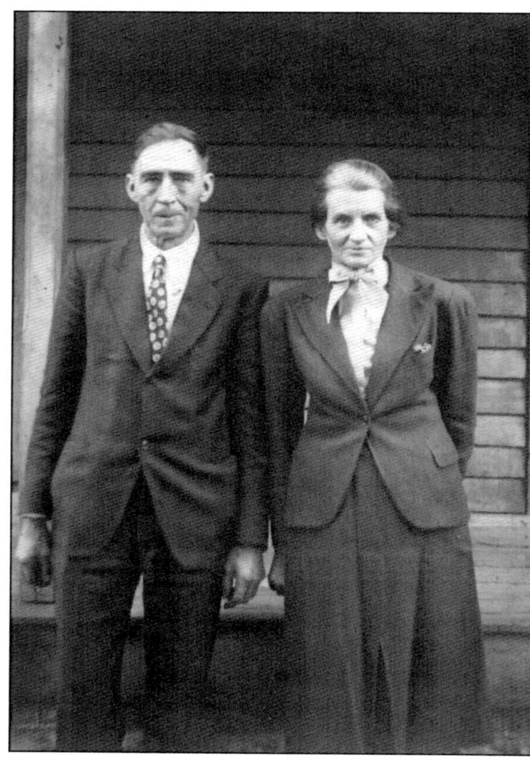

Posing for another of Paul Buchanan's photographs are Marve and Sude Dellinger. This photograph appears to date from the late 1930s. Marve was the third person to run the family mill. After he passed away in 1955, the mill was idle until son Jack Dellinger restored the mill to operation in 2000. (Longleaf Media.)

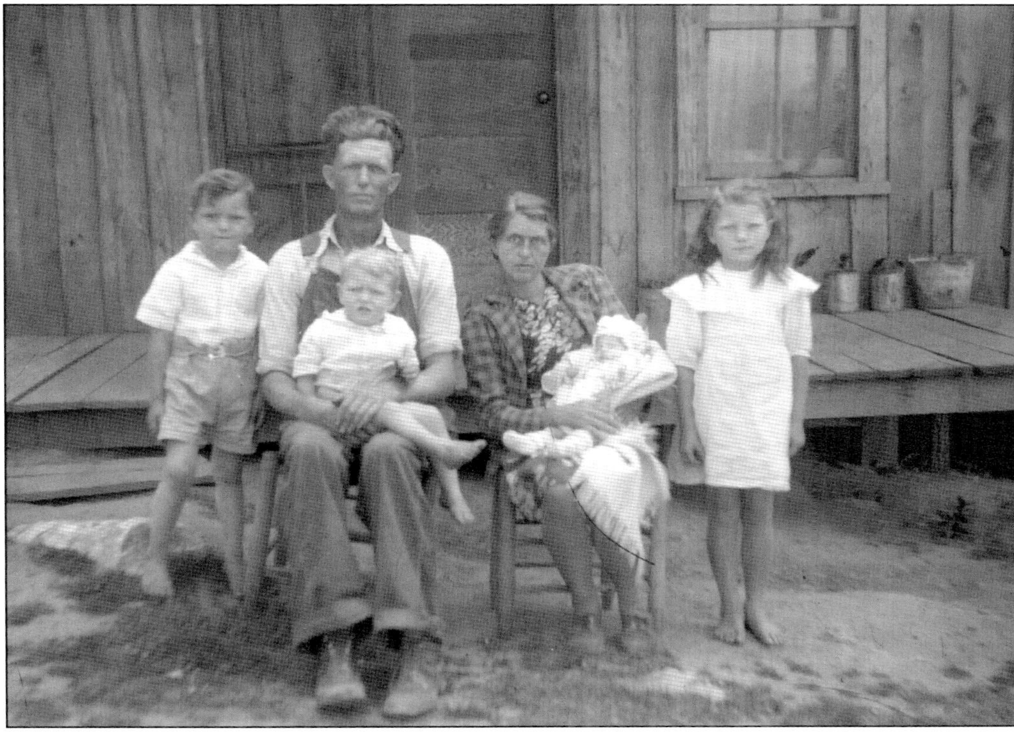

The family that posed for this Paul Buchanan photograph has yet to be identified, but the striking image presented by this apparently poor but very proud family is quite compelling and paints a wonderful portrait of a strong, self-reliant mountain family. (Longleaf Media.)

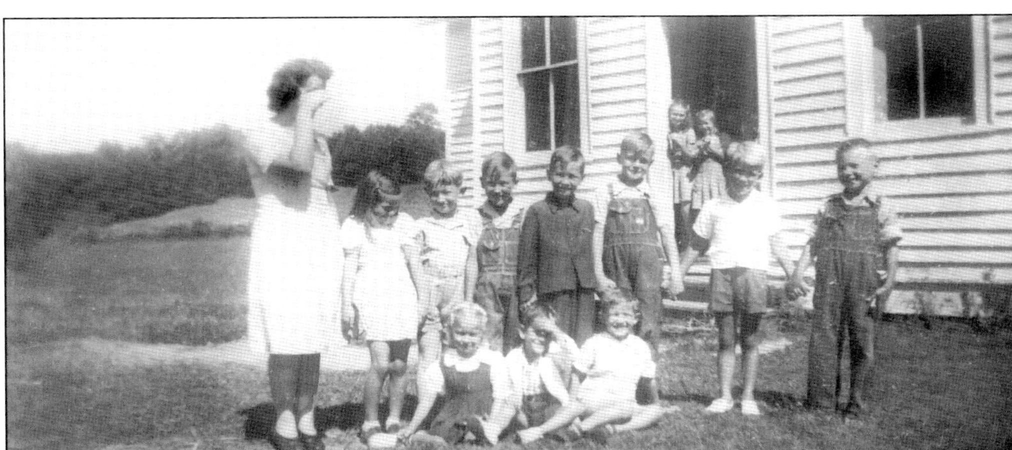

This wonderful 1944 photograph from the Bible school at McKinney Cove Baptist Church features teacher Mary Helen Berry (squinting in the sun) and her amused students. Note that the dress of the students runs the gamut from bib overalls to shorts and tennis shoes. (Faye E. Griffith.)

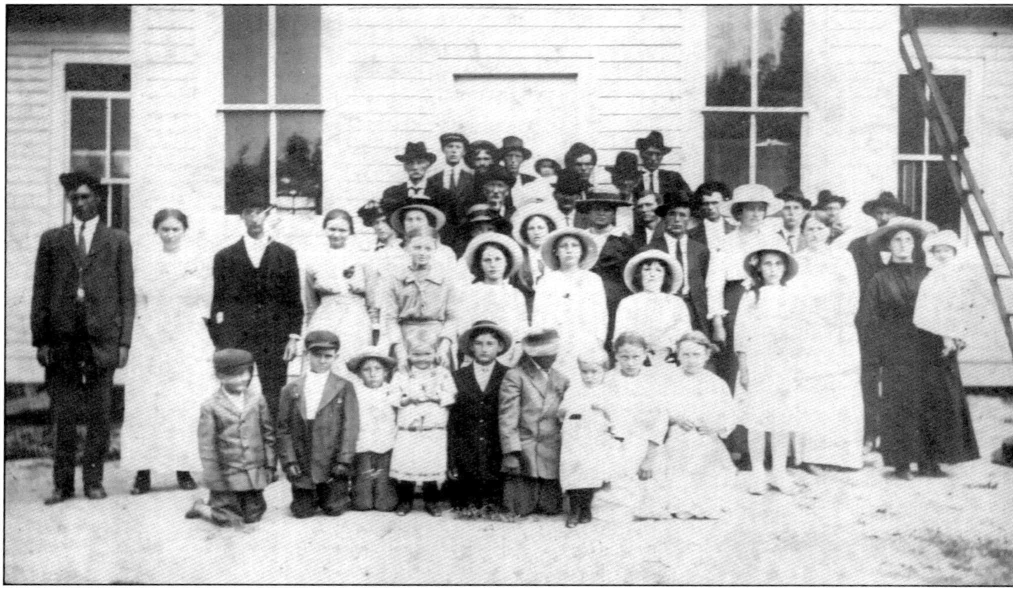

These two photographs, separated by 30 years, are from McKinney Cove Baptist Church. The church was founded in 1888 with a congregation of 40 members. Rev. Charles H. McKinney was a pastor of the church from 1894 until his death in 1934. The picture above was taken in 1915 and shows a Sunday school standing in the snow at the front of the church. The photograph below shows a singing school from the year 1945 as the members pose in front of the church building. These singing schools, which taught shape-note singing, were very popular throughout Mitchell County during the early 1900s. (Both, Faye E. Griffith.)

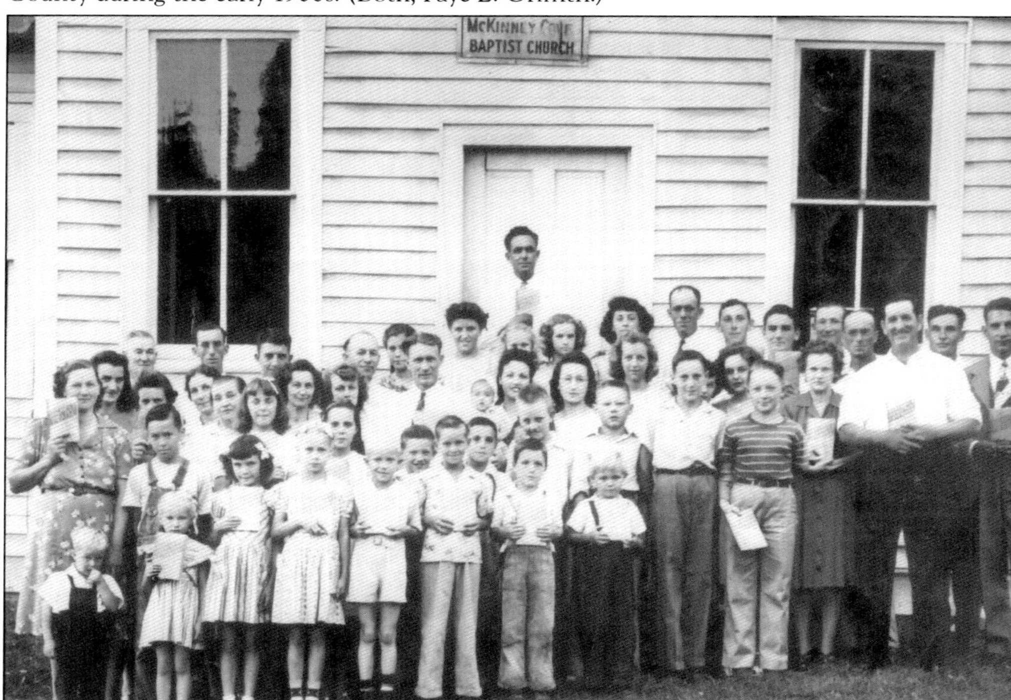

Four
BAKERSVILLE

Bakersville became the county seat of Mitchell County in the 19th century, and for the rest of its history has remained the county's legal center. Like many other early families in the area, the Bakers have continued to be part of the village to this day. One son carried the mail by walking from Asheville to Bakersville, and another was a state senator. A grandson, Joe Baker, ran a mill and a farm. In 1890, Josiah and Jane Pannel Baker bought the house that John Heap built when he started mining here. The house remained in the Baker family for well over 100 years.

Chosen as the county seat in 1863, Bakersville was incorporated in 1870, defining its boundaries as extending one mile east, west, north, and south from the courthouse. It was destined to be one of the largest towns of the area. There were many businesses here, basically taking care of all the needs of the citizens. Doctors operated from cottages near their homes, and pharmacists took care of medicinal needs. The *Mitchell County Banner* informed its subscribers of local, regional, and national news in 1918 and continued until 1936. General businesses like Brown's Shoes, mills, and dry goods and general stores lined the main streets. Add to that the work of the courts, and Bakersville had become a busy place. In the 1880s, Bakersville led the move to get railroads to locate there, but that failed. When the rails were laid, some 20 years later, the village was not on the route.

But Bakersville was still the county seat.

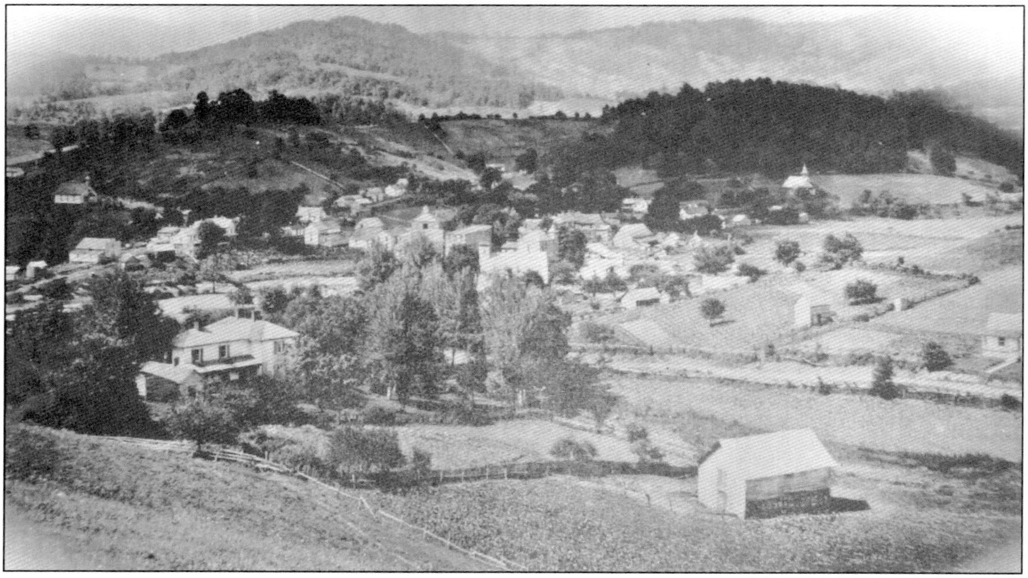

This photograph was also taken before the construction of the 1907 courthouse. The original 1868 courthouse can be seen in the center of the picture. This view is from the south, looking towards Cane Creek and the town. The T-shaped home in the foreground, the Baker home, is the only building in the photograph still standing in 2011. (Daniel Barron.)

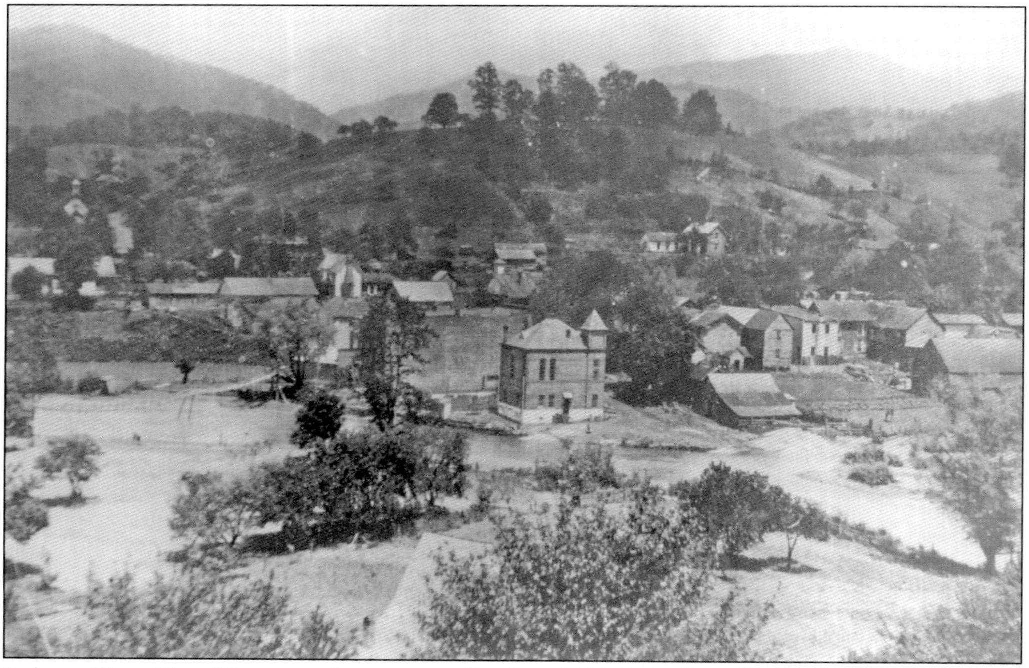

Bakersville suffered its most devastating flood in 1901. Locally called "the May Freshet," it destroyed at least 15 homes and the Bakersville Baptist Church, originally where the Henline Funeral Home is today. Note the footbridge across the creek in the left center of the photograph. The creek waters lap at the jail, and another branch joins the creek in the right side of the picture. (George Morgan.)

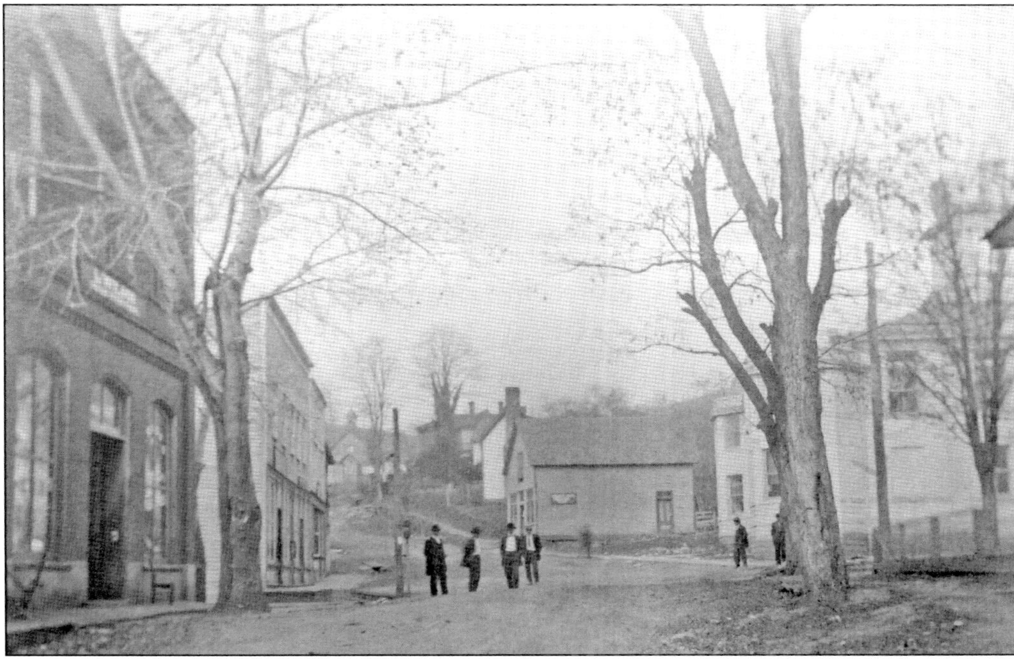

This photograph was taken just after the completion of the new courthouse in 1907. This image looks toward the present road to Glen Ayre. In the background is the Northern Methodist Church. To the left is Lynn Wilson's store and the building that housed George Baker's store and the City Drug Company. (Photograph by Jim Jones; private donor.)

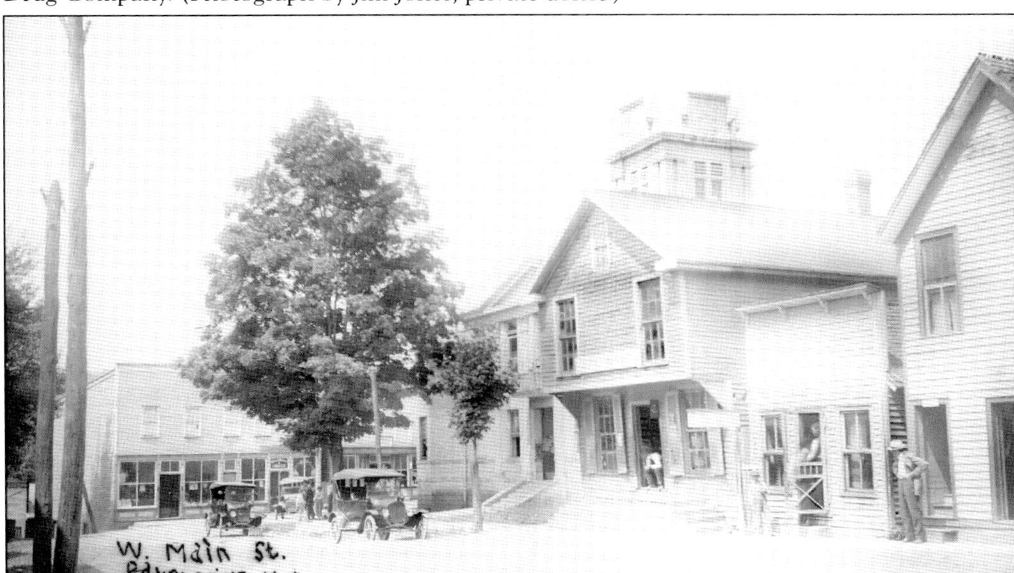

This photograph of West Main Street (Mitchell Avenue) was probably taken around 1918. In the foreground, with the open screen door, is Claude Bowman's barbershop. The large building with the steps is the original building of George Young's store. The building in the background is the City Drug Company and the future location of Brown's Shoes. This building would be destroyed in the fire of 1923. (Photograph by Jim Jones; private donor.)

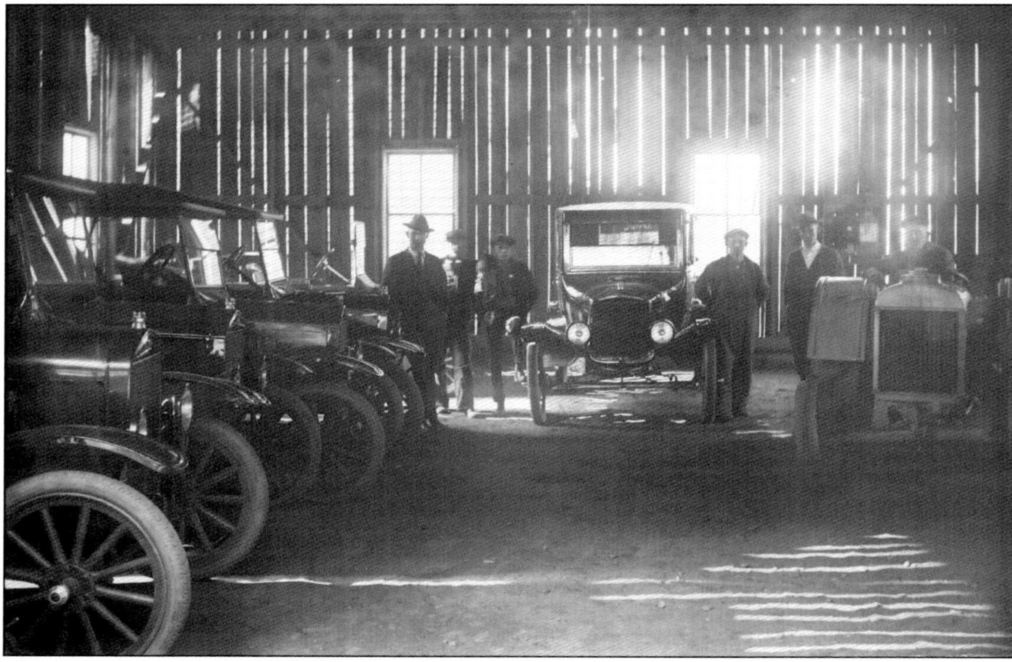

The Baker Motor Company was located at the present site of the Bakersville Town Hall and was owned by George and Frank Baker. Frank can be seen at the far left standing beside a row of shiny Ford Model Ts. This photograph was probably taken shortly before the 1923 fire that completely destroyed the building. (Photograph by Jim Jones; private donor.)

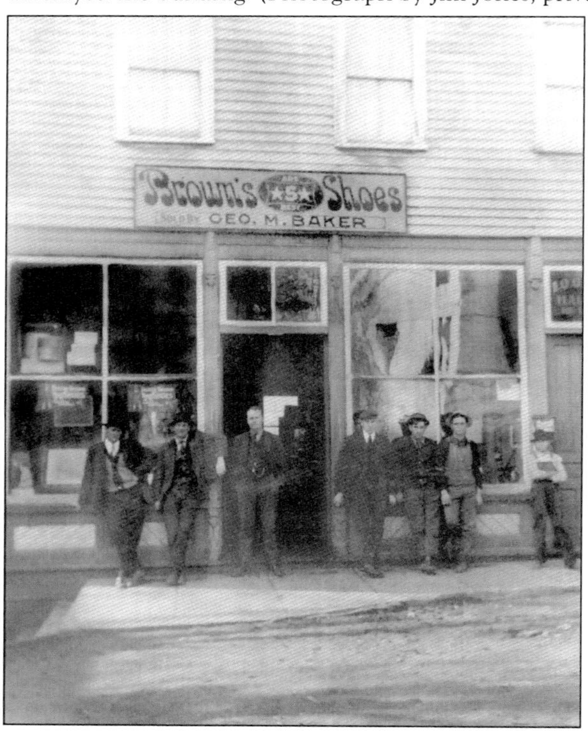

George Baker was co-owner of Baker Motor Company and also sold shoes. This building was located around the corner from Baker Motor Company. The sign on the store reads "Brown's Shoes sold by Geo. M. Baker." Brown's Shoes is a large company based in St. Louis and was well known for its Buster Brown brand of shoes. This building also was destroyed by the 1923 fire. (Daniel Barron.)

The City Drug Company was owned by the Greene family and was originally located in the same building as Brown's Shoes. The gentleman on the left is probably Dave Greene. After the fire, he built the Greene Building down the street and reopened the City Drug Company. This rare photograph was actually found in the 1980s, inside the wall of the present Crimson Laurel Gallery. (George Morgan.)

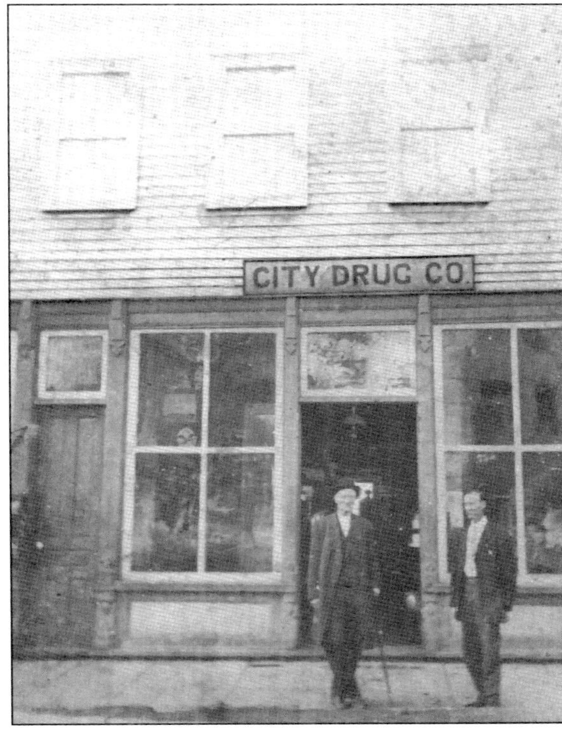

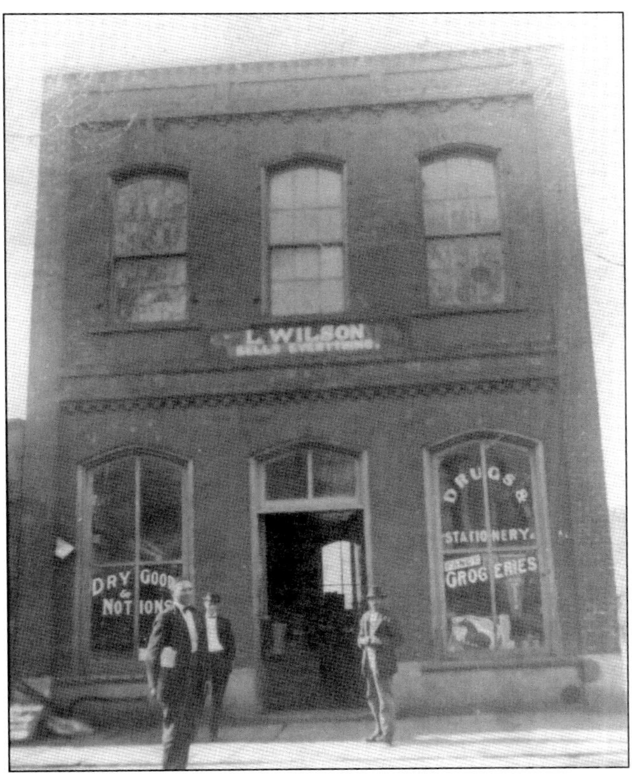

"L. Wilson Sells Everything" claimed the sign in front of Lynn Wilson's general store. Built in 1885, Wilson's store sold "dry goods and notions," drugs, stationery, and "fancy groceries." Wilson's store was located at the corner of today's Crimson Laurel Way and Mitchell Avenue, across from the town hall. (Bud McKinney.)

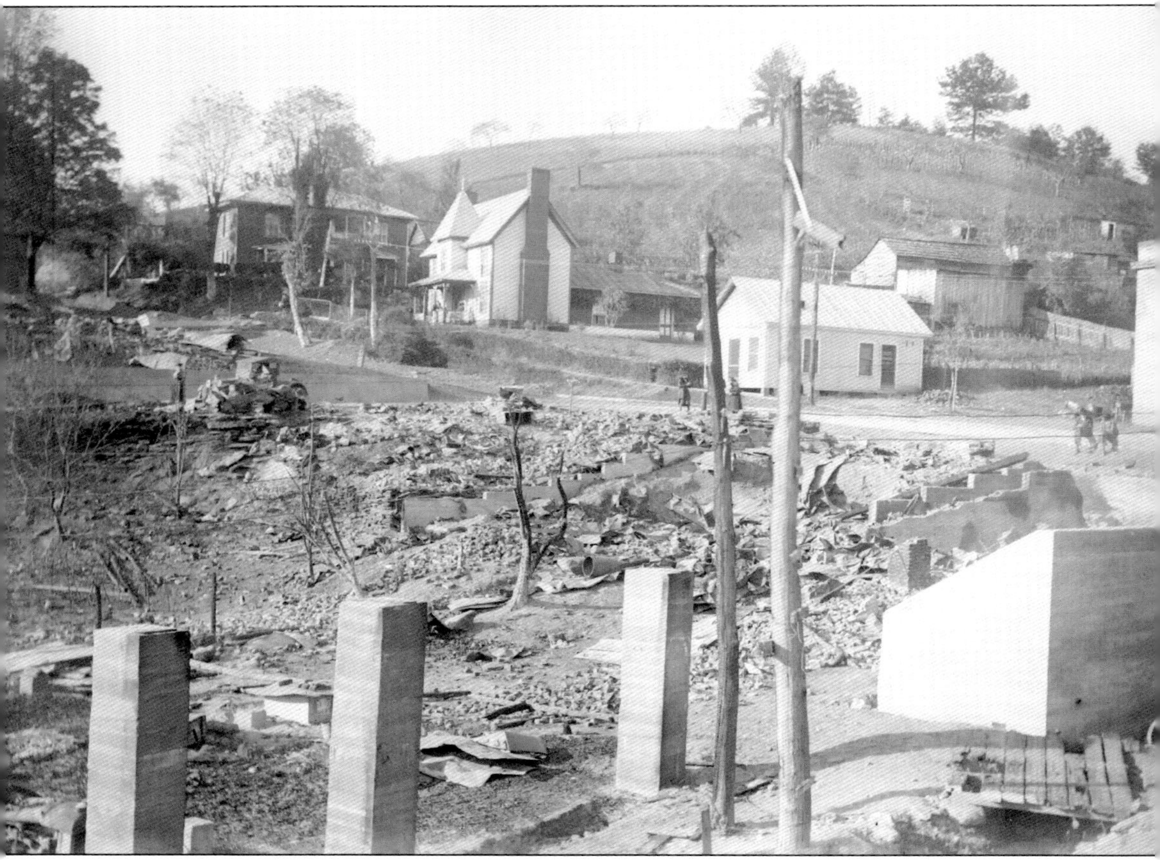

The fire of October 1923 destroyed a large section of downtown Bakersville. This photograph appears to have been taken immediately after the event. The photographer is positioned in front of the present-day Bakersville Town Hall. The fire began after midnight on October 17 at the rear of the City Drug Company and destroyed at least two blocks of buildings, including the house of J.P. Craigmiles, editor of the *Mitchell County Banner*, and several others. The businesses that were destroyed include Baker Motor Company, George Baker's Brown's Shoes, the City Drug Company, and Garland's Store. The roof of the Mitchell County Courthouse caught fire, and only a furious effort by Bright Woody saved the building. None of the businesses were insured. In the lower-left corner of this photograph is the destroyed tractor that was seen in the previous photograph of Baker Motor Company (page 50). Eventually, the Craigmiles family rebuilt their home, the City Drug Company was reopened in the Greene Building on the same block, and Baker Motor Company moved further down Main Street. (Photograph by Jim Jones; private donor.)

This is a photograph of the original Bakersville post office, originally built in 1874. This photograph was probably taken around 1900. The post office was located on the west side of the courthouse. Frank Greene, postmaster and business owner, can be seen in the doorway. This building was razed a few years later and the post office was relocated to Main Street. (Photograph by Jim Jones; private donor.)

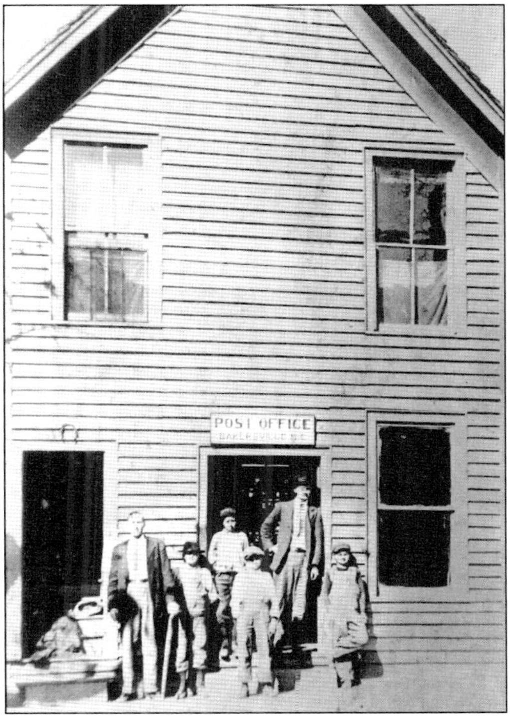

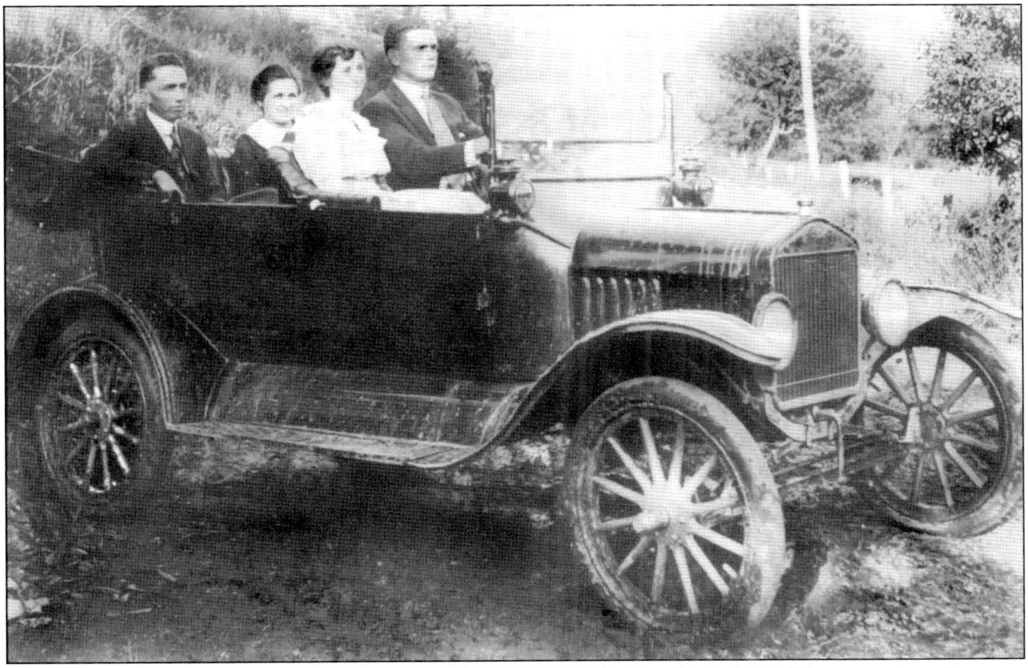

Pictured above is Ed Blevins driving an early version of the Ford Model T. Blevins, a hotel owner and businessman, is showing off the vehicle, which is said to have been the first automobile in Bakersville. Blevins was owner of a coal yard that was transformed into Bakersville Fuel and Supply Company, a business that continued into the 1950s. (Mitchell Historical Society.)

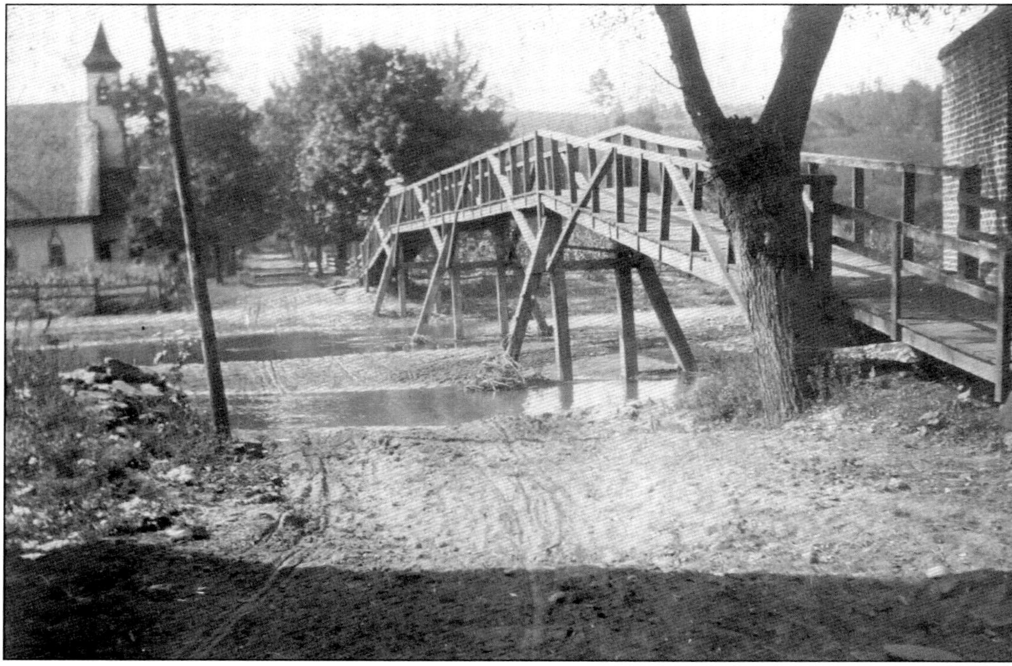

The above photograph shows the original wooden bridge that crossed Cane Creek in Bakersville. The photograph, taken around 1919, is shot from the north side of the bridge near the current town hall. In the background is the original building of the Southern Methodist Church. Below is a photograph that taken several years later showing the construction of the concrete bridge that was part of the new state road building program that included the first paved road in Mitchell County, the concrete road from Toecane to Bakersville. (Above, George Morgan; below, photograph by Jim Jones; private donor.)

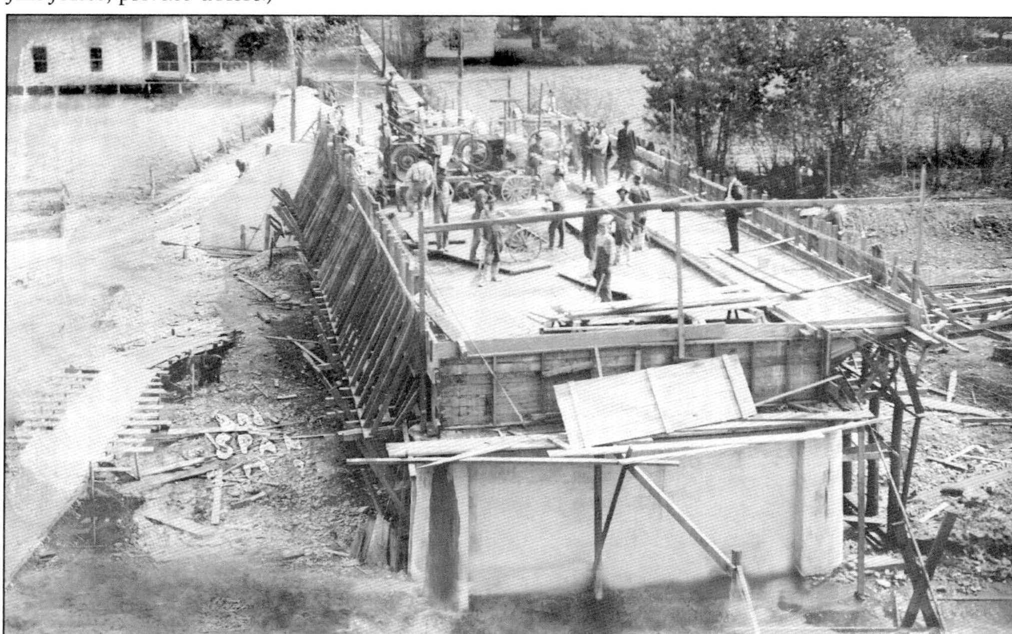

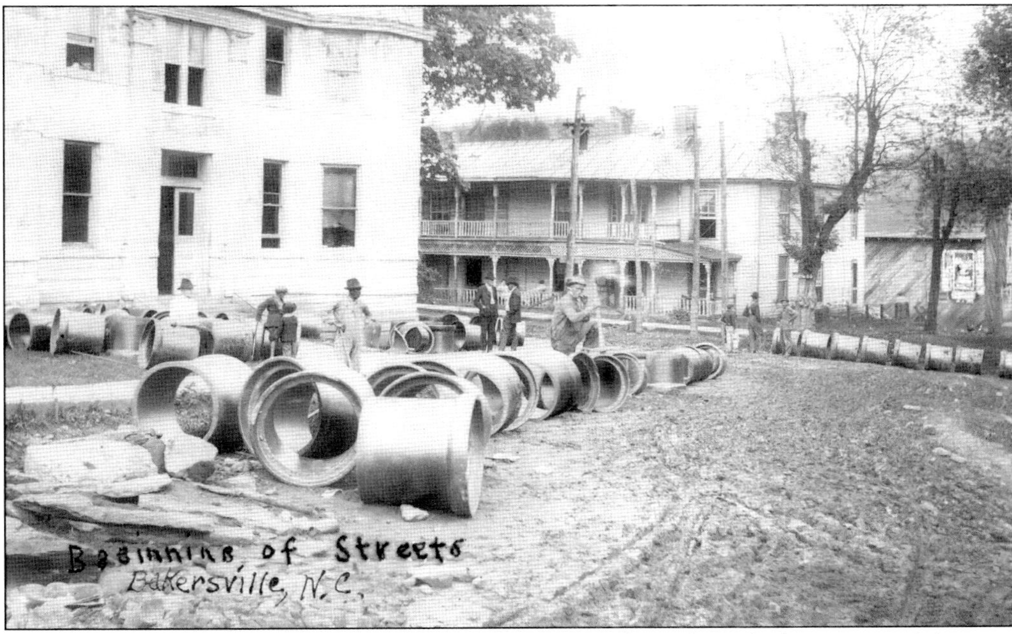

After the Toecane Road was paved, the City of Bakersville undertook the paving of the main streets of Bakersville and the installation of a sewer system. This photograph, taken in the late 1920s, shows the south side of the courthouse. In the background, on Main Street, is Blevins's boardinghouse. (Photograph by Jim Jones; private donor.)

The barbershop in Bakersville was located on Main Street next to George Young's store. Although this photograph probably dates from the 1920s, the barbershop was a town fixture for many more years. The photograph shows owner Claude Bowman, left, and an unknown assistant. (Photograph by Jim Jones; private donor.)

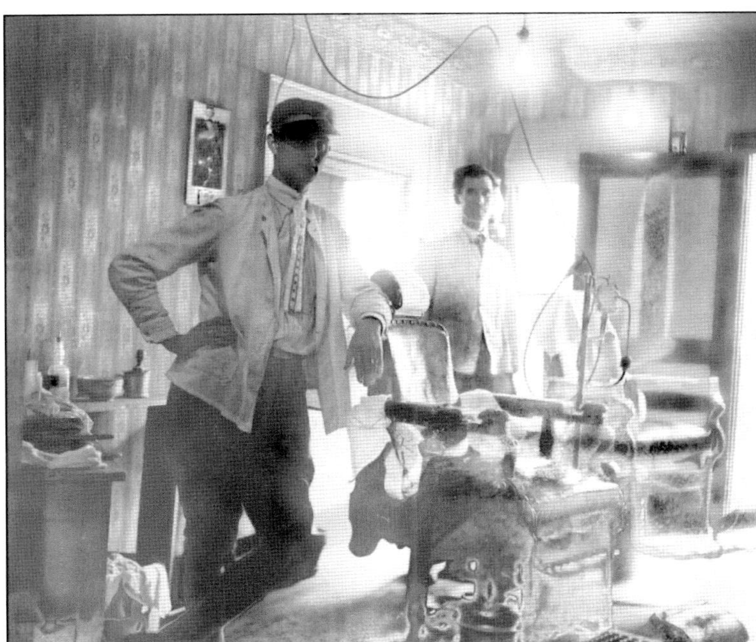

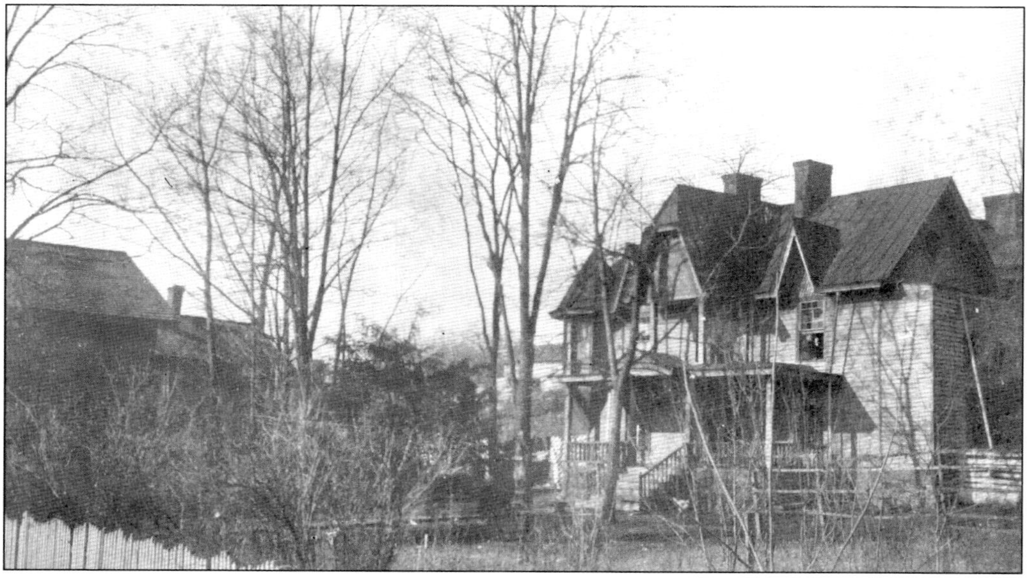

Isaac Bailey was a Civil War veteran who served in the 58th North Carolina Infantry. After the war, Bailey returned home, opened a sawmill and lumberyard in Penland, and built this fine house for his family. The house was located on Main Street (Mitchell Avenue) where the house of Dr. Arthur Gouge (now a bed and breakfast) stands. This photograph dates to 1878. (North Carolina Collection, UNC Library at Chapel Hill.)

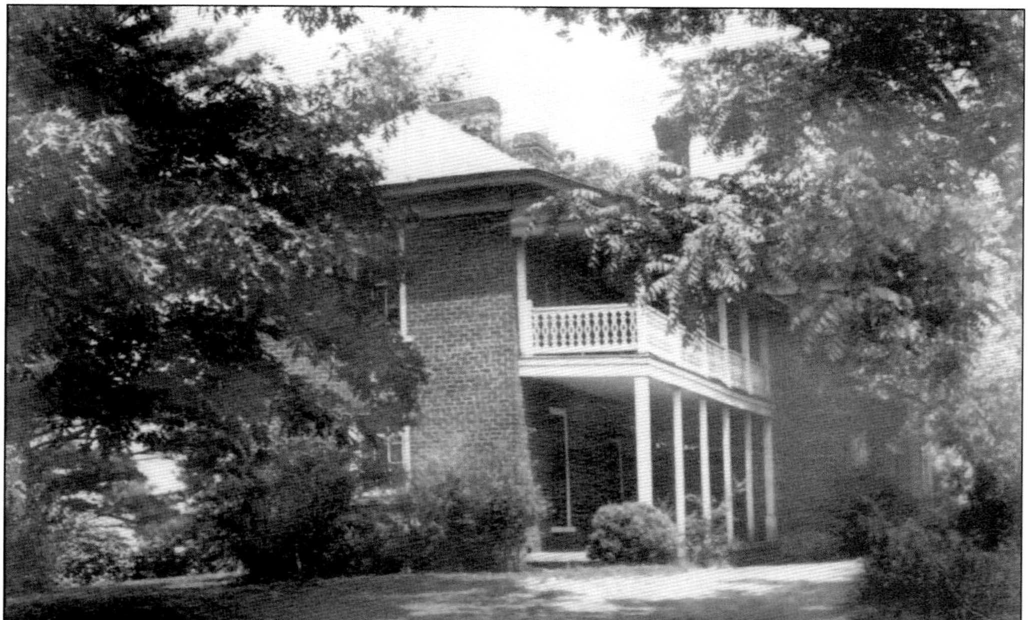

The Green-Sharpe house was constructed around 1875 by Thomas Carlton Green. Green was a Civil War veteran who was a pioneer in mica mining. Green's Cloudland Mine, near Clarissa, was one of the first successful commercial mica mines in Mitchell. The house later passed to Ed and Beatrice Sharpe in the 1930s, when this photograph was taken. (Eddie Sharpe.)

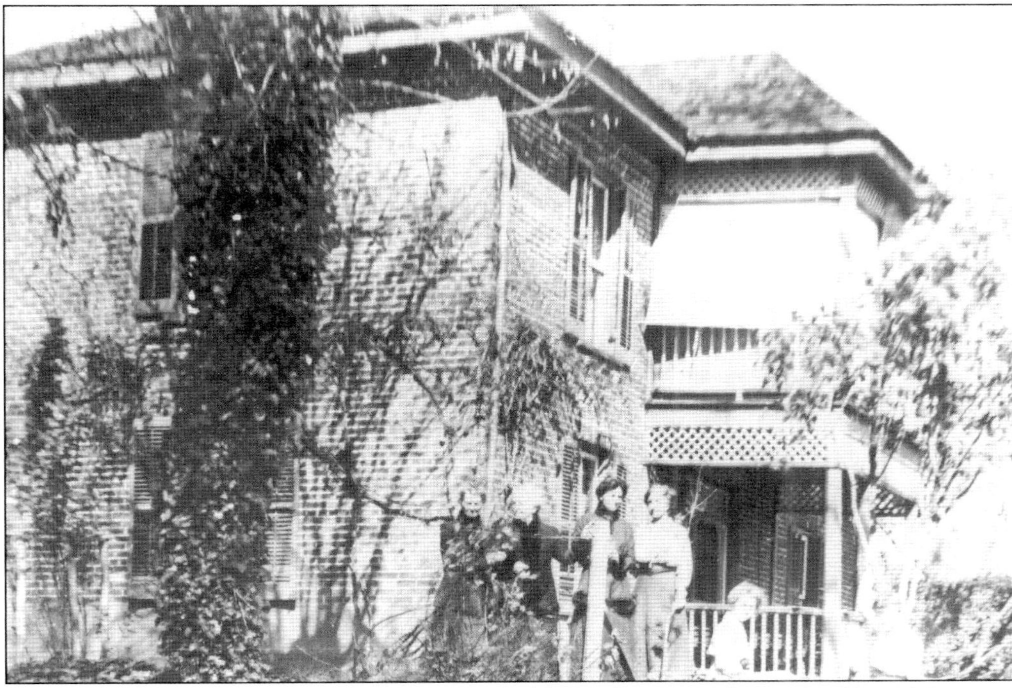

The Gudger House was located just west of the old courthouse on the road to Roan Mountain. Built in 1880 by businessman John Gudger, the story goes that Gudger's fiancé would not consent to marriage until he built her a fine house modeled after the Green-Sharpe House. The Gudger House became a boardinghouse in the 1920s, when this photograph was taken. The house is a private residence today. (George Morgan.)

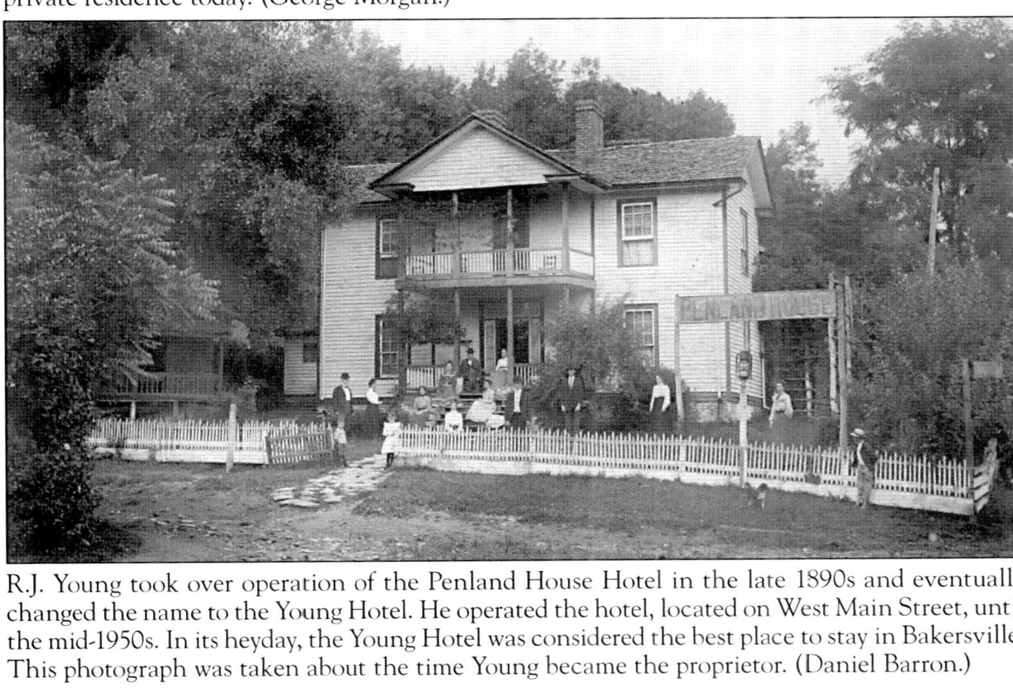

R.J. Young took over operation of the Penland House Hotel in the late 1890s and eventually changed the name to the Young Hotel. He operated the hotel, located on West Main Street, until the mid-1950s. In its heyday, the Young Hotel was considered the best place to stay in Bakersville. This photograph was taken about the time Young became the proprietor. (Daniel Barron.)

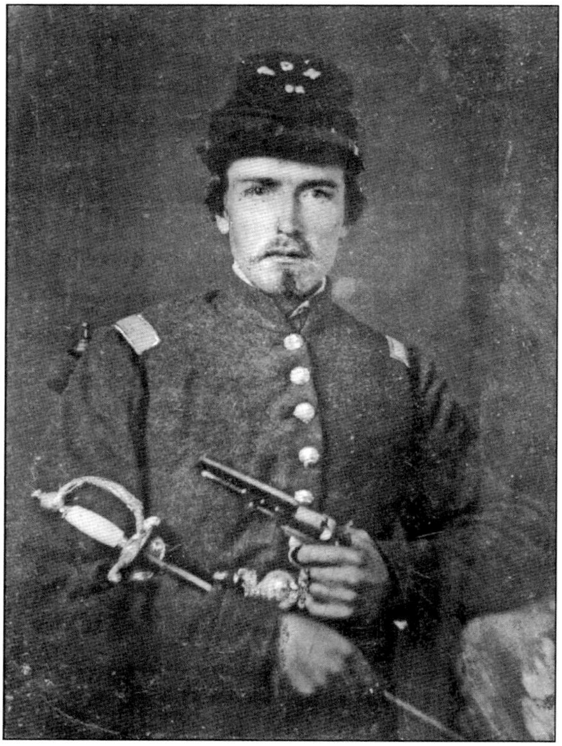

David Mack Young, from Bakersville, served in the 29th North Carolina Infantry as a captain during the Civil War. After the war, Young entered politics and was sent to Raleigh as a state representative. After his death, Young was laid to rest in the Green Young Cemetery. (Mark McKinney.)

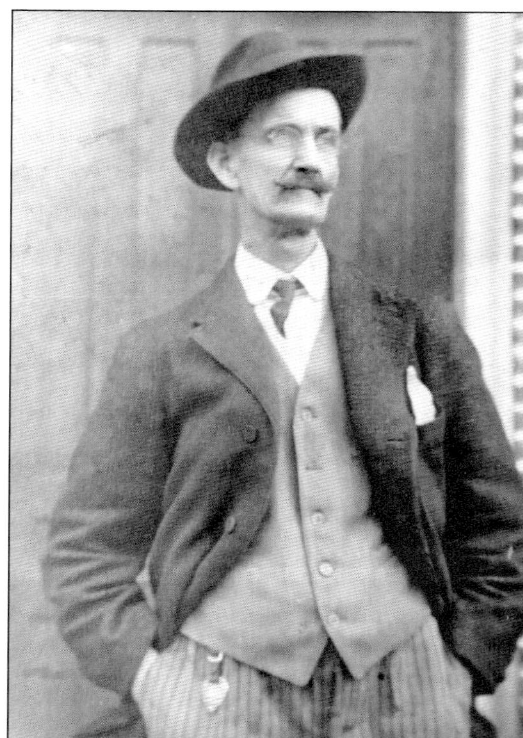

J.B. Craigmiles came to Bakersville from the area of Brevard in 1914. Craigmiles was the founder and editor of the *Mitchell County Banner*. The *Banner* was the newspaper of record for Mitchell County. As of 1918, the *Banner* had a circulation of 800 and continued publishing until 1936. Craigmiles also served as a justice of the peace. This photograph was probably taken during the 1920s. (Photograph by Jim Jones; private donor.)

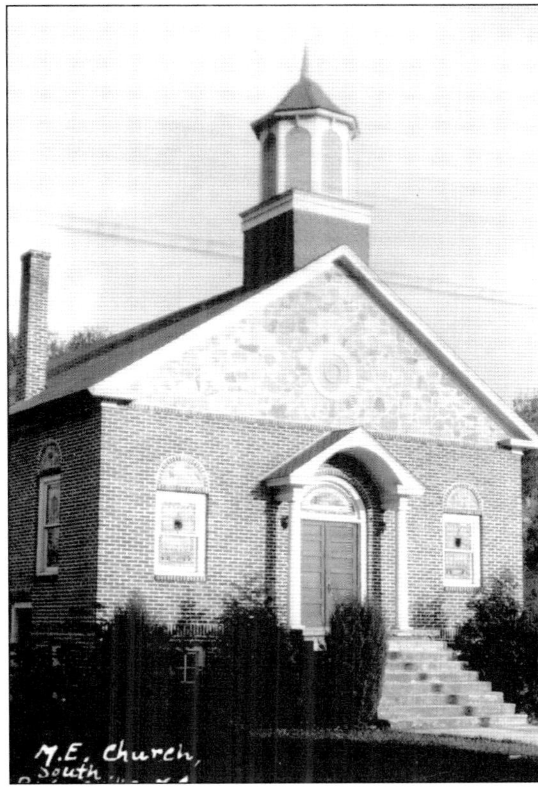

This photograph shows the Southern Methodist or Methodist Episcopal Church, located just south of Cane Creek on South Mitchell Avenue. This photograph dates to the late 1930s. Bakersville also had Northern Methodist Church, located just west of town on the road to Roan Mountain. These two Methodist branches merged in 1939. (Photograph by Jim Jones; private donor.)

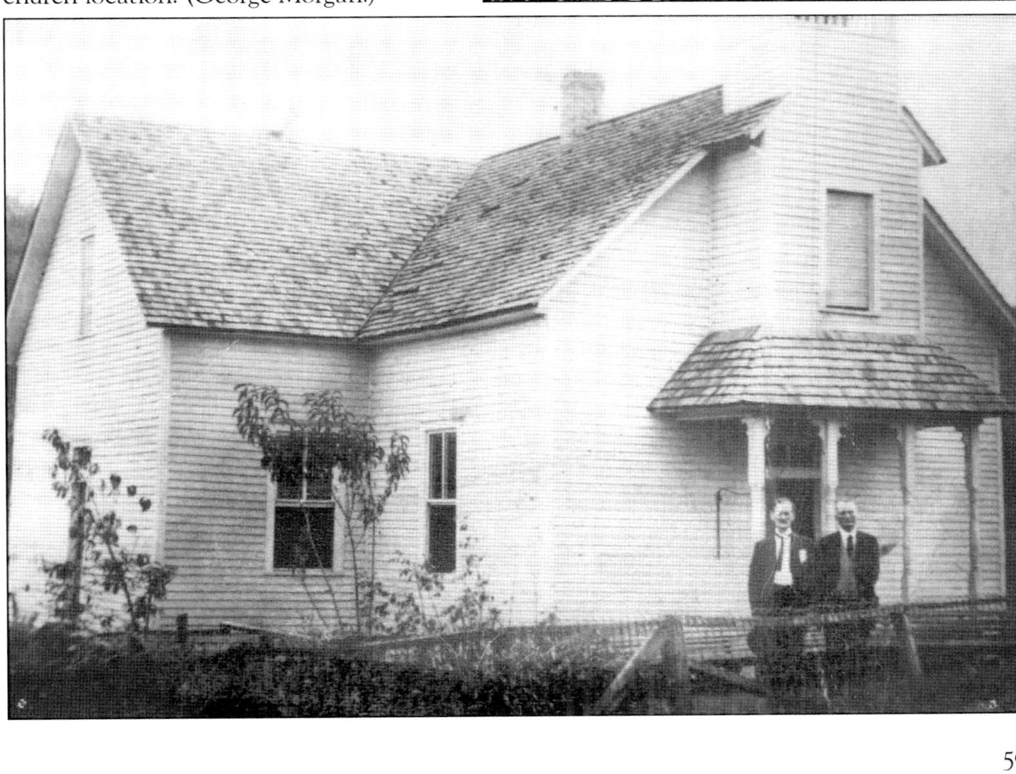

Bakersville Baptist Church was founded in 1869, and the congregation erected its first building about 10 years later. The first building was swept away by the flood of 1901, with the church bell tolling as the building floated away. Shown here is the second structure that was built in 1902 and replaced in 1928 by the present building on South Mitchell Avenue, across the street from the old church location. (George Morgan.)

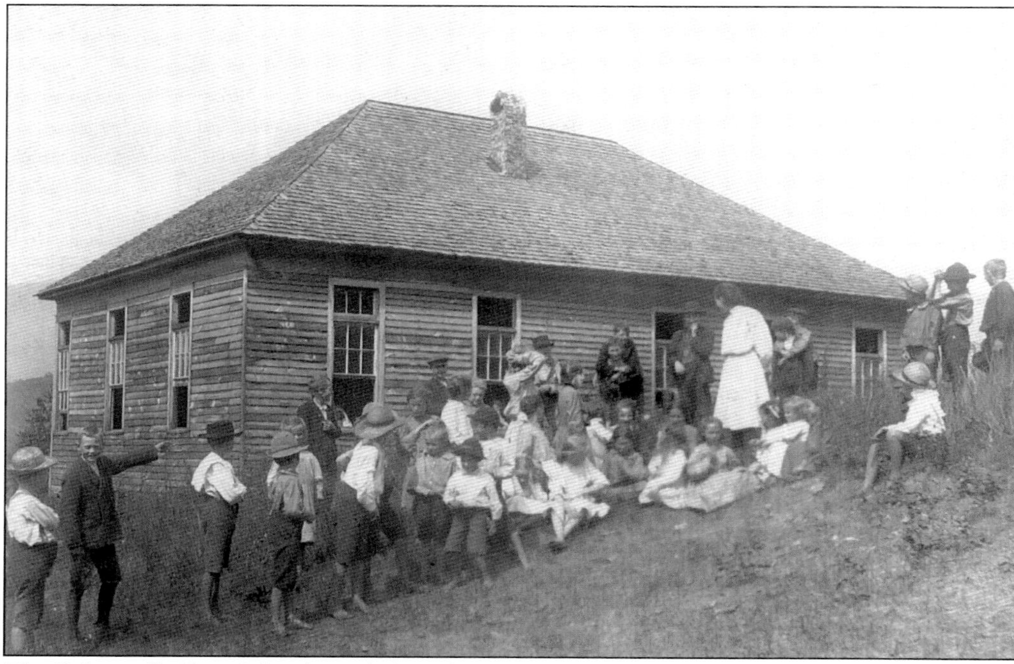

The Bakersville Free School was believed to be located on White Oak Road near Bakersville. It was a private school that did not charge students but did accept donations. This photograph dates from 1908. Some of the school's teachers included Pearl Pritchard, Clara Lambert, and Gene McKinney. (Mitchell Historical Society.)

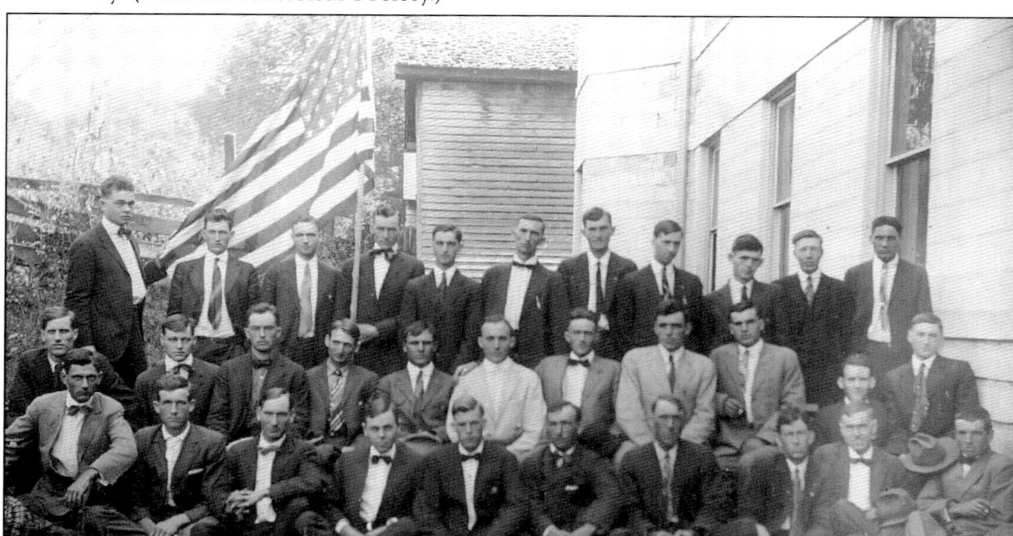

World War I resulted in three drafts of men between the ages 21 and 30. A total of 4.3 million men were mobilized. This 1917 photograph shows a group of patriotic Mitchell County men as they began their journey into military service. This group is believed to consist entirely of volunteers. (Daniel Barron.)

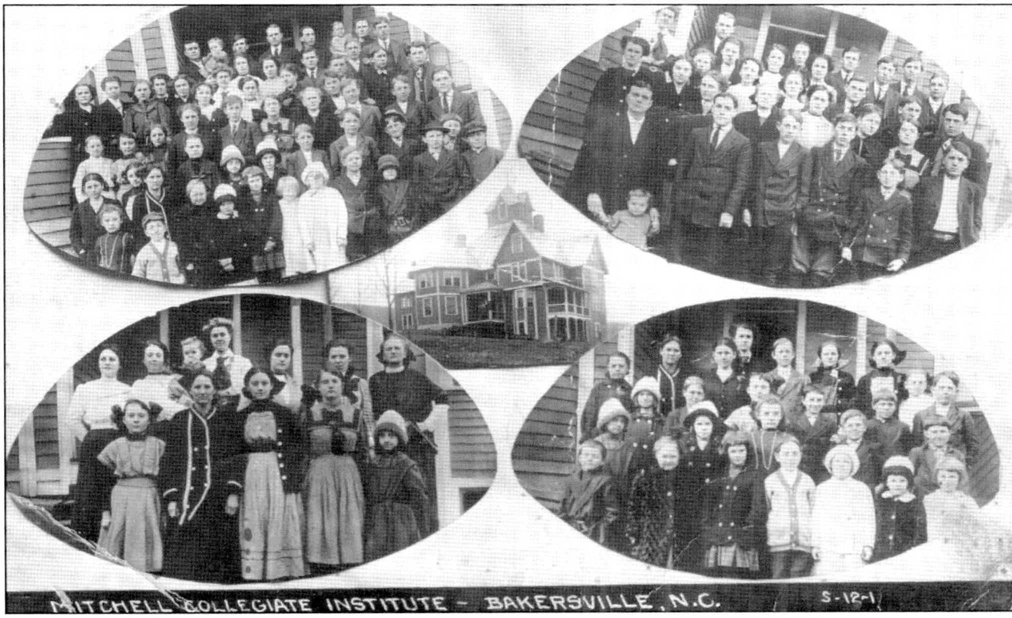

J.C. Bowman founded the Bowman Academy in the 1870s as a private school but gave the school to the Southern Baptist Convention. It continued to run as the Mitchell Collegiate Institute until 1923 when it was sold to the Mitchell County Board of Education. The school was named Bakersville High School, but six years later it was renamed after J.C. Bowman. The above photograph is from a postcard that appears to show the classes of 1901. The 1920s photograph below shows the original buildings. An elementary school building was completed in 1926. Ten years later, in 1936, the old high school building was finally replaced, but it caught fire in 1940 and burned to the ground. Finally, in 1942, a stone building was completed that housed all grades. (Above, Wayne Ledford; below, photograph by Jim Jones; private donor.)

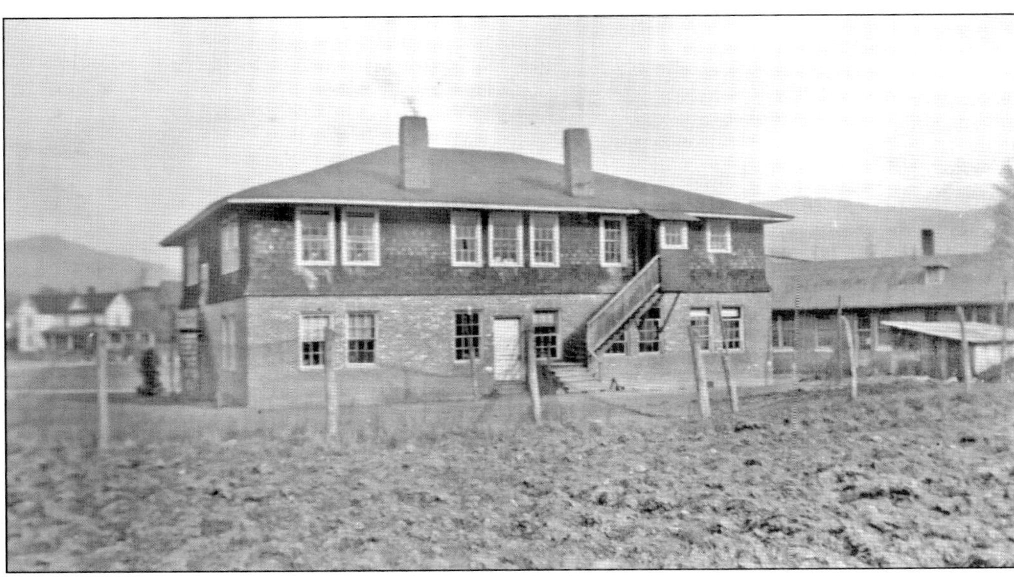

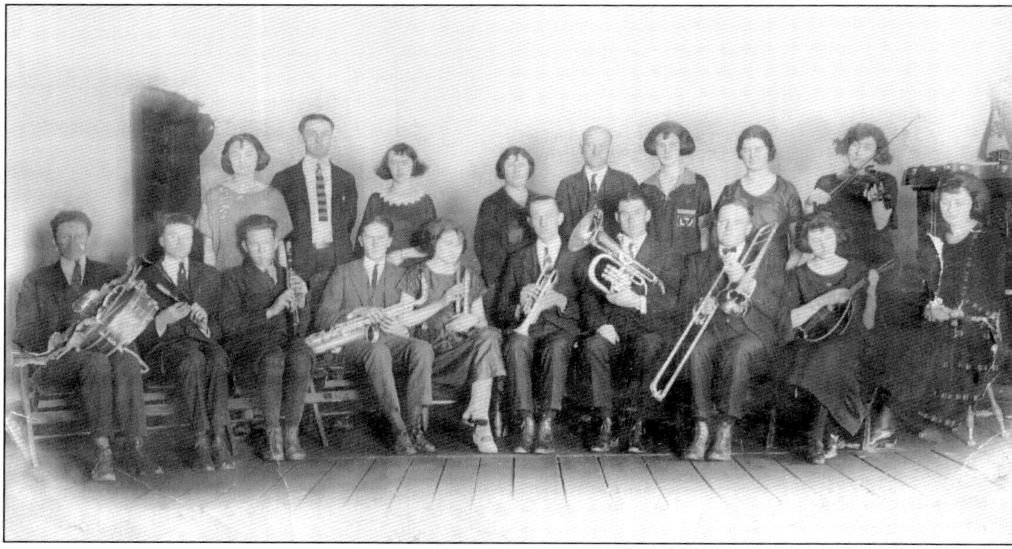

The first graduating class of Bakersville High School was in 1924. There were seven proud recipients of high school diplomas. Even though there was a small student body, Bakersville students participated in a wide variety of student activities and even published a yearbook. This photograph shows the members of the glee club and orchestra. Unfortunately, the yearbook does not disclose the names of the participants. (Carolyn Townsend.)

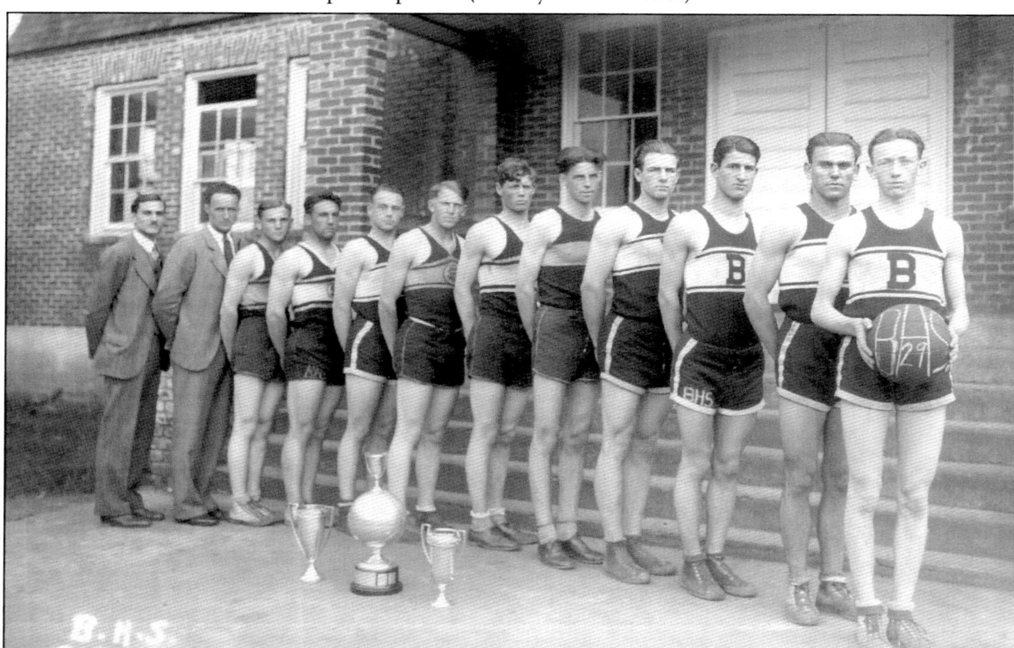

This photograph shows the Bowman High School basketball team from 1929. Seen from left to right are school principal Jamel L. Burnette, coach Essie Gouge, Frank Phillips, Lou Hughes, Lane Wilson, Audie Silvers, Ray Wilson, Harry Phillips, Harry Greene, Fred Stanley, Richard Baker, and George Willis. Two years later, the 1931 team won the North Carolina Class B State Championship. (George Morgan.)

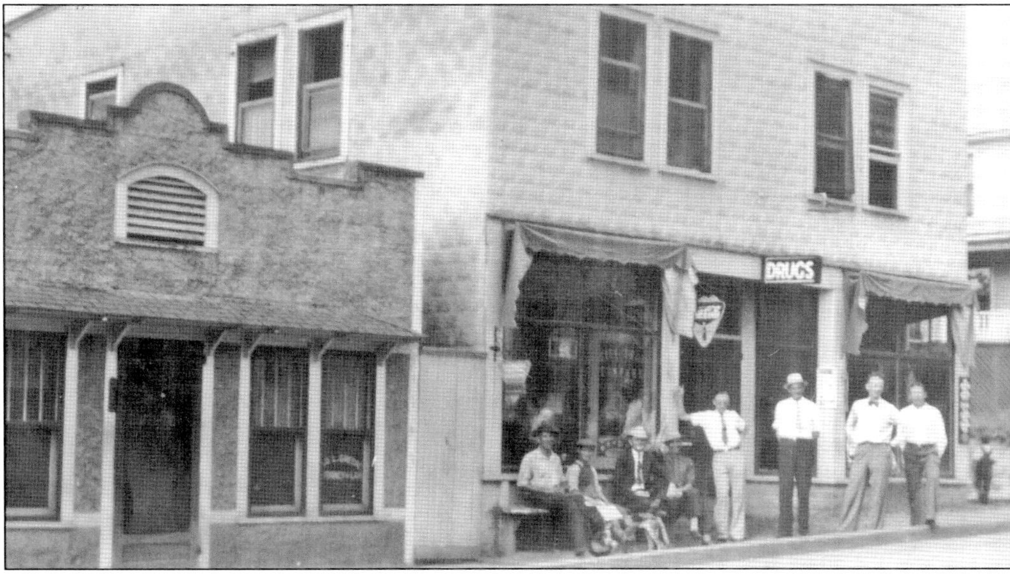

After the fire of 1923, Frank Greene moved the City Drug Company next door to the brand new Greene Building. He eventually hired Charles Richard Vinson to run the establishment. Vinson received his pharmaceutical licensure after attending two years of professional college in Miami, Florida, in the early 1930's. He served as Bakersville's pharmacist for over 30 years. Around 1940, Vinson purchased the business and moved it to a location on West Main Street. Pictured above is the Greene Building and the City Drug Company in the early 1930s. Below is the inside of the City Drug Company as it appeared in the late 1930s. Vinson is on the left and photographer Jim Jones is on the right. The name of the woman is unknown. (Above, Daniel Baron; below, George Morgan.)

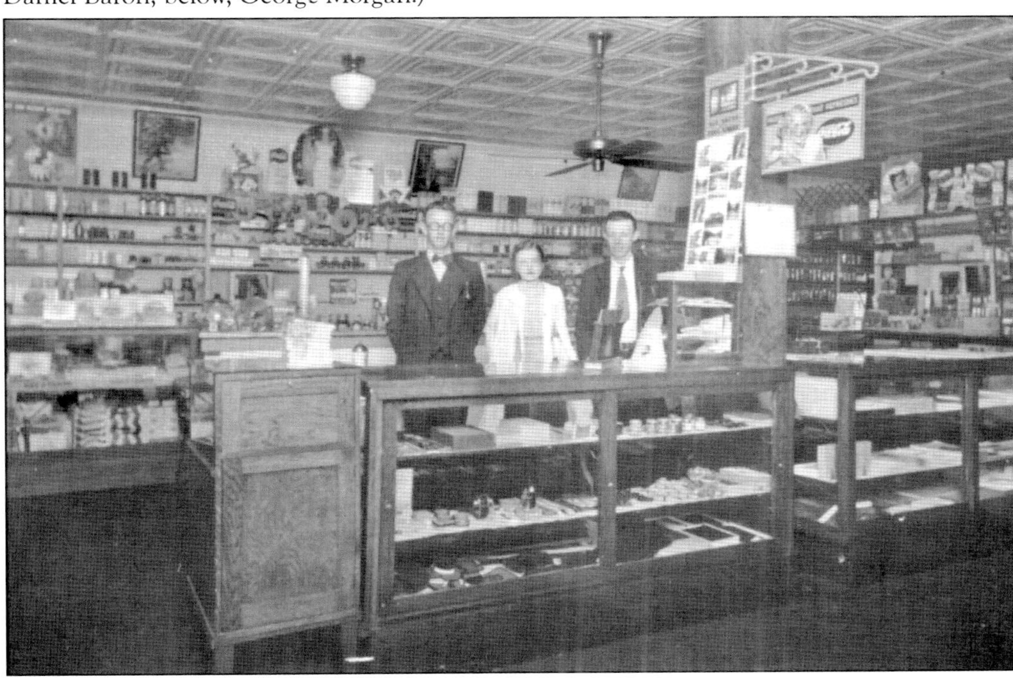

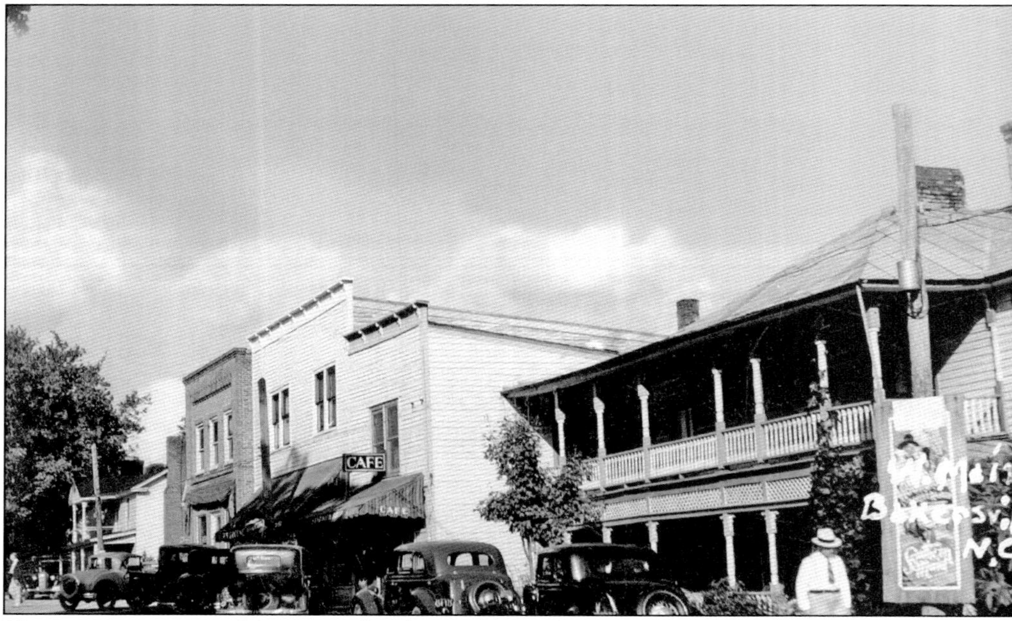

Here is a great view of the east side of Main Street (Mitchell Avenue) as it looked in the 1930s. On the far right is Blevins's boardinghouse. Next is White's Café, owned by Mack White. To the left is the Green Store, which sold general merchandise. The solid-looking brick building next door was the Merchants and Farmers Bank. (Photograph by Jim Jones; private donor.)

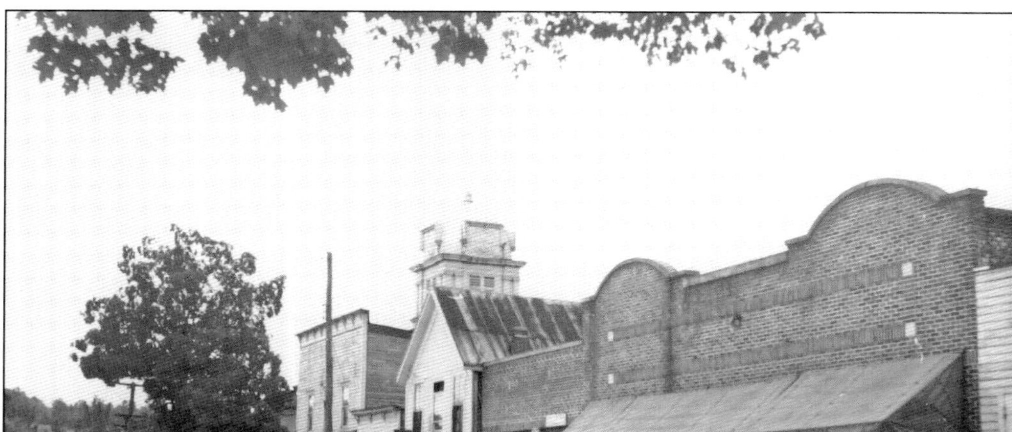

This photograph of the west side of Main Street is also from the 1930s. From left to right is George Young's store, Bowman's Barber Shop, a café, the Bakersville Post Office, and the general merchandise Hughes Store. Interestingly, Young's store looks very different than it does in the older photograph of West Main Street on page 49. (Photograph by Jim Jones; private donor.)

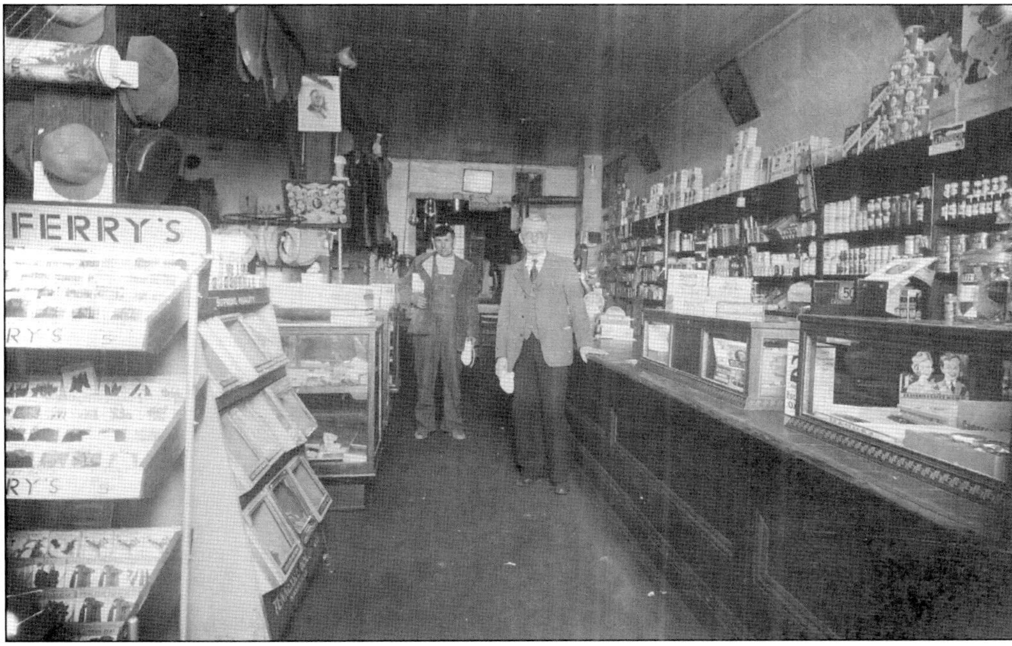

Here is a photograph of George Young with a customer inside his store, probably from the late 1930s. Young's store was a fixture in Bakersville for almost 50 years. As seen in the photograph, the store was filled with all sorts of merchandise and groceries. Young operated his business well into the 1950s. (Daniel Barron.)

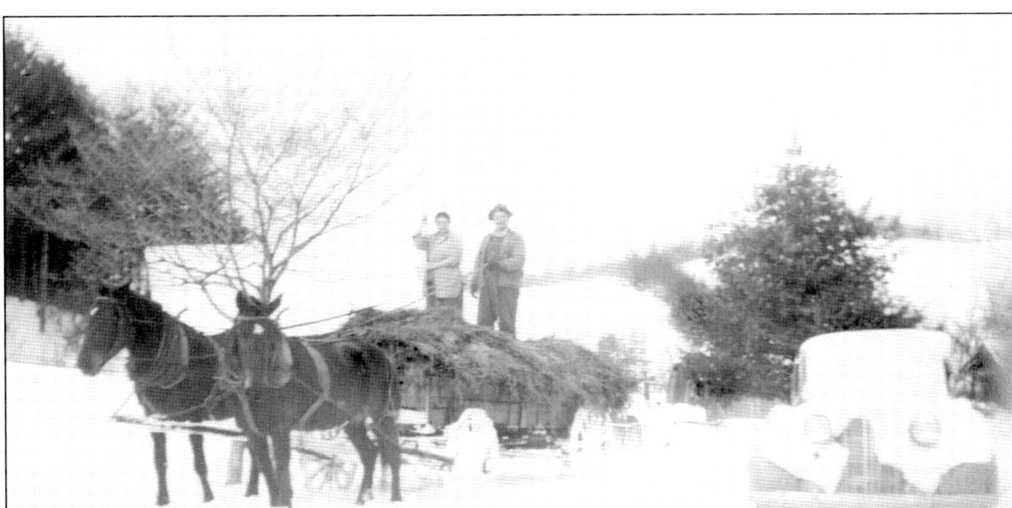

Bob Hughes had a farm at the head of White Oak Road during the 1940s. This photograph was taken during the winter of 1942 and shows Hughes and his sister Beatrice Sharpe as they prepare to fork hay for the cattle on the farm. The Sharpe family lived in Bakersville but was left snowbound by the heavy drifts. (Eddie Sharpe.)

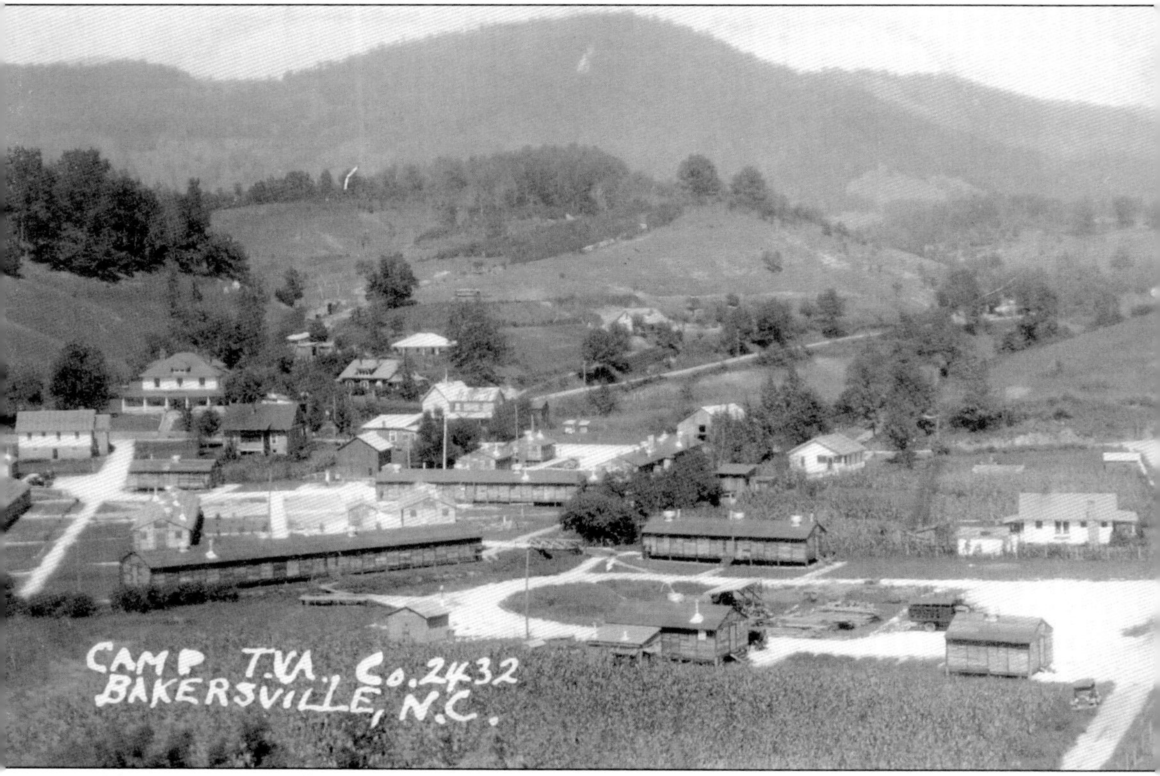

The Tennessee Valley Authority (TVA), was created by the Roosevelt administration to bring electricity and modern improvements to a large area of the American Southeast. This photograph from the 1930s is identified as Company 2432. Maple Street is on the right. In addition to bringing electricity to rural areas, the TVA taught farmers ways to improve crop yields, helped replant trees, and improved habitats for fish and wildlife. They sponsored demonstration farms, and work crews helped improve local conditions. While the TVA was responsible for the displacement of more than 15,000 residents and was controversial for years, Mitchell County benefited greatly from the government assistance. (Photograph by Jim Jones; private donor.)

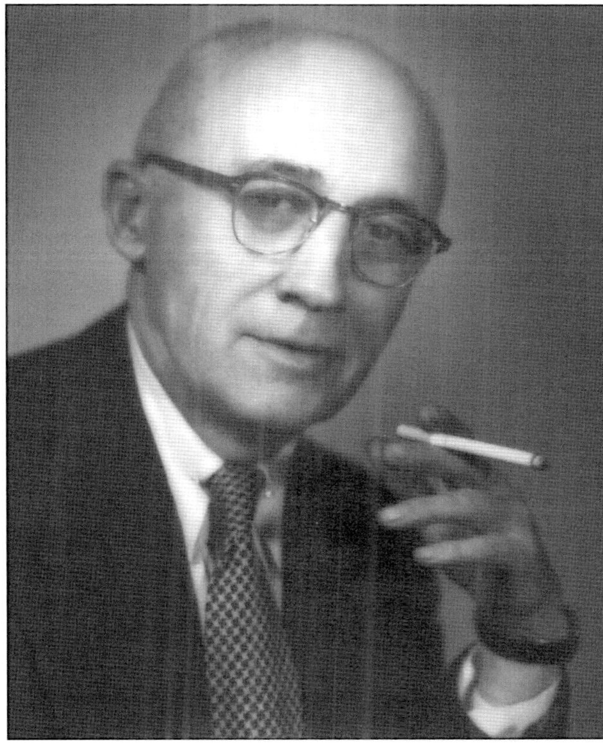

Dr. Arthur Gouge and his wife, Ruby Sisk Gouge, were fixtures of the Bakersville community for more than 50 years. Gouge, right, began his practice on horseback in 1919 and retired in 1969. During his 50 years in practice, he was the family doctor for most of the town. He delivered more than 4,000 babies in Mitchell County and also served as county medical examiner. Ruby Gouge, below, was an educator and school administrator in Mitchell County for more than 40 years. Gouge Elementary School is named in her honor. She also helped found the Mitchell County Library. (Both, George Morgan.)

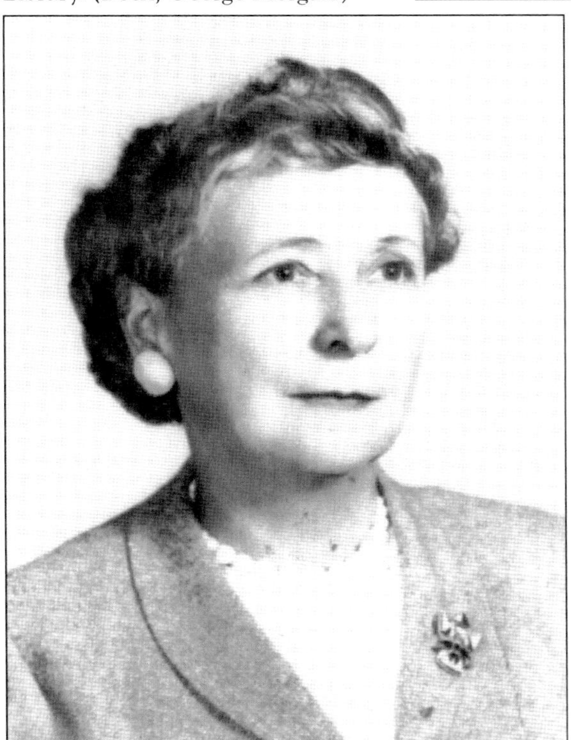

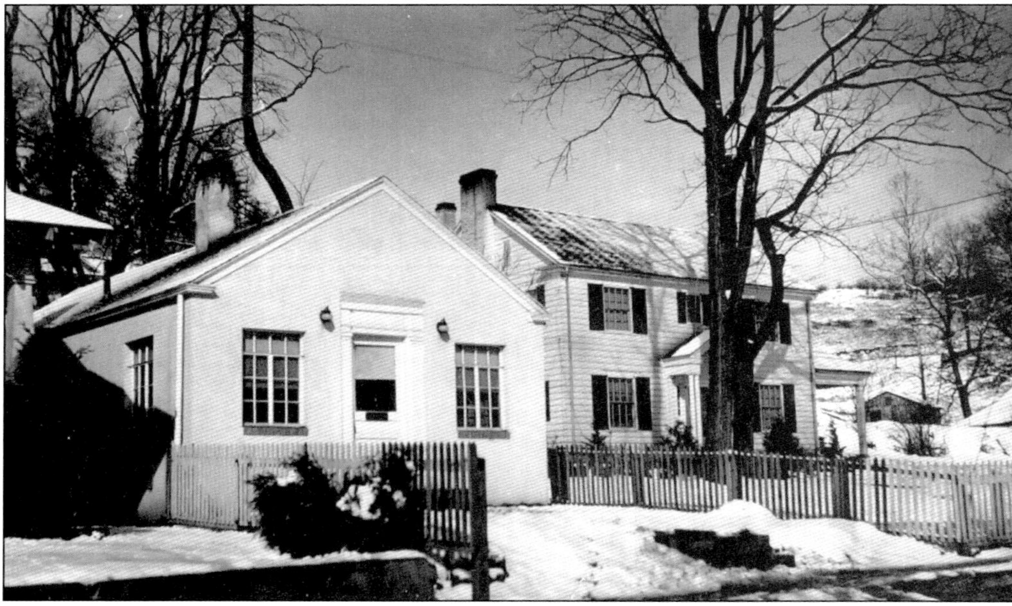

The above photograph shows the office of Dr. Arthur Gouge and the house that was built by he and his wife, Ruby, in 1924. The office was the center of medical activity in Bakersville for 35 years. Upon his retirement, Gouge donated his equipment to the Bakersville Community Health Center. (Photograph by Jim Jones; private donor.)

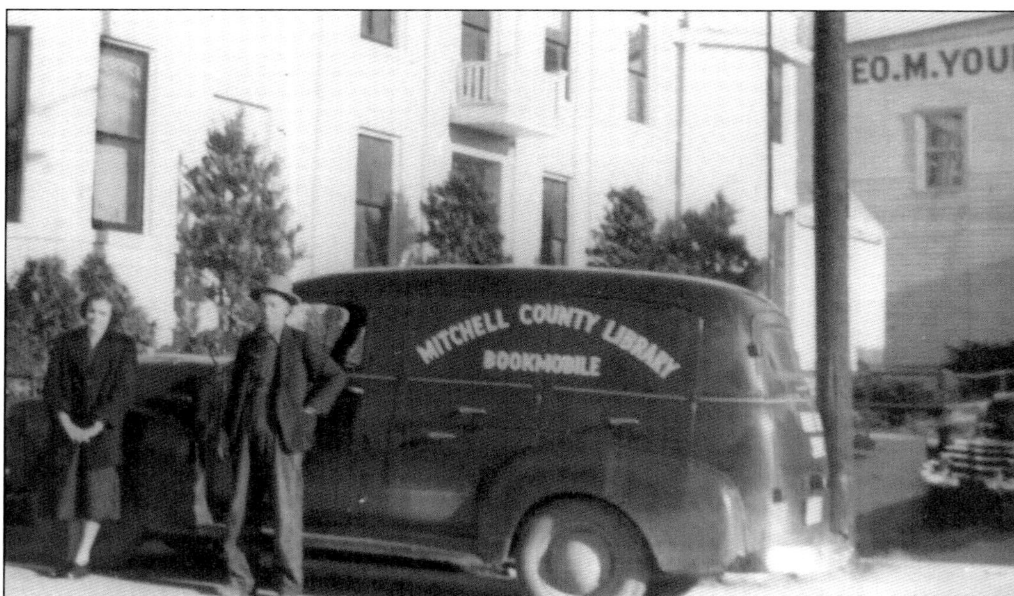

The Mitchell County Public Library was founded in 1948, but did not have a permanent home in the beginning. As a temporary solution, the North Carolina State Library in Raleigh purchased a vehicle that was converted into a bookmobile. In this c. 1952 photograph are Dorothy Lee Anderson, the second librarian, and an unidentified man standing. Anderson drove all around Mitchell County delivering books two days a week. (Daniel Barron.)

Five

Loafers Glory and Toecane

The building of the Carolina, Clinchfield & Ohio Railway (CC&O) through Mitchell County led to the establishment of the Toecane community. Located near the junction of Toe River and Cane Creek, Toecane was the nearest depot to Bakersville. Built largely upon land originally owned by William Johnson, Toecane became a thriving community in the early 20th century after Johnson donated land to the Clinchfield Railroad to build the depot. Toecane sported as many as nine stores, two hotels, several restaurants, Frank Canipe's movie house, and a Baptist church. It is said that the population of Toecane, at its height, exceeded 300 people. Almost all passengers and commerce bound for Bakersville passed through here. Local merchants realized large profits from the buying and shipping of wood and other products.

Loafers Glory is less than a mile from Toecane. Originally called Vian's Valley, the new name was inspired, around 1900, by the sight of several local farmers resting on a bench in front of Nathan Deyton and Joe Wilson's country store as the sun went down. According to one version, Jonathon Burleson, himself a farmer, passed by and commented, "This is just a loafer's glory."

Never a large community, Loafers Glory was the home of a bobbin mill that manufactured wooden bobbins for textile factories. It was also the final location for Bill Master's mill, a prominent gristmill, which ground both wheat and corn.

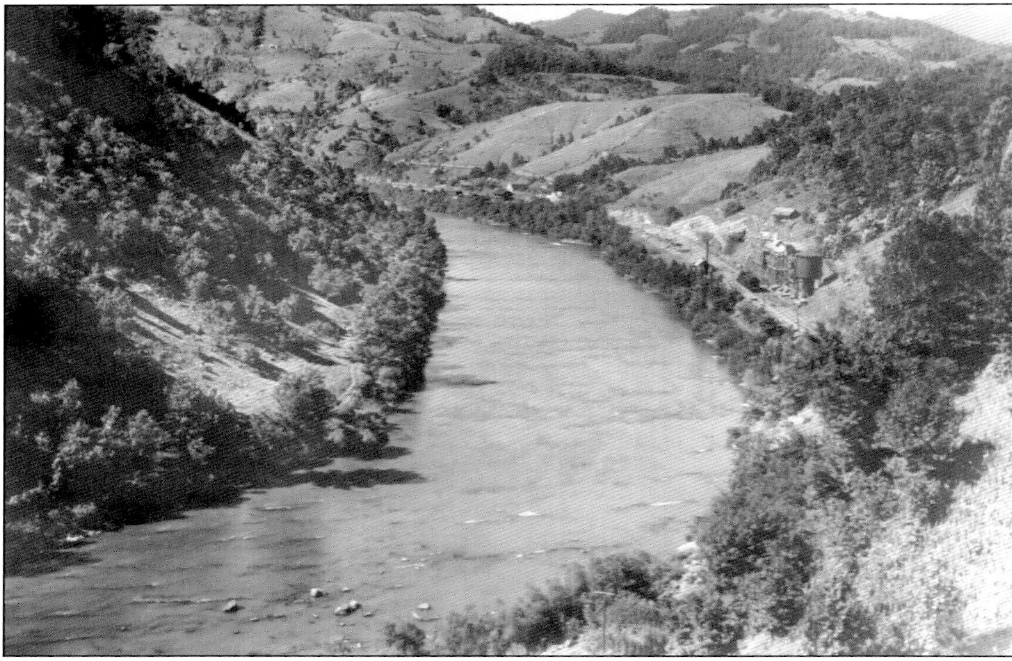

This photograph shows Toecane in the early 20th century. At the right, along the tracks, is a steam engine under the coal tipple and water tank that was operated by Lat Callahan. The depot can be seen to the left of the tracks with homes, hotels, and shops across the tracks. (Appalachia Archives, ETSU, James Goforth Collection.)

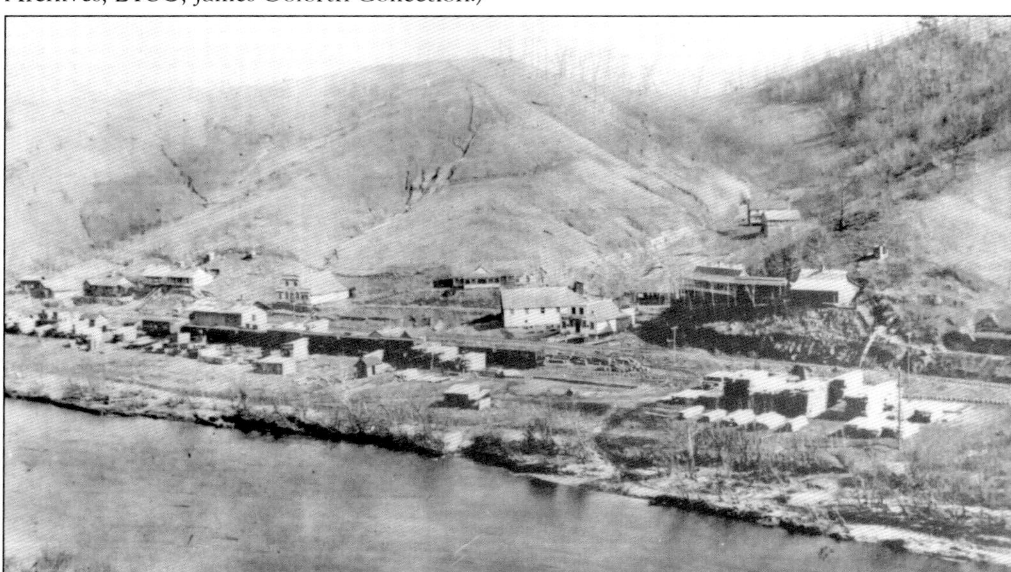

This photograph shows the Toecane riverfront as the town began to show signs of development around 1910. The railroad depot can be seen, as well as a number of stores and other structures. The building that became the Garvin Hotel after renovation can be seen behind the depot. The connected buildings on the right are the residence of William Johnson, founder of Toecane. (John Burn.)

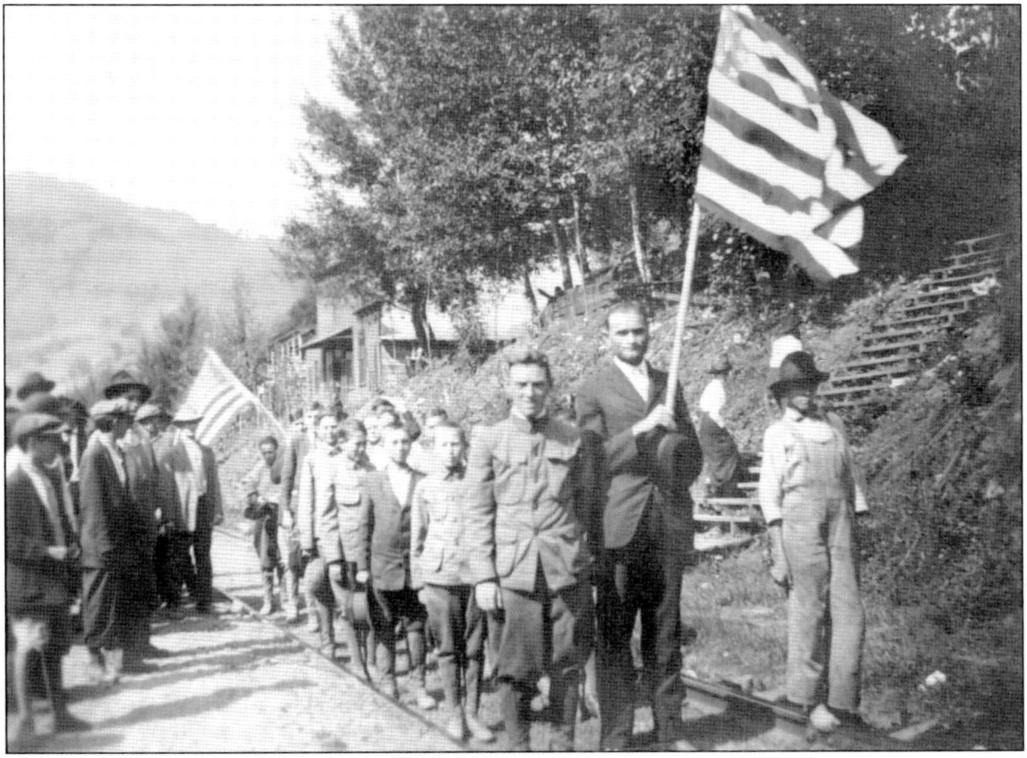

The celebration of the ending of the Great War was a major event across North America and Europe. This photograph from 1920 shows an Armistice Day event on the Clinchfield tracks in the center of Toecane. Townspeople watch as a group of uniformed young men, possibly Boy Scouts, pass by. In the background are a pair of women climbing the steps to the Garvin Hotel. (Photograph by Jim Jones; private donor.)

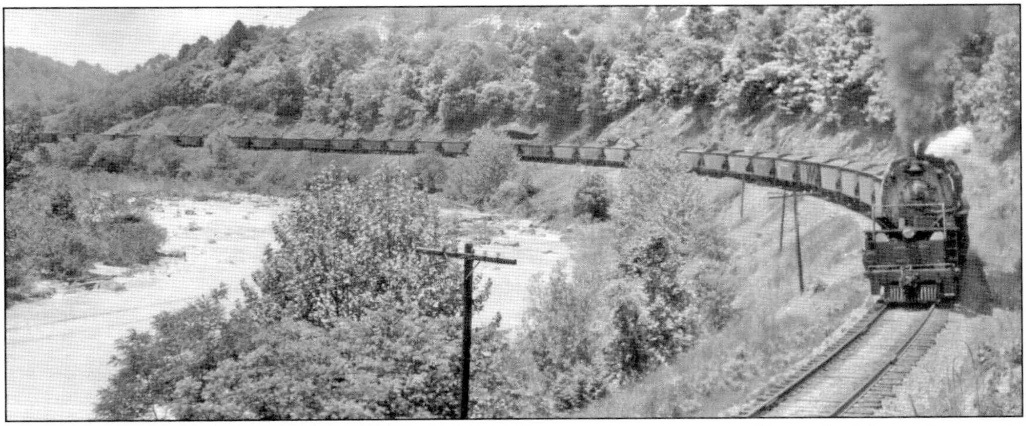

A Carolina, Clinchfield & Ohio Railway (CC&O) steam locomotive pulling a freight train travels alongside the Toe River near Toecane. The CC&O line was a primary route for the transportation of Appalachian coal to the Southern states. In addition to coal, the railroad supplied freight and building supplies to the relatively isolated mountain communities that were not yet served by good roads. This photograph from 1950 shows a CC&O locomotive pulling a line of coal cars alongside the Toe River (John Burn.)

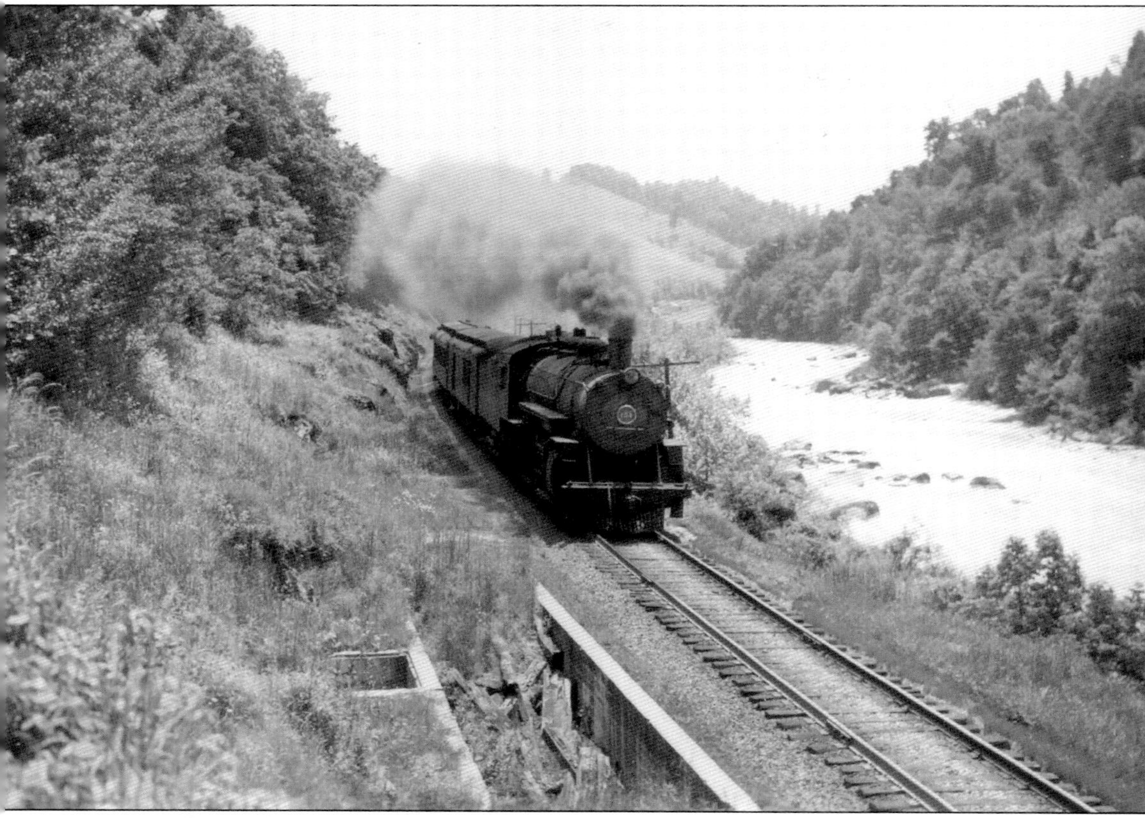

A Carolina, Clinchfield & Ohio Railway (CC&O) steam locomotive travels alongside the Toe River toward Toecane. The line that became the Clinchfield was a successor to several railroads—notably the South and Western Railroad that had completed tracks from Cincinnati, Ohio, to Spruce Pine, North Carolina, in 1905. In 1915, the CC&O was finally complete from Cincinnati to Spartanburg, South Carolina. The Clinchfield made numerous stops in Mitchell County and offered an economical and easy way to travel across a region lacking paved roads. At least two passenger trains a day made scheduled stops in Toecane until the mid-1950s. Northern Mitchell County residents could easily spend the day experiencing the amenities of towns like Marion and Spruce Pine. Johnson City, Tennessee, was a favorite destination for an overnight excursion. Passengers could also easily make connections to Asheville or travel into Tennessee and destinations farther north. (John Burn.)

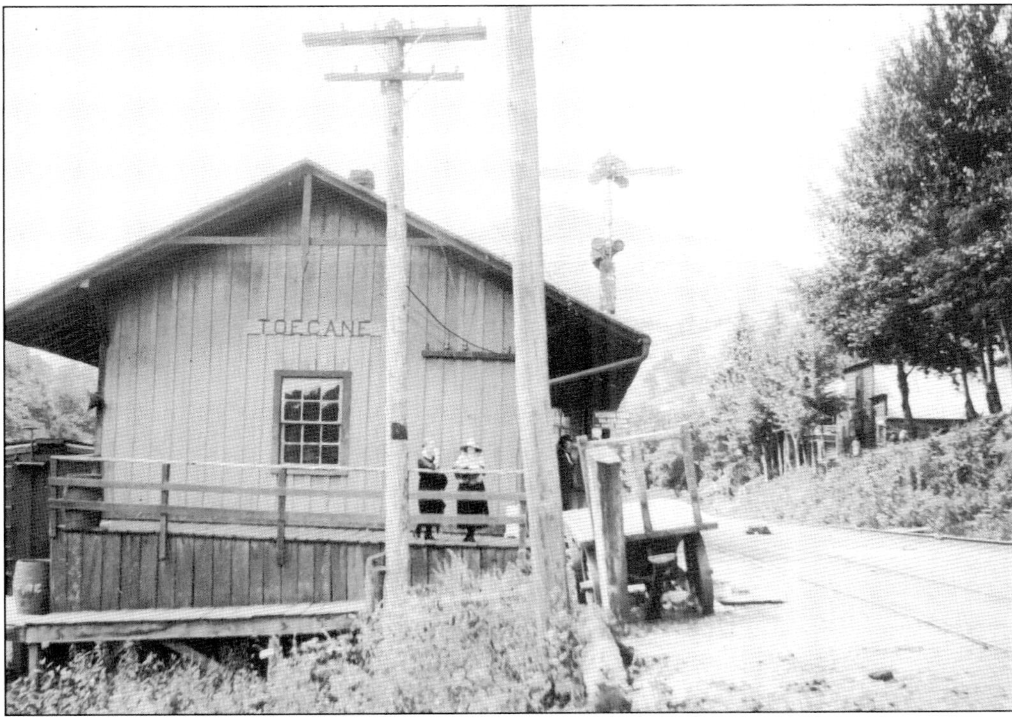

This Clinchfield depot was the center of passenger and freight traffic for northern Mitchell County. During the heyday of Toecane, tons of freight bound for Bakersville and nearby areas arrived regularly, while wood and agricultural products made their way to the outside world. With the development of the automobile and the advent of paved roads, the need for local rail freight diminished. This led to the closing of the Toecane depot. (John Burn.)

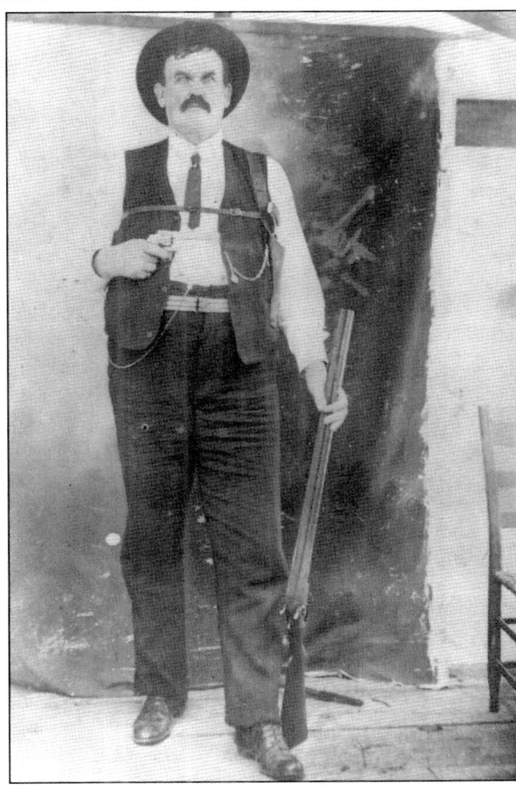

William Johnson is given credit for founding Toecane. In the late 1800s, when Johnson heard about the plans to build the railroad, he agreed to donate land to the Clinchfield line; then it could establish a depot and freight yard in the area that became Toecane. In addition to donating land to the railroad, Johnson sold property to others and operated a store in the early days. (Pam Johnson.)

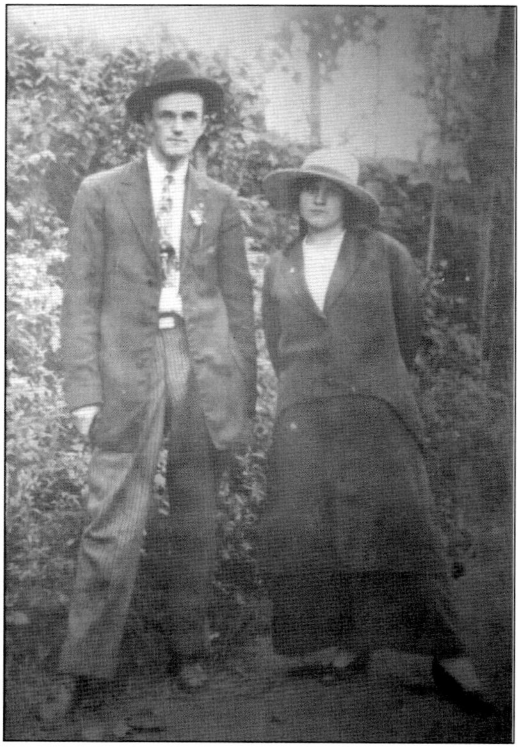

Brown Blevins was a landowner and merchant in Toecane in the days after World War I. Blevins's store was a center of activity in Toecane. Dr. Masters, a dentist, had an office and private entrance on the second floor of the Blevins Building. This photograph shows Blevins with his wife, Molly Deyton Blevins. (George Morgan.)

This automobile bridge across the Toe River was constructed in the early 1950s. It consisted of two bridges that were salvaged from previous locations and formed into a unified span. It replaced a previous span that was washed out by a flood. This bridge has since been replaced by a more modern structure. (George Morgan.)

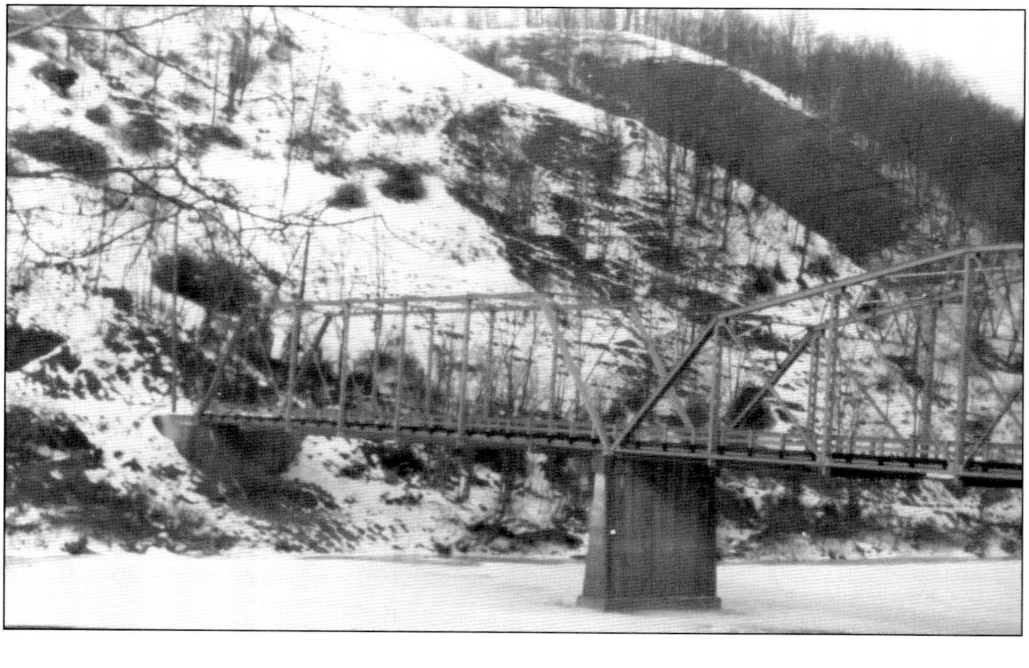

At right is a photograph of William Masters as a young man that is thought to have been taken in West Virginia. He appears quite confident. Masters would go on to open a mill in Toecane and later in Loafers Glory. His mill produced quality wheat flour as well as cornmeal and grits. (Maxie Gouge Buchanan.)

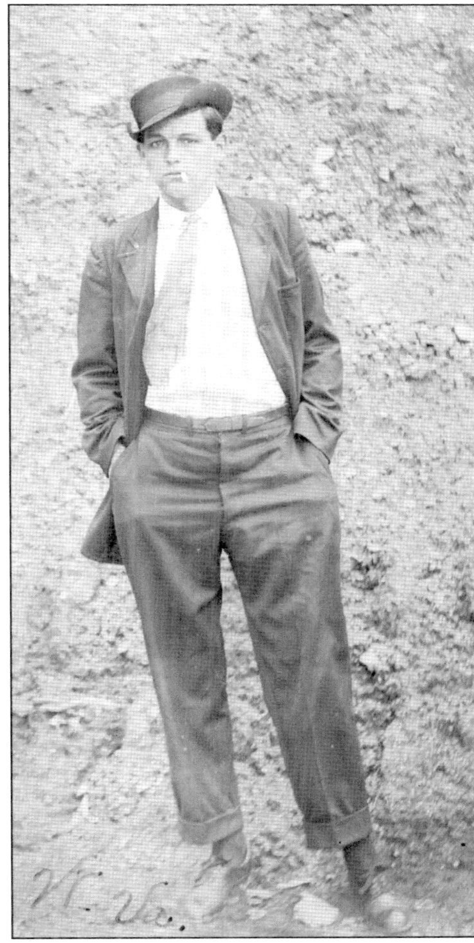

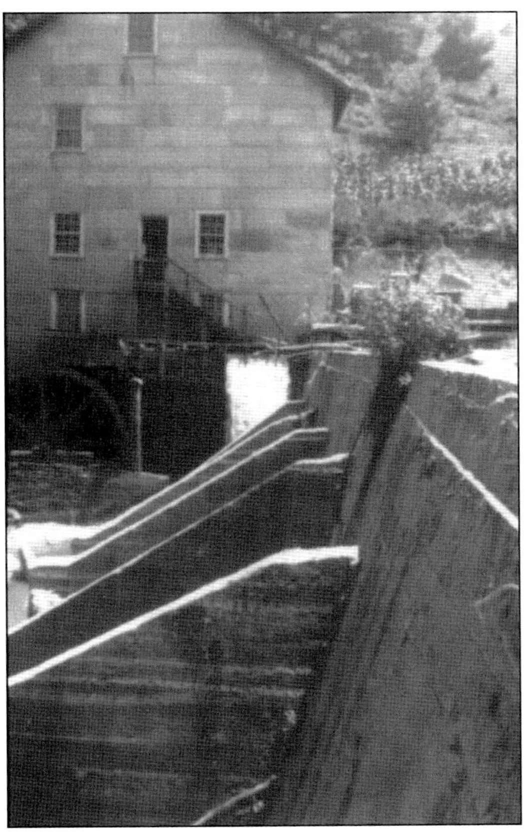

Bill Masters's original mill was near Toecane. However, a fire in the 1930s destroyed the entire structure. Masters moved his mill to Cane Creek near Loafers Glory and built an impressive concrete dam across the creek. He operated his mill at that location for many years. The building that housed the mill, pictured at left, still stands. (George Morgan.)

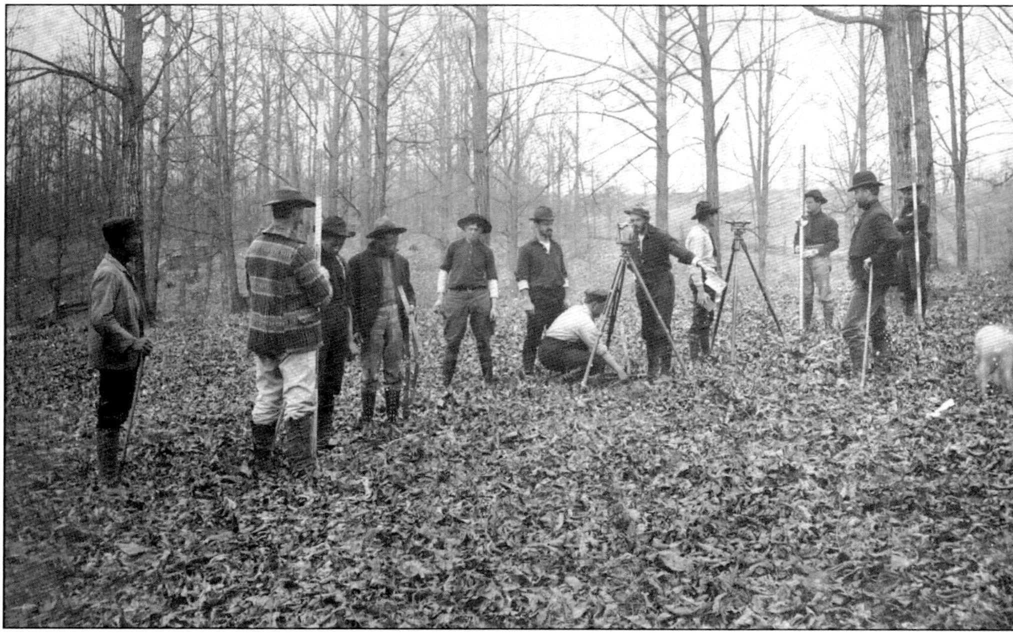

The railroads dreamed of a straight line through from Ohio to South Carolina, and as they began to put dreams into reality, they had to survey the land through which the trains would run. This photograph was taken just east of Toecane near the Toe River. (North Carolina Collection, UNC Library at Chapel Hill.)

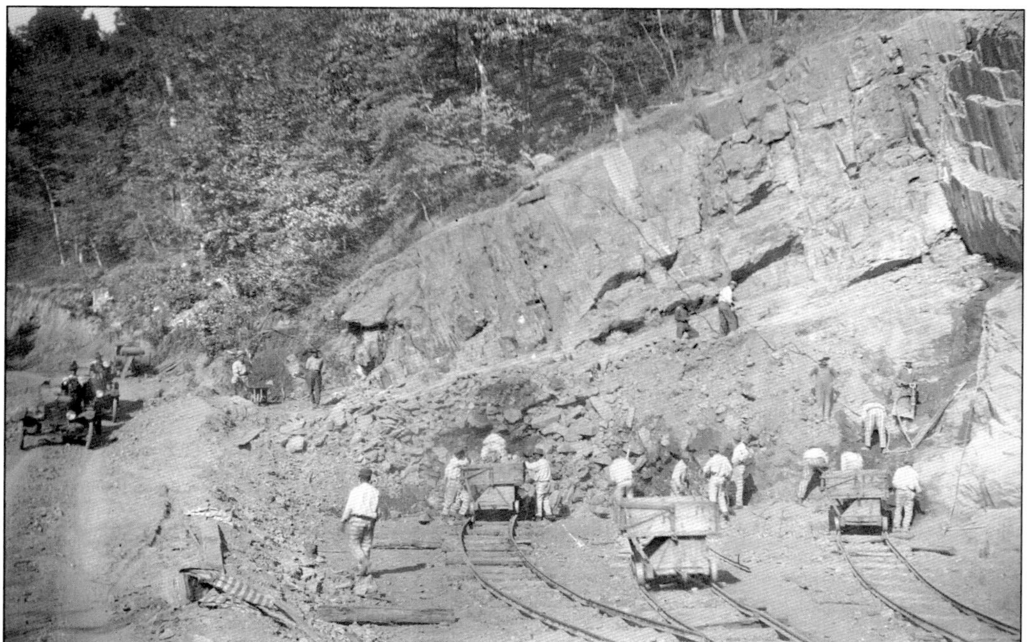

This 1922 photograph shows construction workers and convict laborers as they toil, under primitive conditions, to clear the way for the concrete road from Bakersville to Toecane—the first major road-building project in Mitchell County. (Photograph by Jim Jones; private donor.)

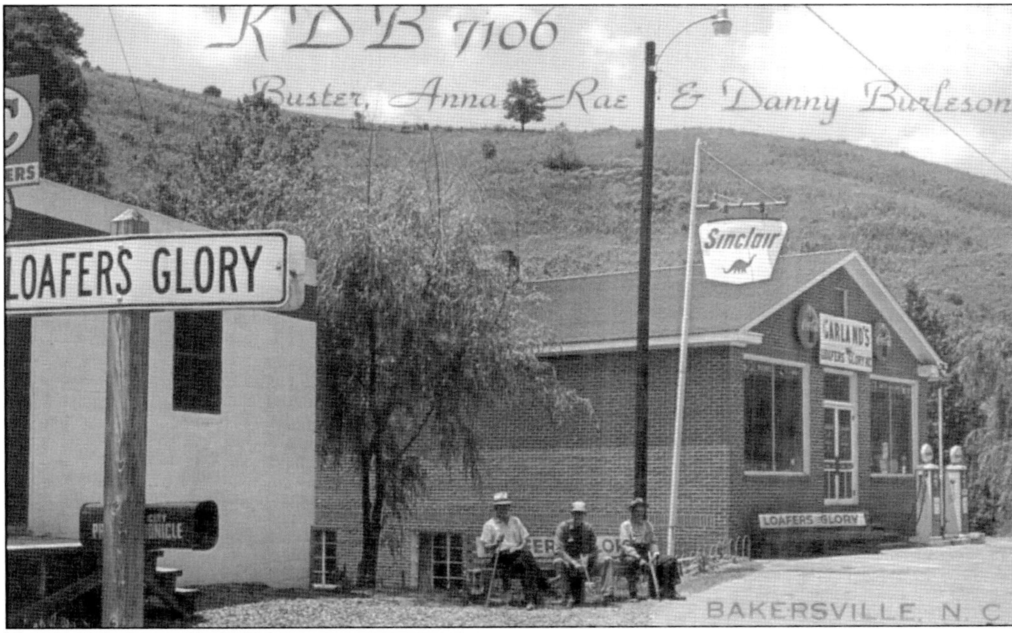

This photograph, originally used for a postcard, shows "downtown" Loafers Glory, complete with three "loafers" on a bench. Downtown Loafers Glory still supports several businesses, but Garland's store has long since closed its doors. (George Morgan.)

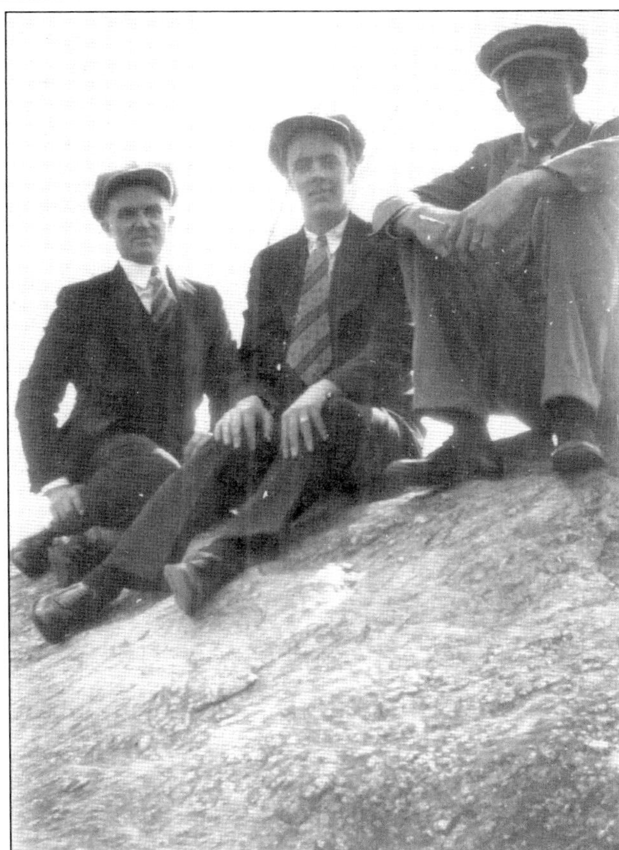

Pictured from left to right are Garfa Griffith, Park Edwards, and Holden Griffith. All three young men became educators, and all three taught in schools throughout northern Mitchell County. While most of the teachers in grammar school were women, by junior high, men were included as faculty. (Gail Bryant Griffith and Scott Griffith.)

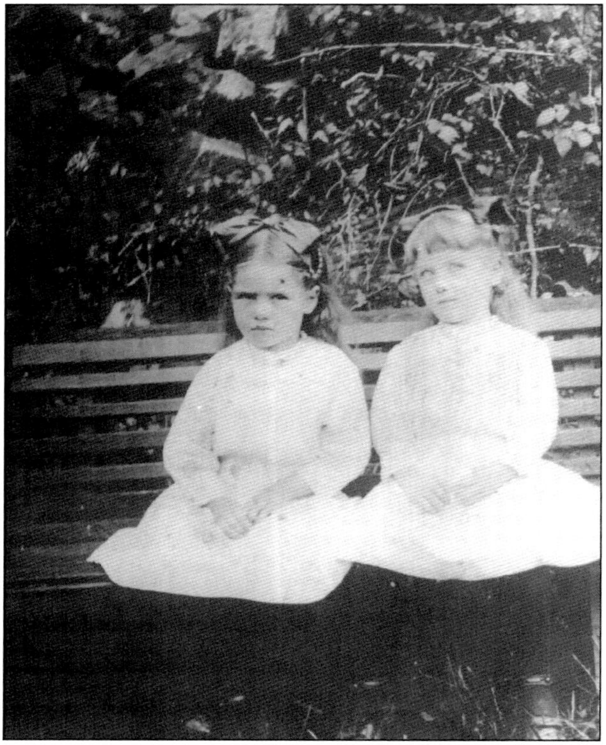

The family of Don and Lidia Bailey lived on Pumpkin Patch Mountain near Loafers Glory. Don was a farmer and rock mason while Lidia served as a midwife and tended to the couple's 15 children. The c. 1920 photograph at left shows the Baileys' twin daughters, Nola (right) and Iola. Nola became ill and passed away at the age of five. The photograph below shows the Baileys' daughter Bertha Bailey Byrd in the 1930s at the age of 23. On the far left of the photograph is a "bee gum," a hollow log transformed by farmers into a man-made beehive. (Both, James Byrd.)

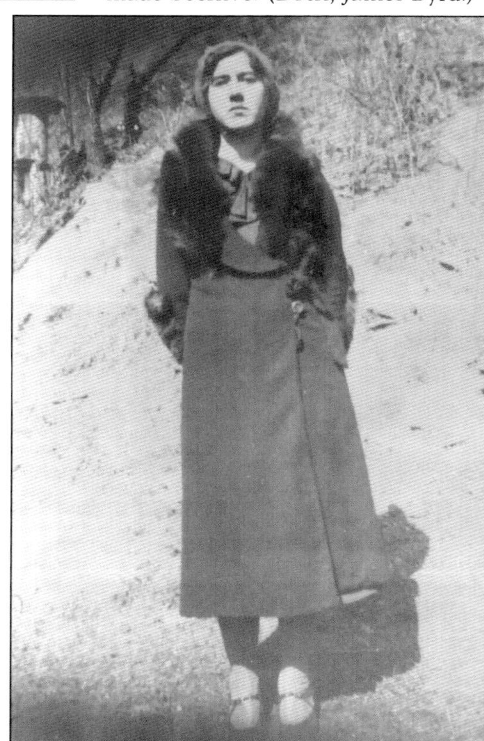

Six

Tipton Hill, Red Hill, Harrell Hill

In the mountains northwest of Bakersville lie the towns of Red Hill, Harrell Hill, and Tipton Hill. Closest to Bakersville, Red Hill was a place where, reputedly, a family over-farmed the area and when excessive rains came, the soil eroded, leaving red clay. Thus, the village became, "Red Hill." Tipton Hill was named after the community's first settler, John Tipton. Harrell Hill was named after the family whose ancestors first settled in the area in the late 1700s.

Post offices dotted the countryside in the days prior to rural mail delivery. They, like country stores, were places to exchange gossip and receive mail. Once mail deliveries were extended to rural routes in the late 1930s, local post offices closed. Later, they were consolidated into larger districts.

Frank Griffith, a local historian, states that the main income crop in his early years in Tipton Hill was tobacco. During the late 1800s, Americans were smoking fewer than 40 cigarettes per year, but with the 1880s invention of the cigarette-making machine, tobacco became a cash crop. By World War II, it was making a good income for some of Mitchell County's tobacco growers.

No discussion of these towns would be complete without acknowledging their extreme support of education. As in all towns in the area, schools were important, but in Tipton Hill, the schools were able to produce doctors, lawyers, and many other professionals. They still claim to have many of the best students.

Churches, too, were critical in these rural areas. Singing schools, Sunday schools, and regular worship services were important social outlets for citizens. In times of travail, the church was a form of support. Besides being social supports and social outlets, churches helped to reinforce the basic values of residents.

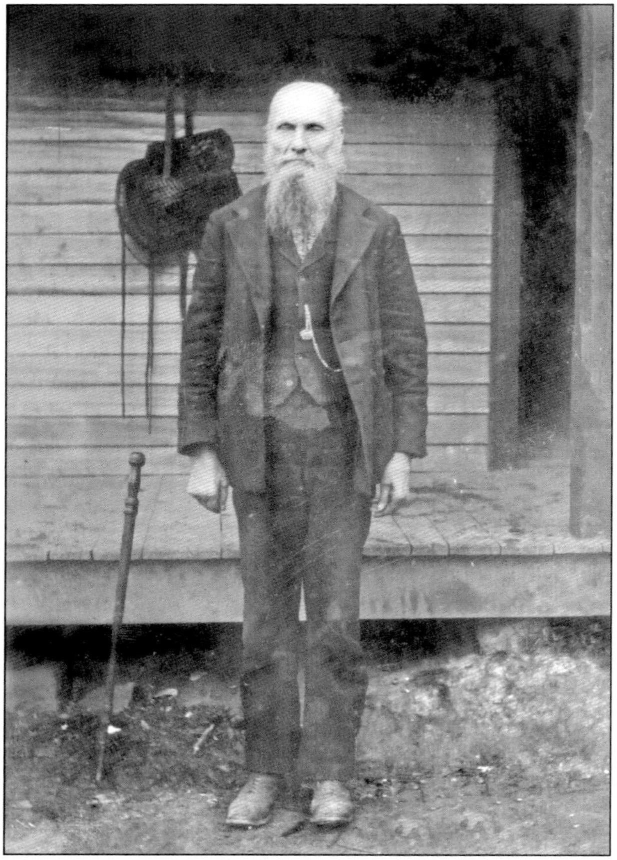

A veteran of the Mexican-American War, John Tipton was the first postmaster at Tipton Hill. Blind in later years, he is the man whose name was given to the town. This photograph dates to around 1915. (Frank Griffith.)

This fine picture from 1920 shows the Byrd family. Arthur, Mary, and son Jack go for a spin in the family buggy. The Byrds lived in Tipton Hill. Arthur made his living as a carpenter and handed that occupation down to Jack. Mary was a homemaker and lived to the age of 106. (Frank Griffith.)

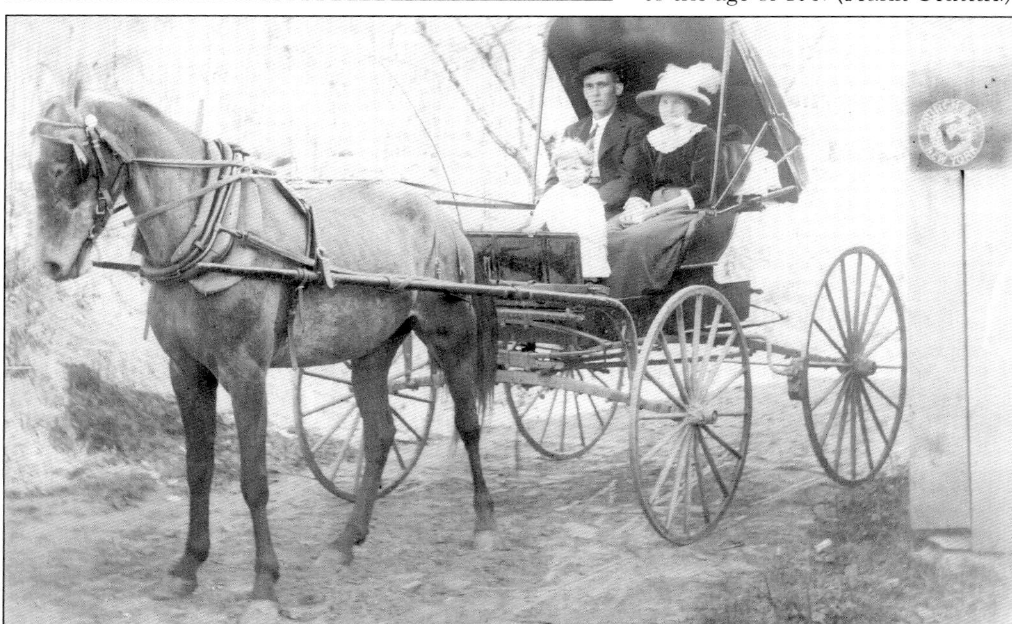

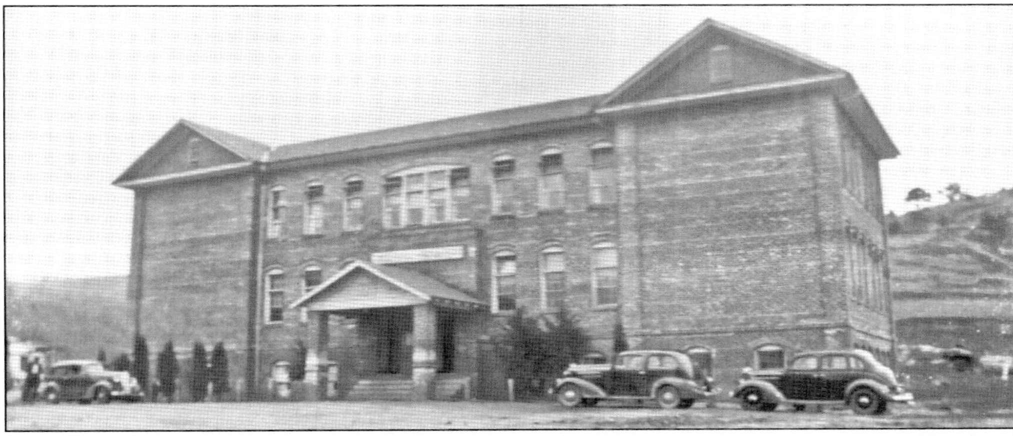

Built to be a Methodist college, this three-story brick building became the Tipton Hill School. Due to a lack of funds for the college, it was turned over to the state to be used for public education. Parents from the area helped to haul the bricks to build it and put in the water line. Education was important in Tipton Hill. The first graduating class (consisting of seven students) was in 1929. Children were transported to the school in a wagon but later rode school busses. Below is the 1937–1938 school picture, showing Frank Griffith, age 14, second from left in the bottom row. Students could bring produce and canned goods to the "soup room" instead of paying 10¢ for lunch. Homeroom with teacher Bertha Yelton focused on moral values, such as abstaining from drinking alcohol. (Above, Longleaf Media; below, Frank Griffith.)

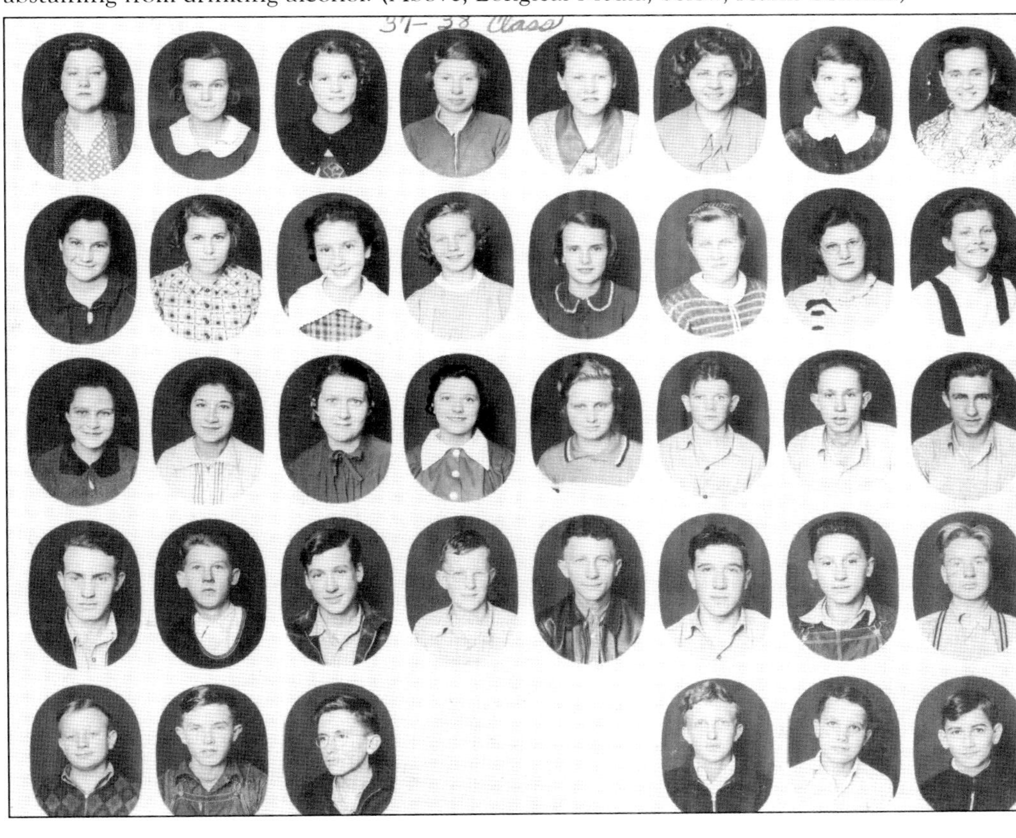

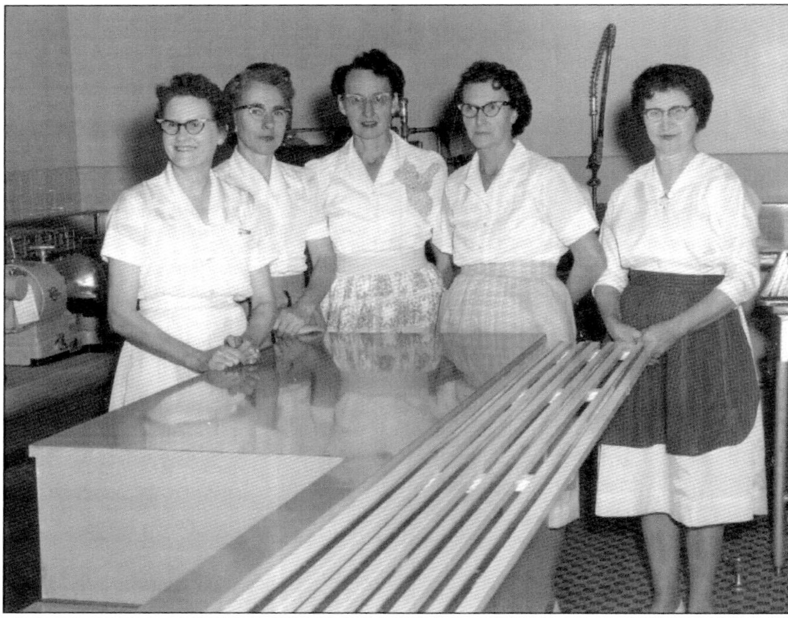

As time went on, on-site cafeterias became an important part of the educational system. These capable lunch ladies excelled at making good food and serving it hot during the school day. From left to right are Jane Harrell, Helen Whitson, Dalie Griffith, Myrtle Byrd, and Etta Mae Whitson. (Frank Griffith.)

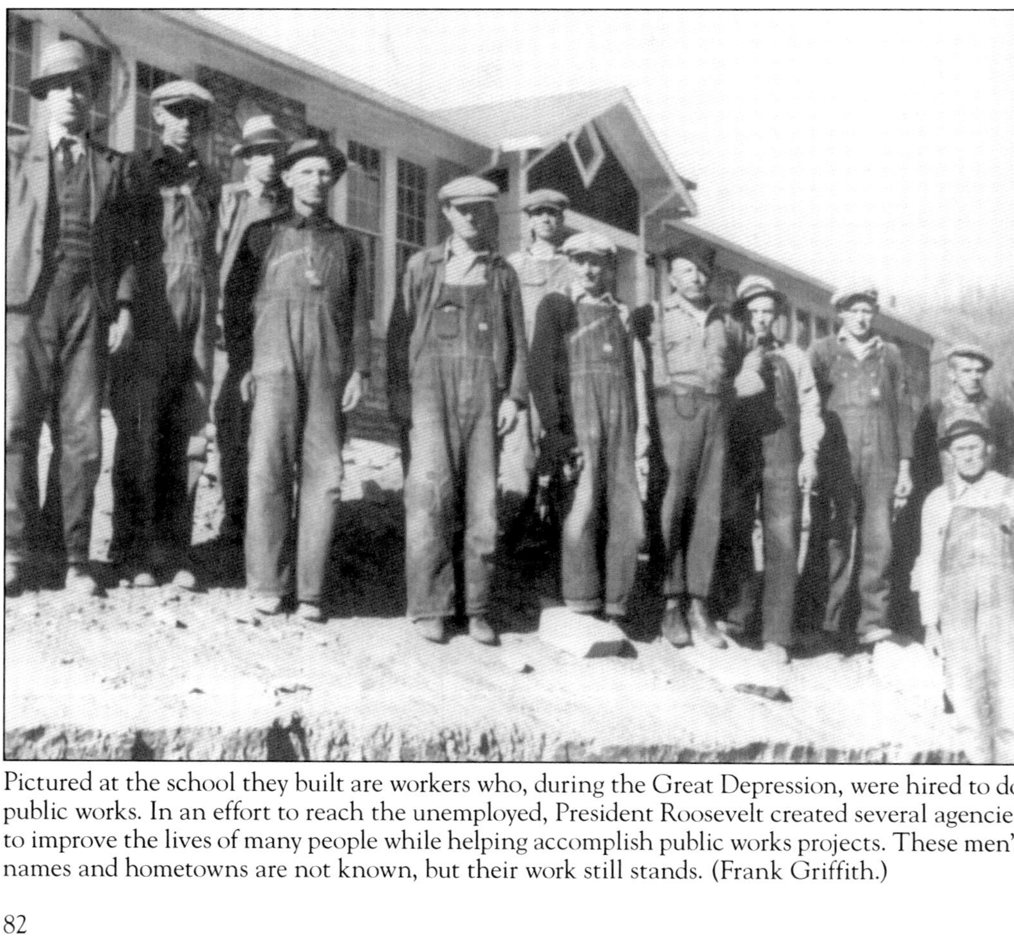

Pictured at the school they built are workers who, during the Great Depression, were hired to do public works. In an effort to reach the unemployed, President Roosevelt created several agencies to improve the lives of many people while helping accomplish public works projects. These men's names and hometowns are not known, but their work still stands. (Frank Griffith.)

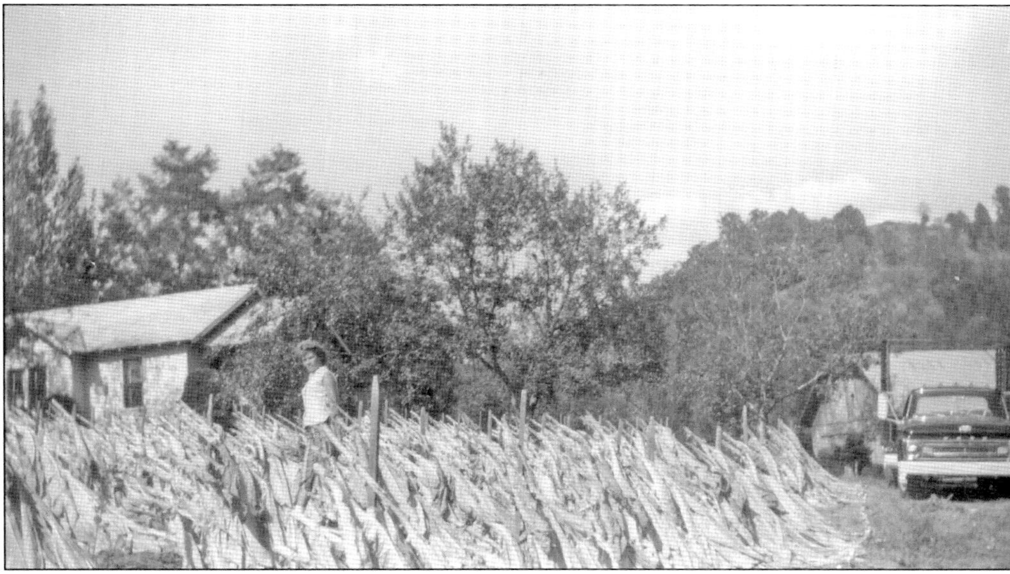

A tobacco crop brought income to many families in the area, including this one in Harrell Hill in 1962. Tobacco became an important product for folks, especially during and after World War II when cigarettes were given to soldiers and home-front advertising targeted women who were becoming more economically independent. (Shelby Street.)

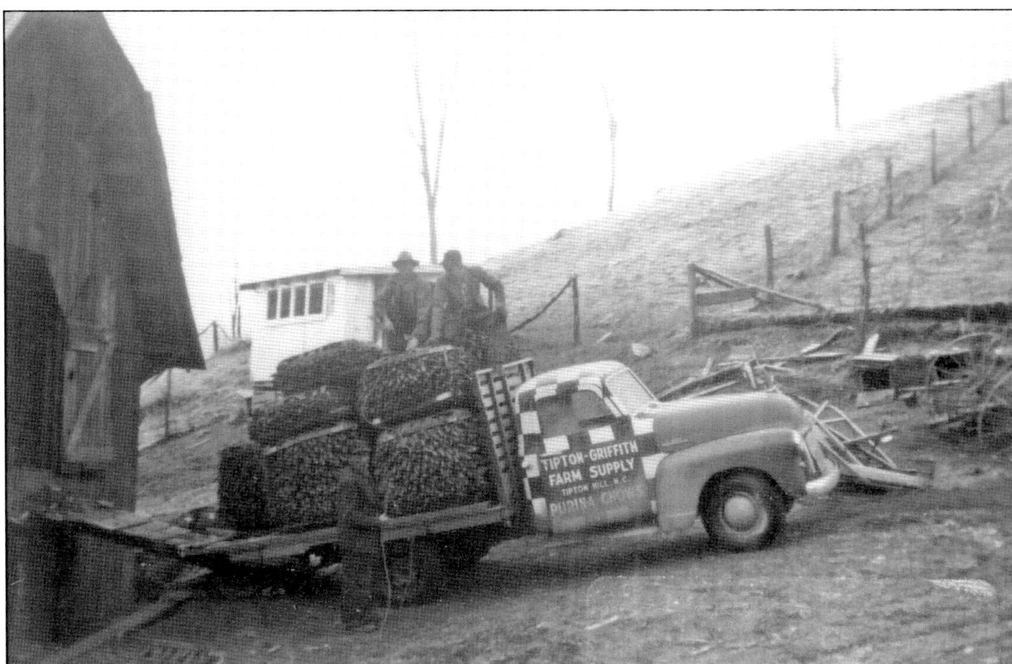

In this picture, men from Frank Griffith's store in Tipton Hill gather up the "hands" of tobacco from the drying barn. Hands are dried leaves wrapped in another leaf, then put in wooden baskets for transport and sale to manufacturers where they are made into snuff, cigarettes, and other tobacco products. (Frank Griffith.)

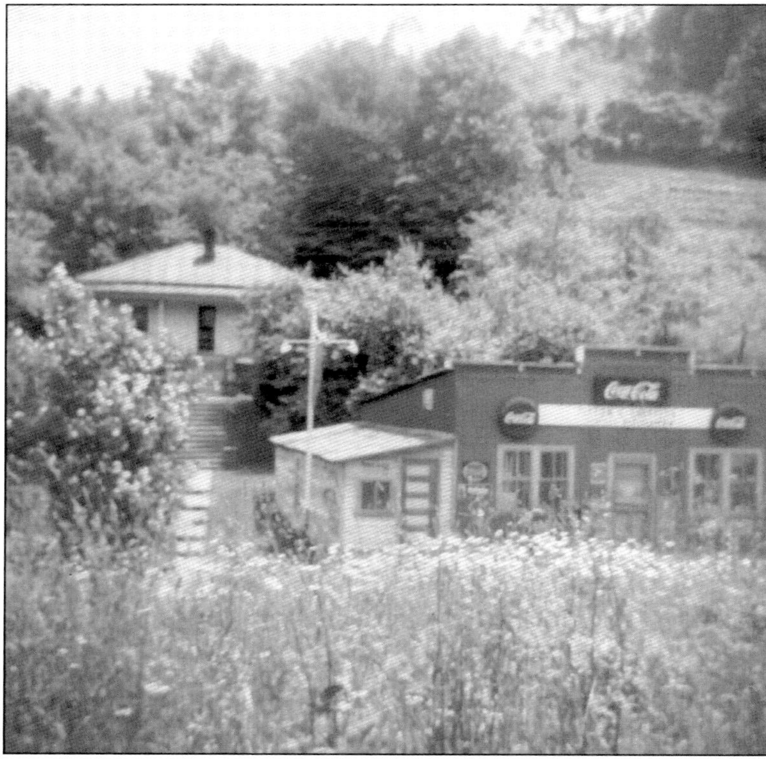

Griffith's store is seen here in Tipton Hill, pictured in 1950 as Tipton and Griffith's store. Country stores were lifelines in rural areas and the mountains. Besides selling everything from feed and grain to groceries, clothing, and pots and pans, the fires from their pot-bellied stoves warmed many customers while they shopped. (Frank Griffith.)

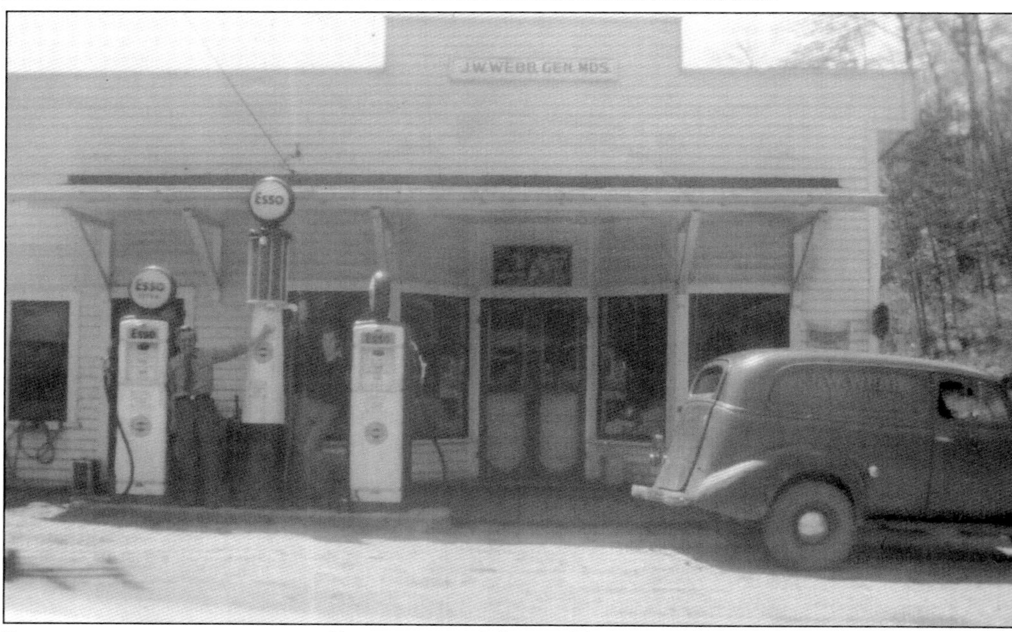

Boasting a service station as well as groceries, John Webb's Red Hill Grocery served area shoppers. Often, the store delivered goods to those who had no way to get there. Shopping then was anything but self-service. One would bring a list of needs to the person behind the counter, who would retrieve the products from shelves behind the counter. (Joyce Boone.)

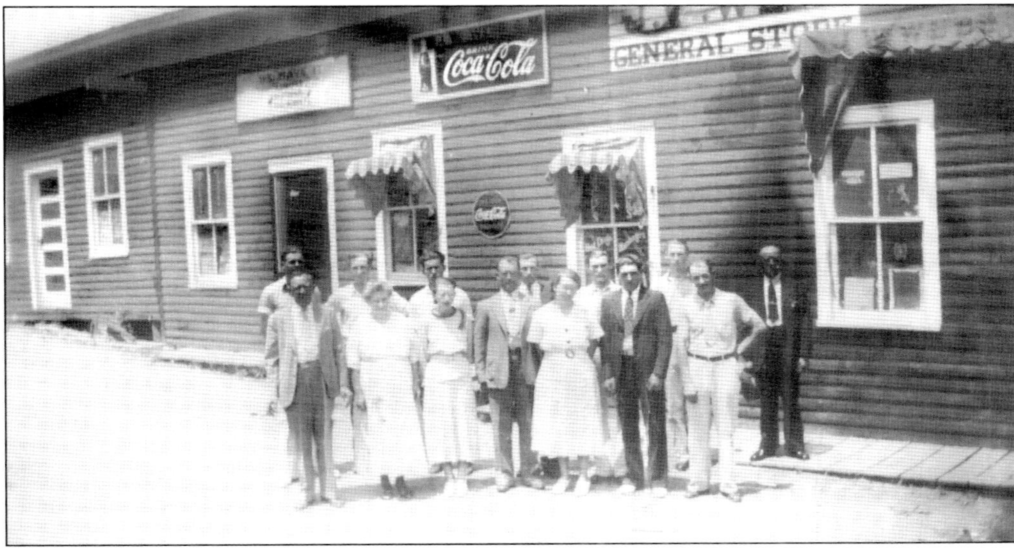

John Webb also had a store located just outside of Tipton Hill, pictured in this photograph in 1936. This was a large enterprise that employed 18 people. Webb was quite a businessman. At one point, he had stores in Red Hill, Poplar, and near Tipton Hill. In addition, he opened Webb Funeral Home, a business that still operates in Spruce Pine. (Frank Griffith.)

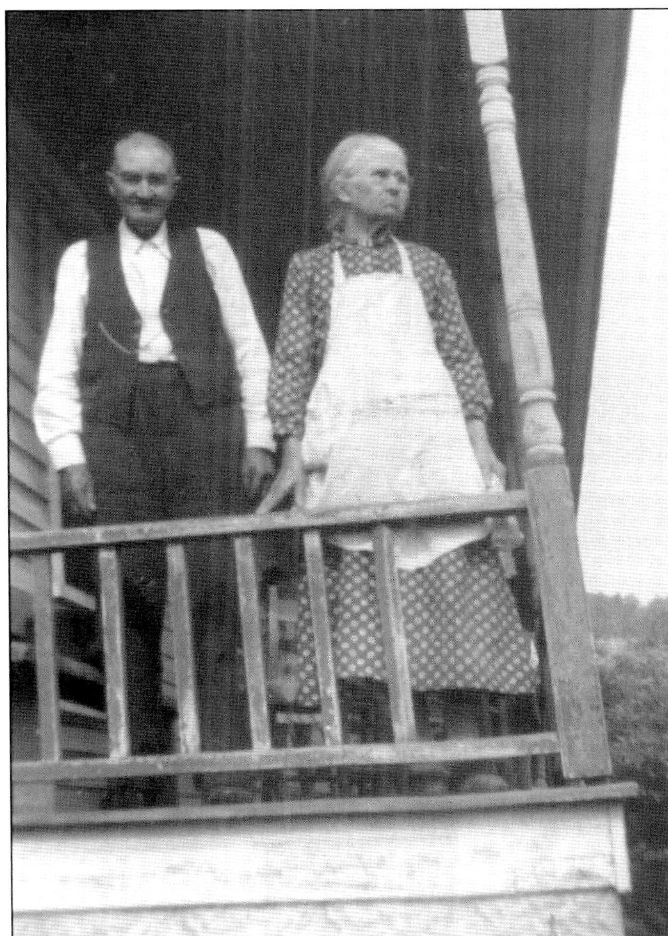

Standing on the porch of their family home in "downtown" Tipton Hill are Clingman and Vicey Whitson. Clingman started out as a tobacco farmer and made enough money to open a general store in Tipton Hill. This photograph was taken in 1936, the same year that Vicey passed away. (Frank Griffith.)

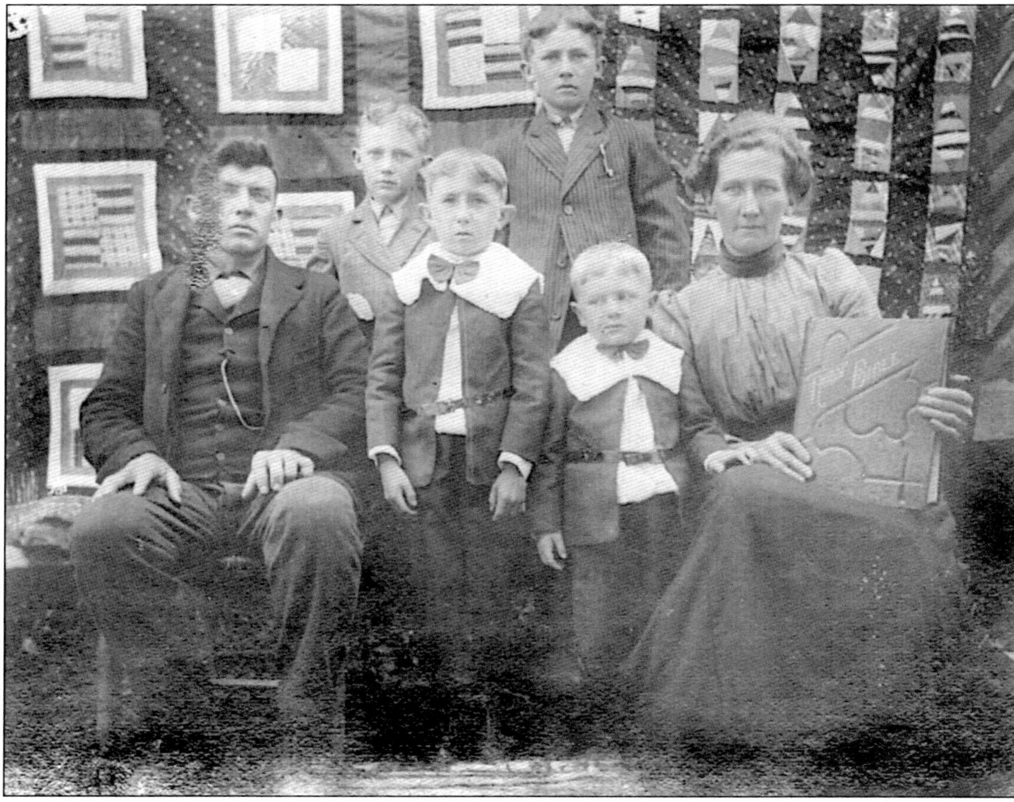

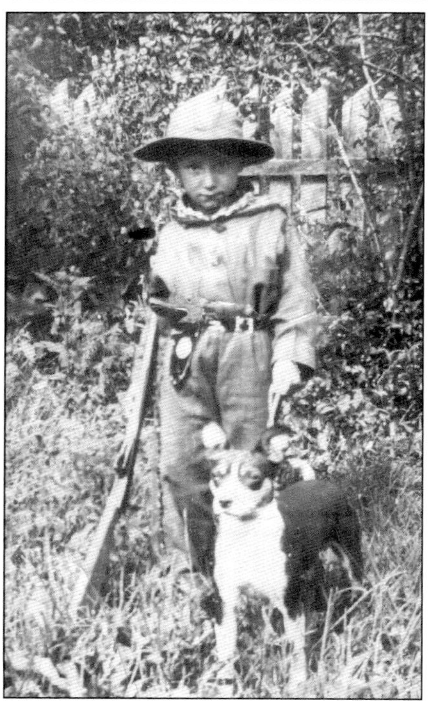

Pictured around 1915 are the Griffiths: a family of four boys and parents young enough to sire several other children. Note the two different quilts that were used as a backdrop for the photograph. Also, note that the mother is proudly holding a large copy of the Holy Bible. Family and religion—these are still important values to most people who live around Bakersville. (Frank Griffith.)

In this picture, Frank "Cowboy" Ellis has stopped to pose with Bob, his faithful companion, and his guns. Children in the mountains made their own fun, sometimes by pretending to be a cowboy hero. (Frank Griffith.)

Seven

Brummetts Creek, Huntdale, Pigeon Roost, Poplar, Relief

The communities making up the northwest section of Mitchell County are relatively distant from its centers of population. The mountainous terrain adds to this isolation even today, but due to the lack of good roads, this was especially true in the 1800s when the area was first settled. Because traveling outside of town was onerous, these communities were largely self-contained. Most rural county residents lived within a few miles of the church, general store, and post office they frequented. As a result, the communities clustered around these gathering places developed their own unique characters and cultures, which in many ways continue to this day.

Agriculture and timber were the most significant sources of income. Mining and activities like beekeeping were important as well, but most people lived off the land. Community churches were a source of both spiritual and cultural fellowship. Church schools were the primary source of education until public schools were established.

Mitchell County eventually established a large network of schools throughout the county. These small schools served an essential purpose and delivered a solid education to these isolated students. A surprising number of students continued their education beyond high school and achieved advanced college degrees.

In Mitchell County, the Pigeon Roost community—especially the area of upper Pigeon Roost—was perhaps the most isolated. It is said that Pigeon Roost and Pigeon Roost Creek were named for a large flock of pigeons that once roosted in the area. Timber was an especially important resource in this area, and several impressive log flumes were constructed to move the timber to a transportation point.

The area around Brummetts Creek, close to Tipton Hill, was also well-settled with farms growing corn, tobacco, and other crops. During the early 20th century, it had a larger population than Tipton Hill.

Closer to the railroad and the Toe River were the communities of Poplar, Relief, and Huntdale. Poplar was originally called "Hollar Poplar Creek." It was named after an enormous hollow poplar tree that was used as shelter for Confederate soldiers during the Civil War. The name Relief is said to derive from a popular patent medicine called Hart's Relief that was sold at Squire Peterson's store in the 1870s. It is said that Huntdale was named after a husband's attempt to "hunt Dale," his runaway wife.

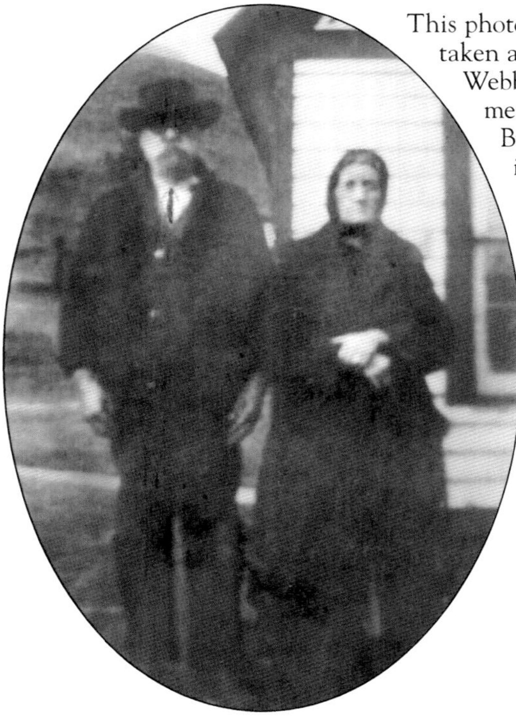

This photograph of Burton and Jane Webb was probably taken around 1900 when Burton was close to 60. The Webb family lived near Relief, where Burton was a member of the Freewill Baptist Church for 70 years. Burton's father, Wilson, was one of the first settlers in the area around Relief. (James Byrd.)

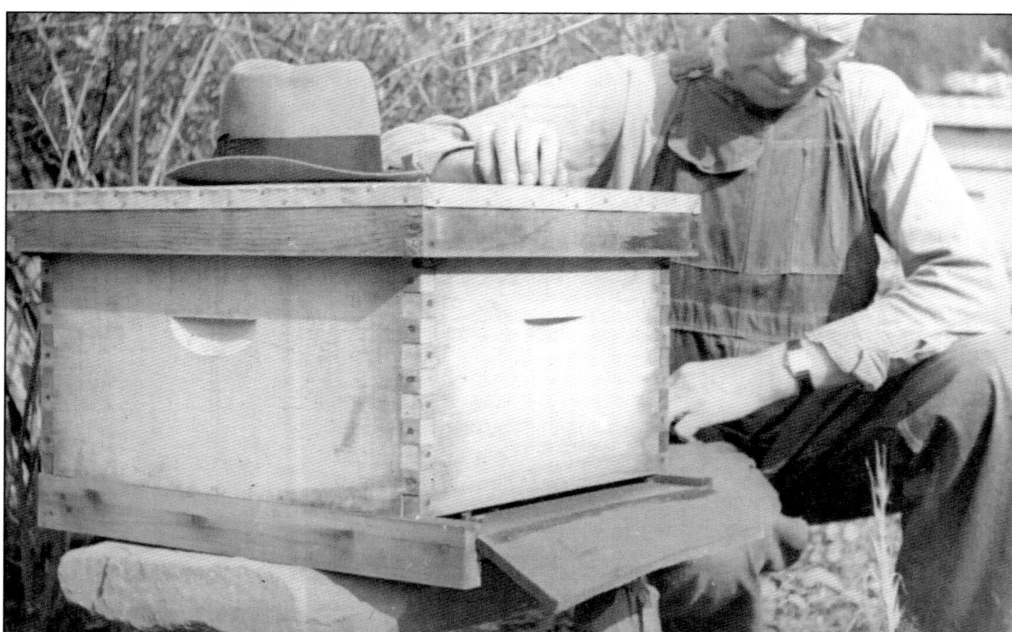

Beekeeping was not an especially common activity, but Ed Bennett from Brummetts Creek was an expert beekeeper, and honey was a good way to supplement income. This photograph from the 1940s captures Bennett as he examines one of his hives. Note that he is not wearing any protective clothing. (Star Bennett.)

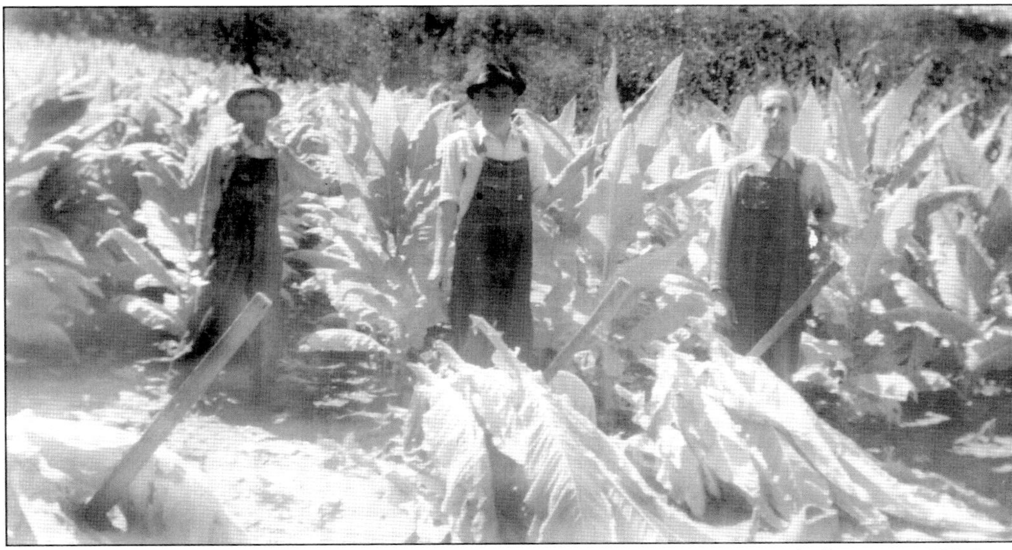

Tobacco was a good cash crop, especially the burley tobacco grown in Mitchell County. Without a government allotment, however, one could not grow tobacco. The Peterson farm near Poplar was one of the fortunate farms that was allowed to grow this valuable crop. Pictured here in 1935 in the tobacco field are, from left to right, Jerry Peterson, Wes Peterson, and Ashley Gouge. (Joyce Boone.)

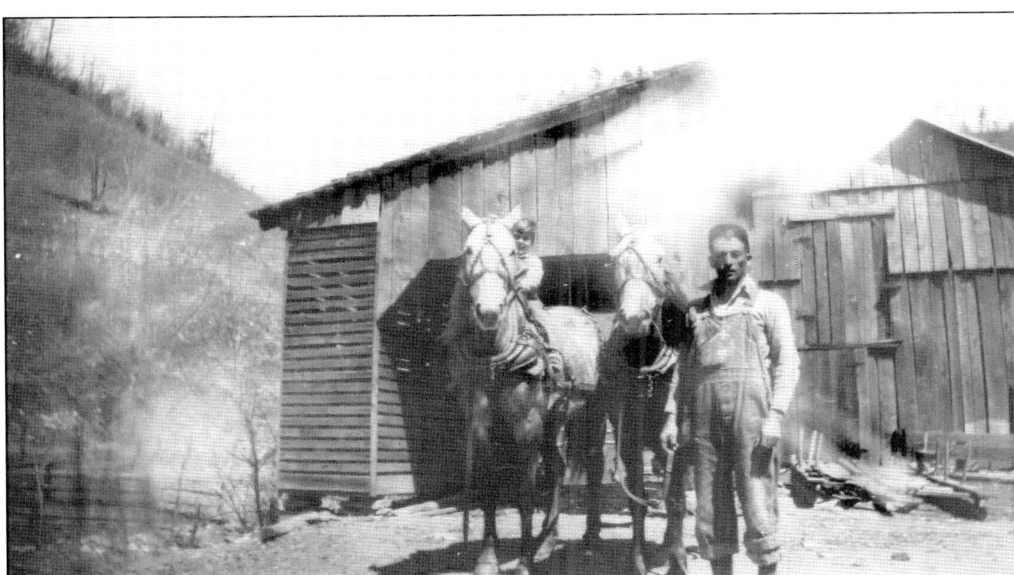

Park Bryant and his family lived in the Brummetts Creek area. This photograph from the 1940s shows Park and his son Bobby in front of their barn. Even in the midst of work, there was still time for a photograph and for Bobby to have some fun. (Star Bennett.)

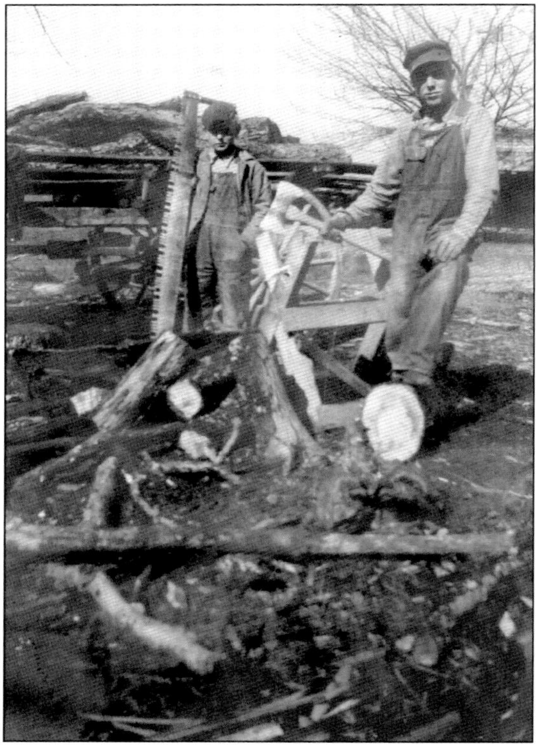

It was always necessary to have plenty of wood on hand for cooking and heating during the winter. This 1920 photograph from the area of Pigeon Roost shows Henry (right) and Levi Edwards with a saw, axe, and wagonload of wood. (James Byrd.)

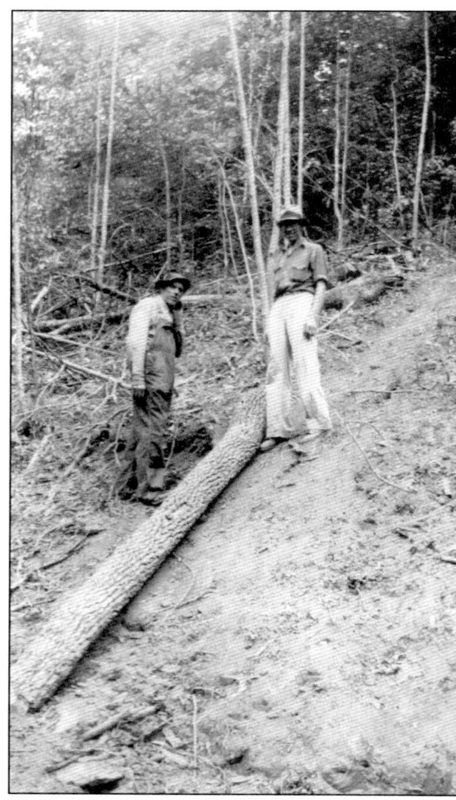

Logging was a good, consistent source of income. It was especially well established in the area of Pigeon Roost where this 1941 photograph captures I.V. Peterson (left) and Ed Bennett standing over a freshly cut tree. (Star Bennett.)

Sawmills were a common sight throughout the area. The many creeks and rivers were abundant sources of waterpower for many of these mills. Often, water-powered gristmills would also have a saw attached to the waterwheel. When they were not grinding corn, mills could cut wood. Sawmills could also be powered by a small steam engine instead of water. The photograph at right is a sawmill located on Pigeon Roost Creek, but historians do not know if it was driven by water or steam. This photograph probably dates to the 1940s, and the exact location of the mill is not known. The photograph below depicts a sawmill located in the Huntdale area in the 1950s. Although this mill also appears to be close to a water source, it is almost certainly steam driven. (Right, Appalachia Archives, ETSU, James Goforth Collection; below, Star Bennett.)

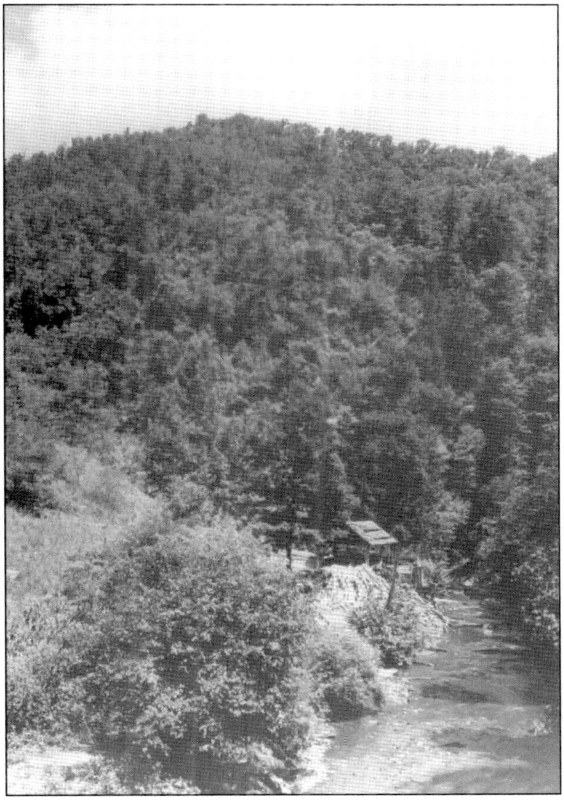

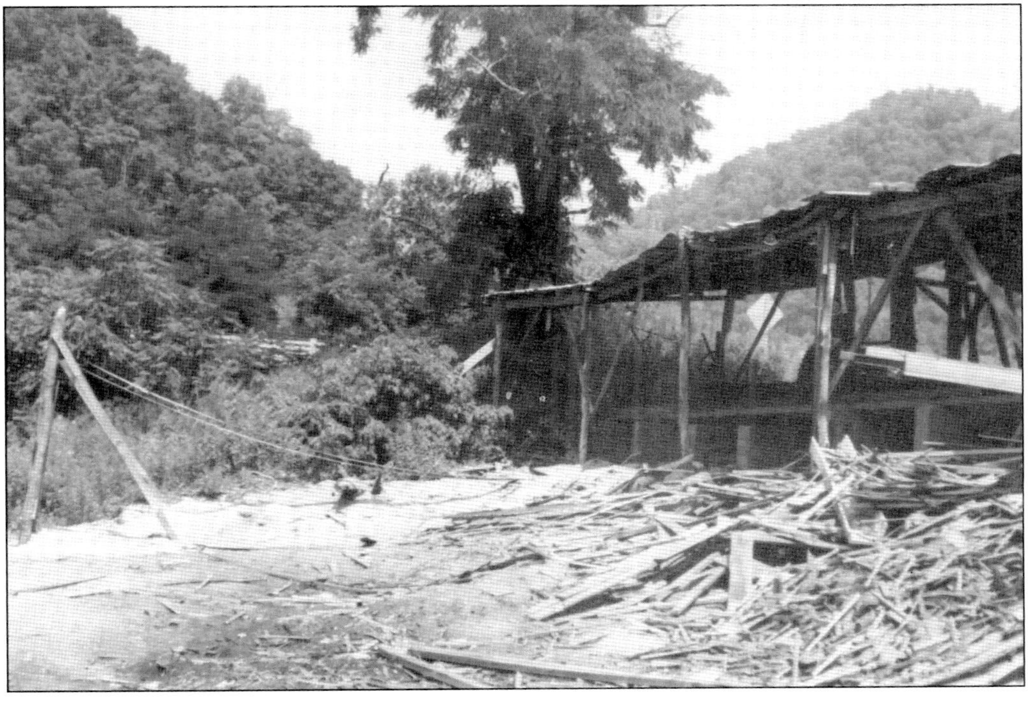

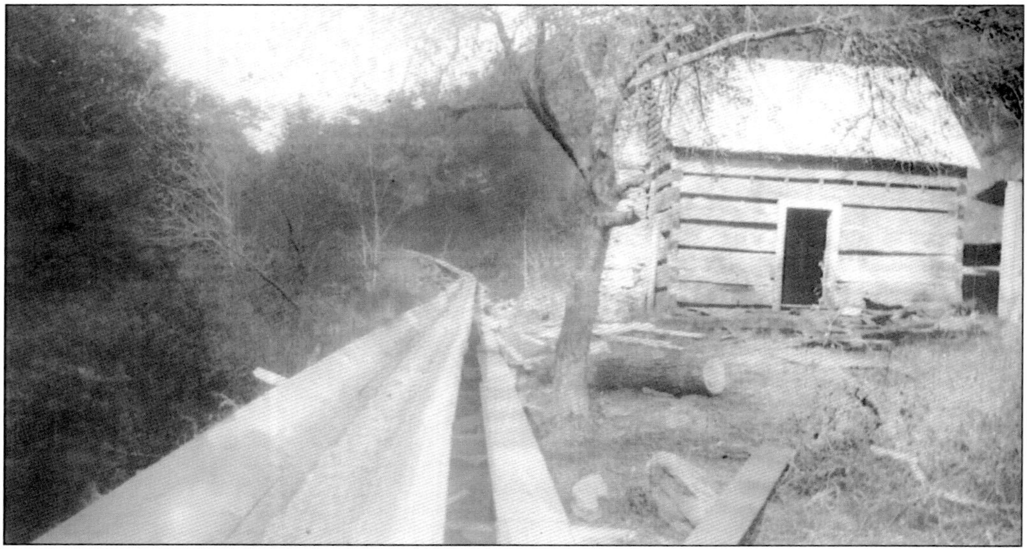

Logging was a consistent source of income for many people in the area. There were several log flumes in the Pigeon Roost area. Using water from the left-hand fork of Pigeon Roost Creek, this log flume ran for miles downhill, transporting logs from the hills to the road for transportation to sawmills. (Frank Griffith.)

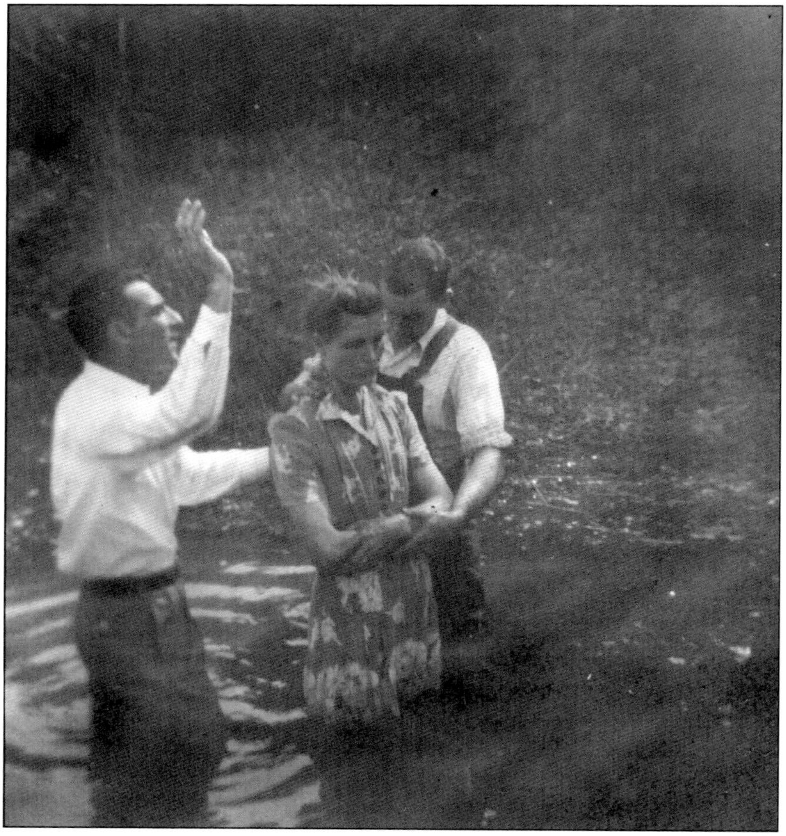

Bob Potter was a local preacher who was not actually affiliated with any specific congregation. This 1940s photograph was likely taken after a revival meeting at Brummetts Creek. The name of the young woman being baptized is not known. (Star Bennett.)

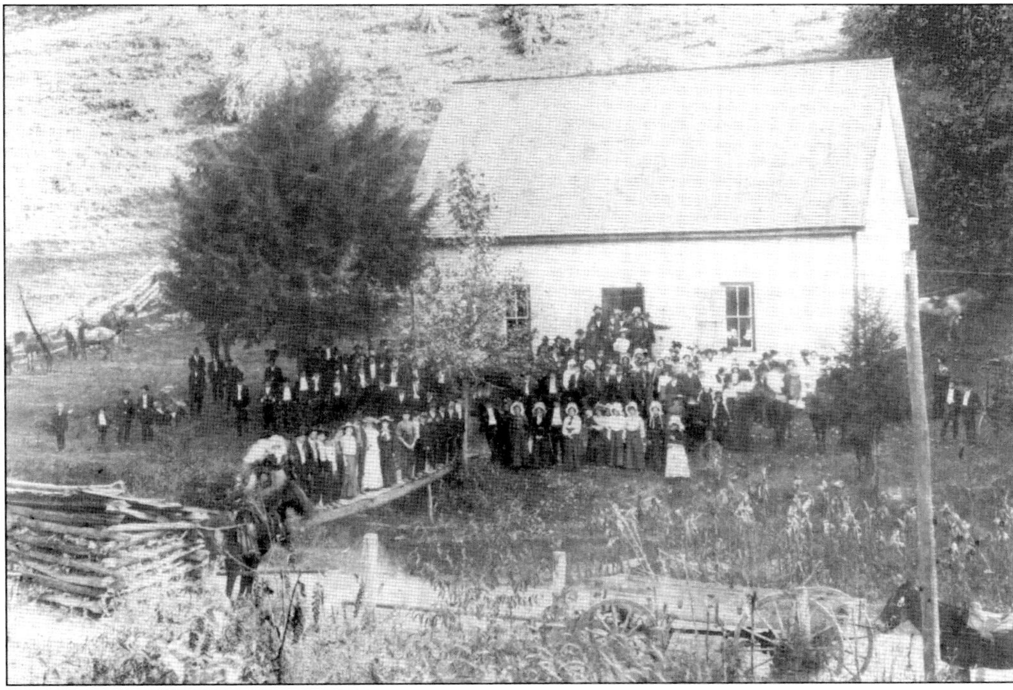

The photograph above, from 1920, shows Brummetts Creek Brethren Church, originally constructed in 1878. The photograph below also dates to 1920. At that time, this building in upper Brummetts Creek was the Lloyd Griffith School, operated by Mitchell County. Below, the students in the photograph are joined by several adults, but it is not clear if they are parents or teachers. When the school was closed, and students were sent to Tipton Hill, the building was converted to the Upper Brummetts Creek Fundamental Brethren Church. The congregation of the church was largely drawn from the Brethren church in Brummetts Creek, apparently over a question of doctrine. The building was eventually demolished in 1939. (Both, Frank Griffith.)

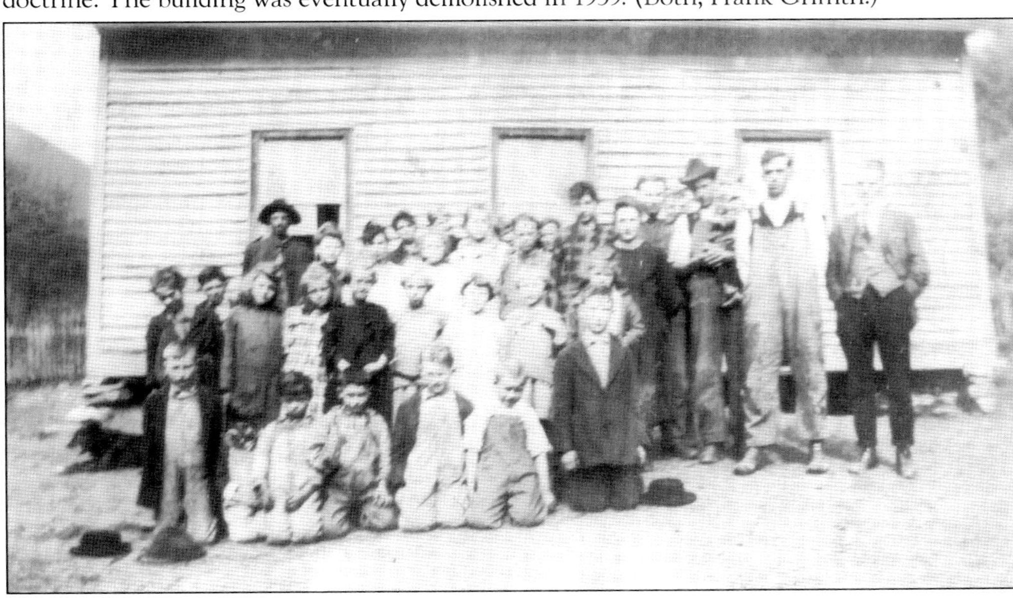

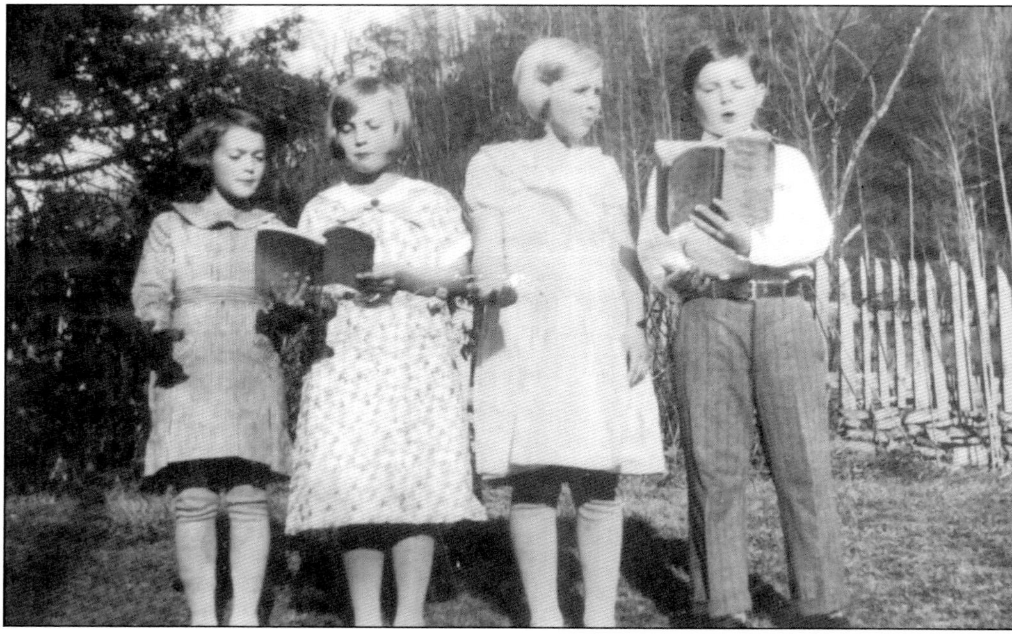

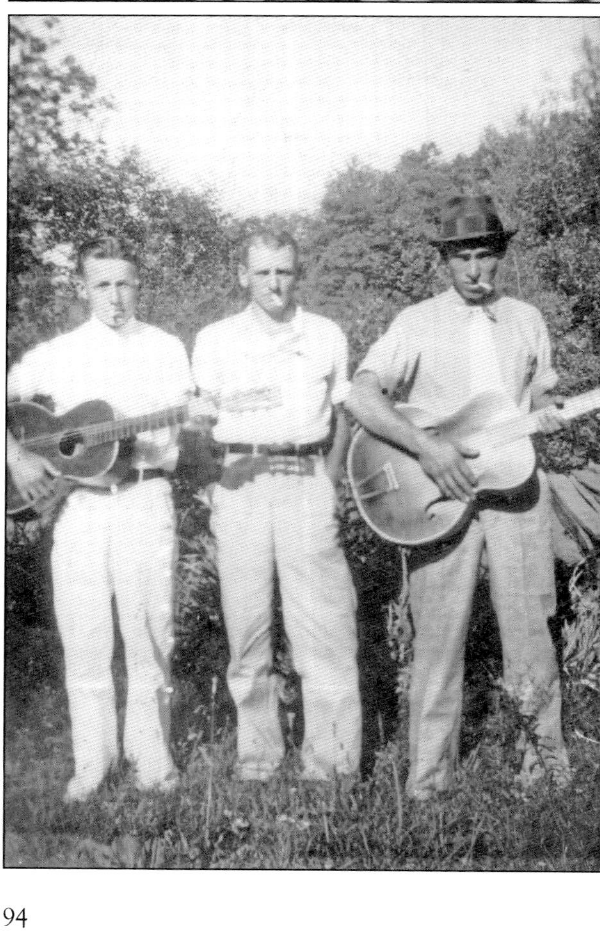

The Zephyr Quartet was composed of (from left to right) Star Bryant, Joyce Bennett, Vaultie Miller, and Vaughn Bryant. Singing Christian songs from the sacred-harp, shape-note tradition, this youthful quartet sang at various locations in Mitchell County during the mid-1930s. People would pass the hat during their performances, allowing the youngsters to obtain a few much-needed coins. (Star Bennett.)

One of the happy by-products of life in the mountains has been the rich tradition of homemade music. This photograph from the Poplar area dates from 1933 and shows, from left to right, Ike Griffith, John Peterson, and Burna Cooper. It is unknown today what sort of music they played (or how they sang with cigarettes in their mouths) but it is unlikely that they were professional musicians. (Joyce Boone.)

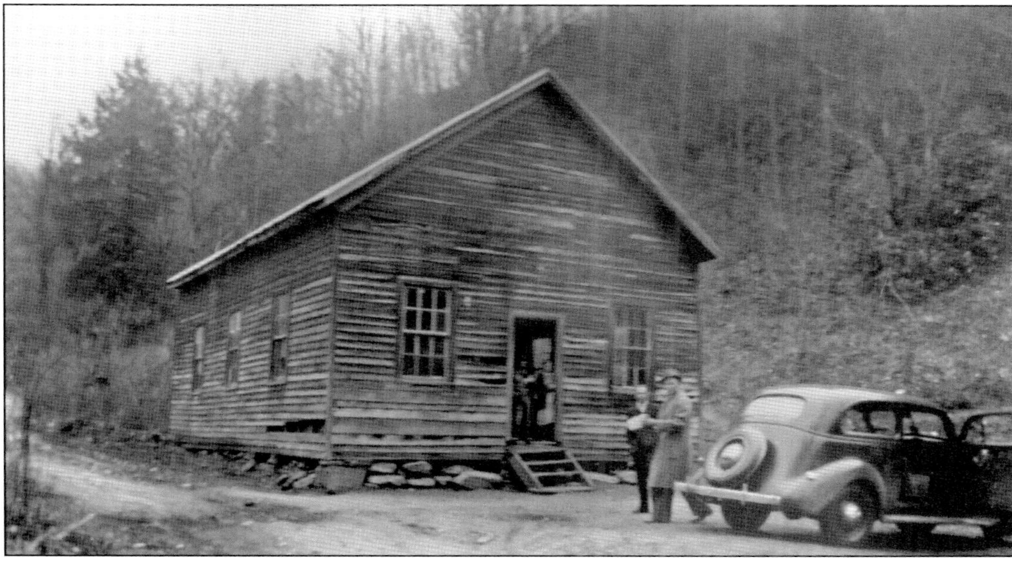

Transportation in areas around Pigeon Roost was particularly primitive well into the 1940s. Roads in the area were not paved and movement, especially in the winter, was very difficult. Even though Pigeon Roost had a school with several classrooms, it was necessary to construct this one-room schoolhouse in upper Pigeon Roost several miles away. This photograph dates from 1938. (Longleaf Media.)

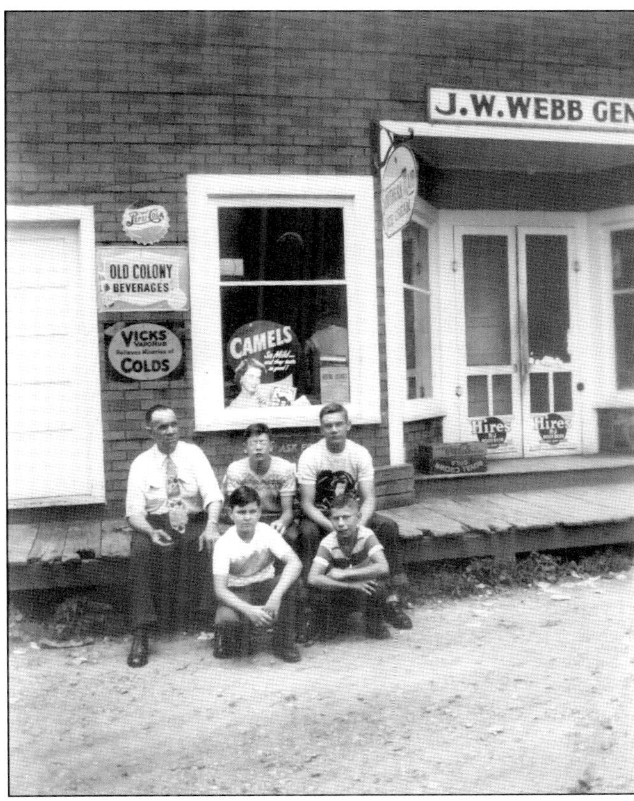

Pictured here are Jake Gouge and his family in front of the J.W. Webb General Store in Poplar around 1939. The Webb store was a true general merchandise store that sold all the necessities of daily life. The store also featured two gas pumps to fuel the growing demand of the automobile. Eventually, the increased use of automobiles and better roads put most general stores out of business. (Joyce Boone.)

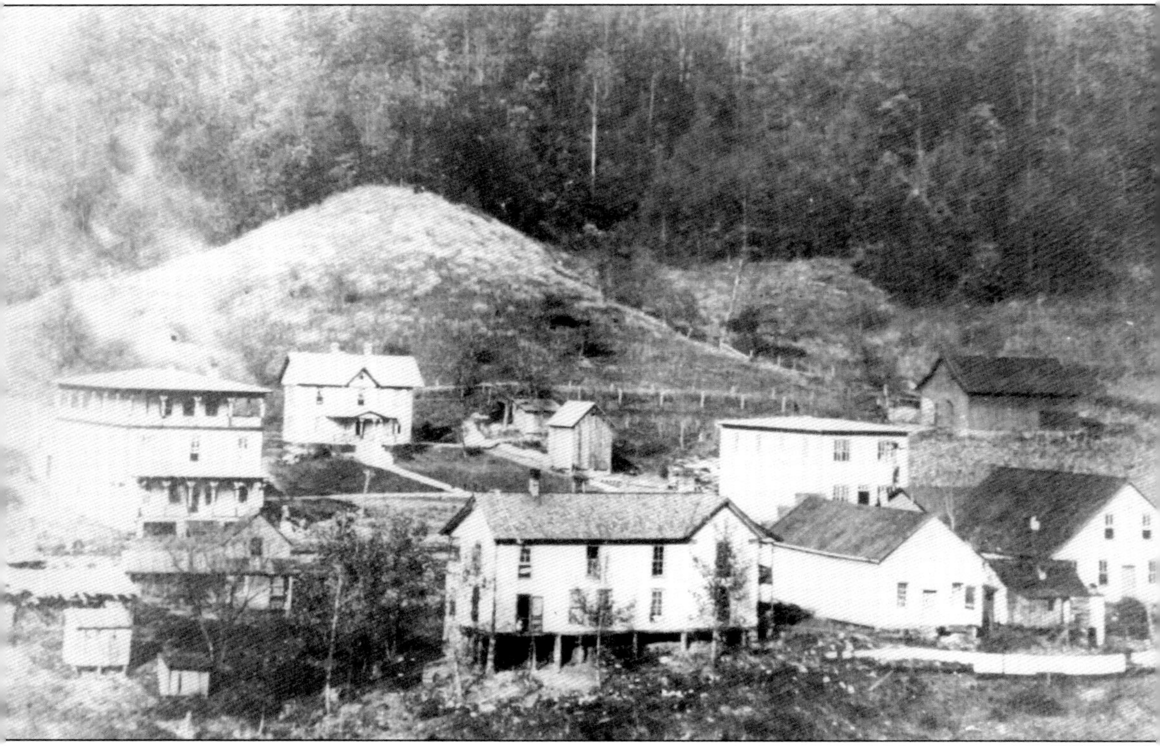

The community of Huntdale was located on the Toe River between Relief and Poplar. This photograph from 1920 shows a good view of the town. While not a large community, Huntdale offered farmers and travelers essential services. The location of the community gave farmers a relatively convenient location for trade as well as access to the railway. The left side of the photograph shows a large hotel for travelers and the residence of Bob Griffith, the principal merchant in Huntdale. The large building in the center was a hostel for railway workers. To the right of the hostel is the CC&O depot. Behind the depot is Griffith's store, a general merchandise shop that supplied farmers with most of their seeds and supplies. On the far right is Griffith's gristmill for grinding corn, which also contained warehouse space for the store. (James Byrd.)

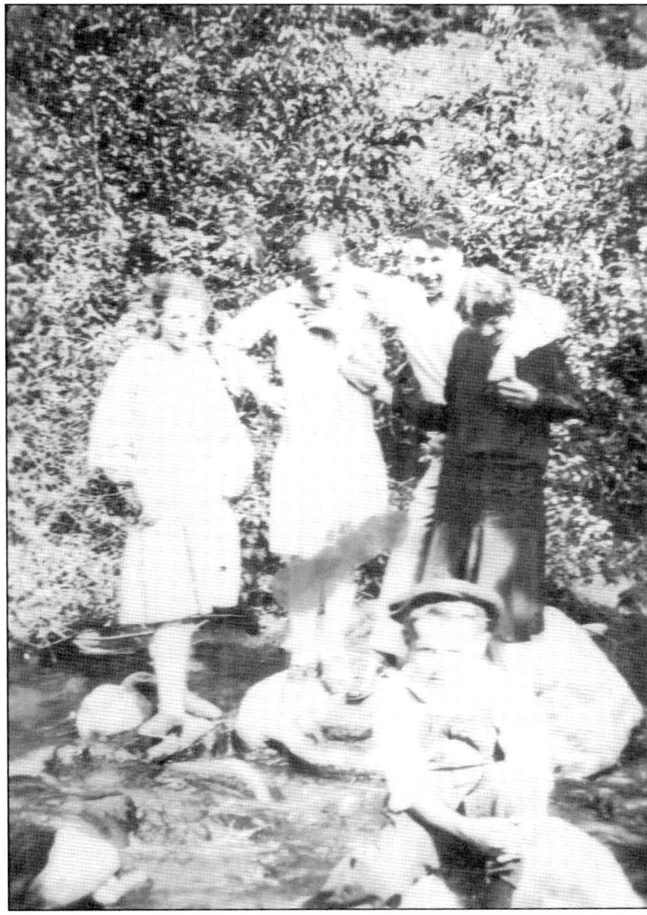

Even in rural Mitchell County, folks knew how to have fun. While there were many church and school sponsored-activities, there were plenty of other diversions along the creeks, bridges, and in the mountains. Whether on a picnic at Carver's Gap, going on a hayride, playing in a nearby creek, hiking in the hills, or poling down the Toe River, life could be good indeed! Pictured at right, this photograph from 1923 shows a family having fun in Poplar Creek. The photograph below shows three friends poling down the Toe River. The photograph appears to date from the early 1930s. (Right, Joyce Boone; below, Star Bennett.)

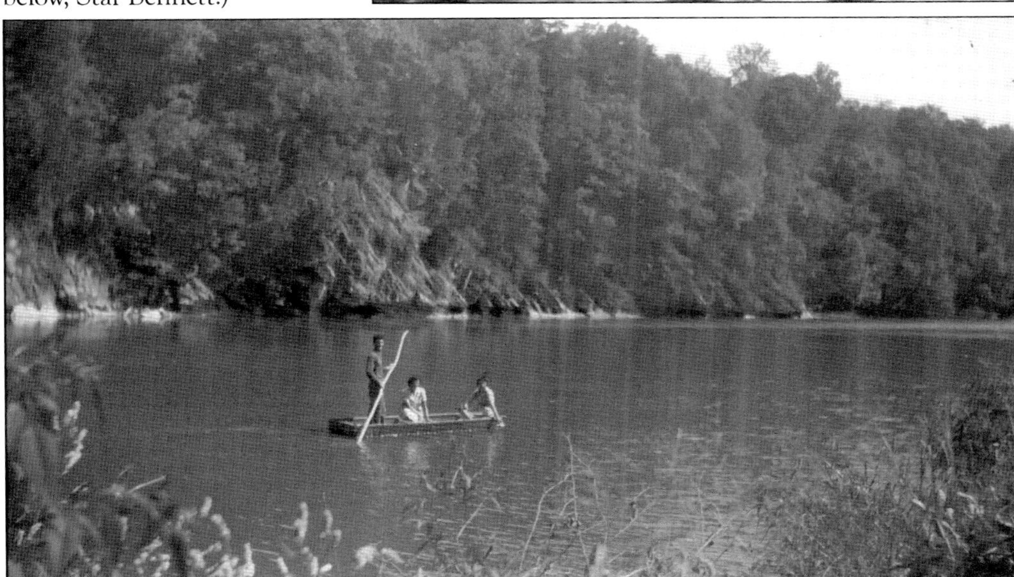

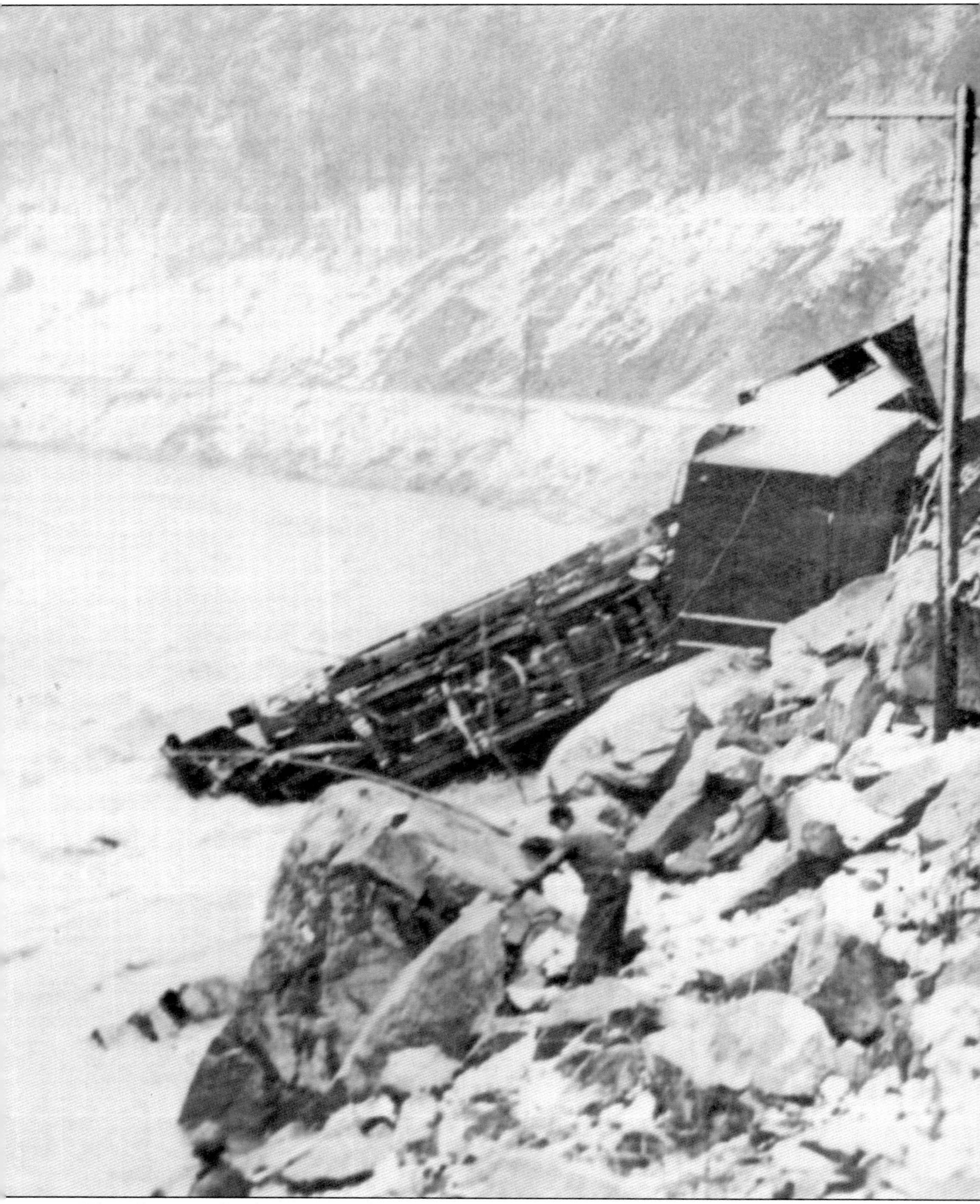

This photograph of a train wreck near Poplar probably dates back to the 1930s. Wrecks along this stretch of the line were not uncommon. One notable wreck in 1935 was caused by a train engine hitting a huge boulder, which killed the train's fireman, injured two others, tossed the tender

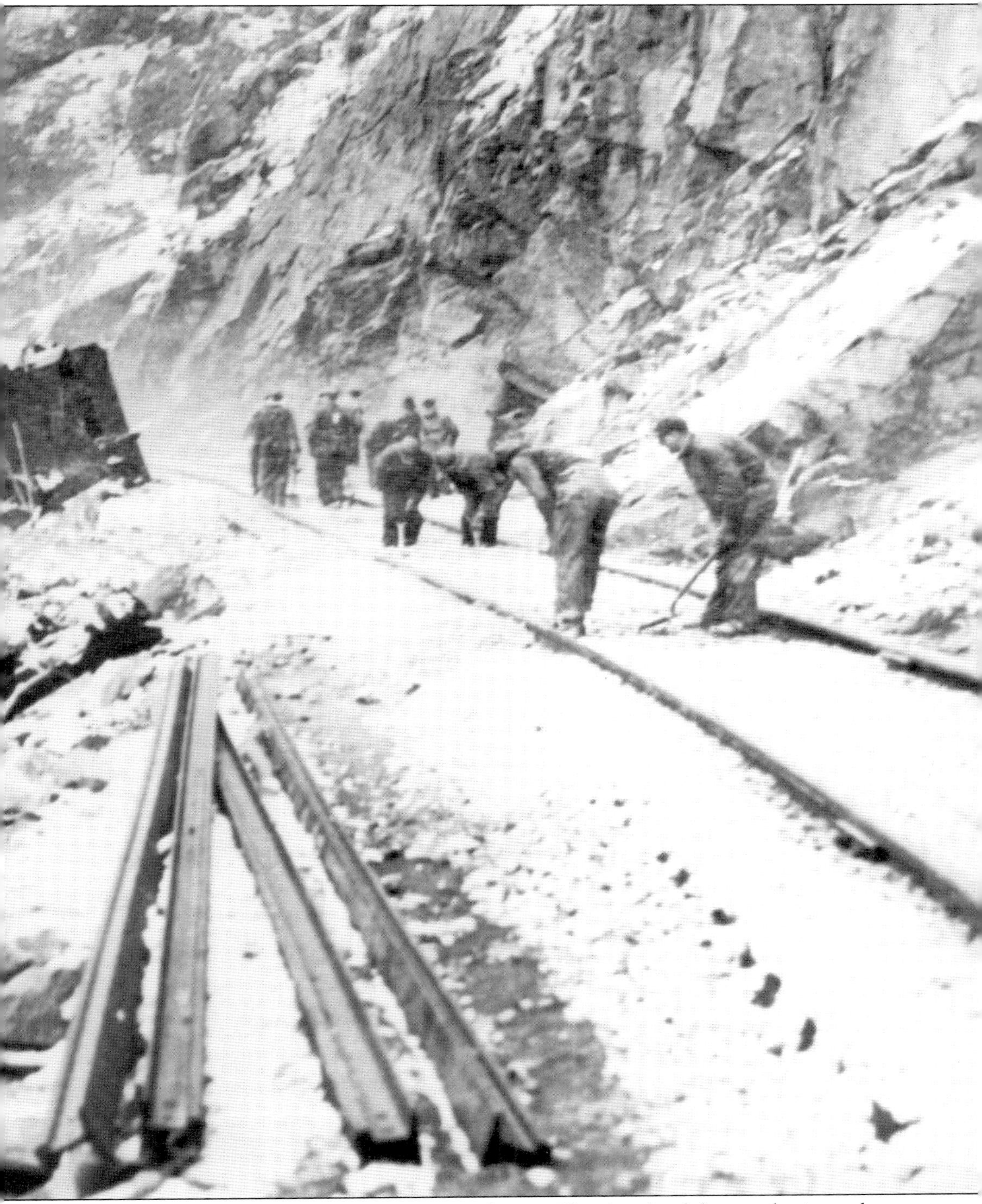

into the river, and derailed an entire 100-car coal train. The details of the wreck pictured are lost, but it appears that a locomotive and several cars derailed and settled into the nearly frozen Toe River. (Appalachia Archives, ETSU, Dorody Collection.)

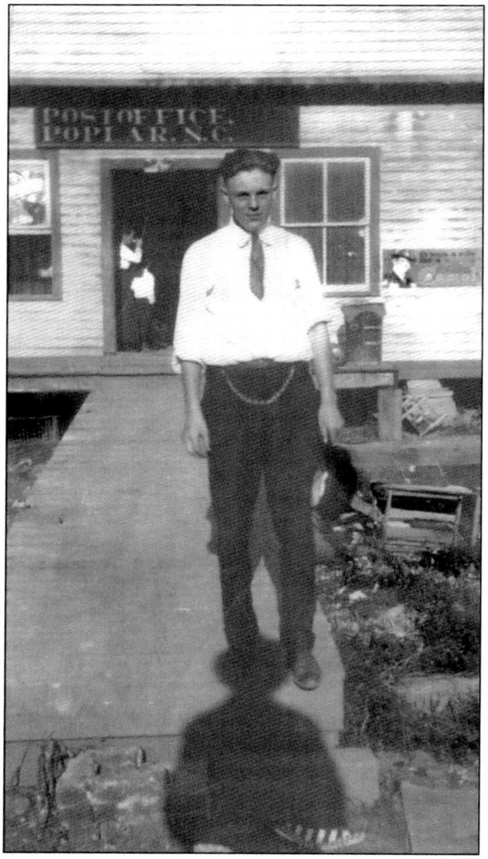

This photograph from the late 1920s shows the post office in Poplar and postmaster Brisco Peterson. Poplar was a flag stop for the CC&O Railroad, and the post office benefited from regular rail delivery. (Pam Johnson.)

This photograph shows Nat Gouge (right) and his son Will as they lie in their caskets. On November 15, 1914, they were ambushed on the bank of the Toe River in Poplar by a man identified as Baxter Bennett. Despite the offer of a $500 reward, Bennett was never apprehended. (Joyce Boone.)

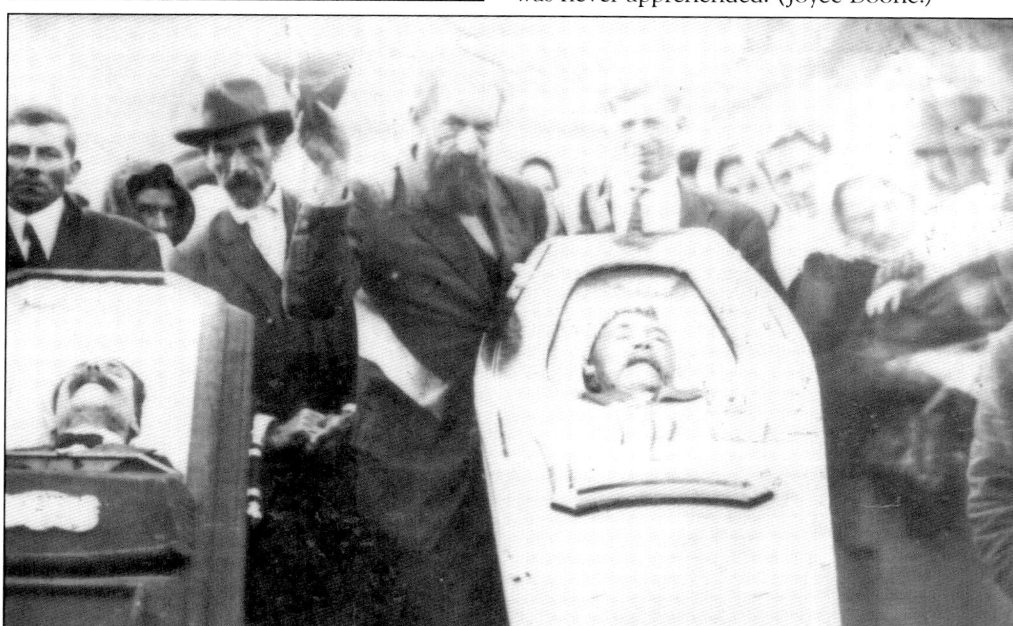

Eight

Buladean

An area on the road to Tennessee was initially called Wilder's Forge. Later, it was dubbed Magnetic City, because of the magnetic iron ore found there. Sometime later, as there was actually no "city" to speak of, the name was changed again. Two stories exist about the naming of Buladean. The first points to the settlers' Scottish-Irish heritage, wherein the word "Beulah" means beautiful and "dean" means dune or hills. The second points to the first postmaster, a Mr. Dean, who had a daughter named Beulah, so the town became "Buladean."

Located on the North Carolina side of Iron Mountain, Buladean citizens often felt more connected to Tennessee than to North Carolina. Though there was a mountain between, Johnson City offered more opportunities than Bakersville or Spruce Pine, which were themselves a long ride away. Today, people in Buladean are still more likely to cross the mountain than go south. One of the economic drivers in the 1930s and 1940s and afterward was the Clinchfield–Blue Ridge Pottery works in Erwin, Tennessee. Women from Buladean painted flowers, animals, and scenes on the dishes, vases, figurines, and whatnots that were shipped to buyers throughout the nation. It provided both an economic support and a creative outlet for the women of the area.

Buladean, as with so many of the other places around Bakersville, used the timber business as a part of its economic income. Pictures of Frank A. Hughes at work in the lumberyard speak of the hard labor involved in cutting wood and getting it ready to ship or use in local construction.

Education in Buladean began at the hands of the Presbyterian church. The original school was housed in the church, an old store. In 1924, the state took over the schools and levied a tax to support the teachers' salaries. Students were eager to learn in their five-month sessions, and teachers had few problems with discipline. One of the best teachers, William Harvey Wise, 70, met an untimely death that had the town wondering if he had been murdered. Wise had gone to Bakersville to get his paycheck, then his body was discovered in the Old Master's Mill on Rock Creek. Though the money was never found, the coroner decided that Wise had died accidentally. Some folks never agreed with that conclusion.

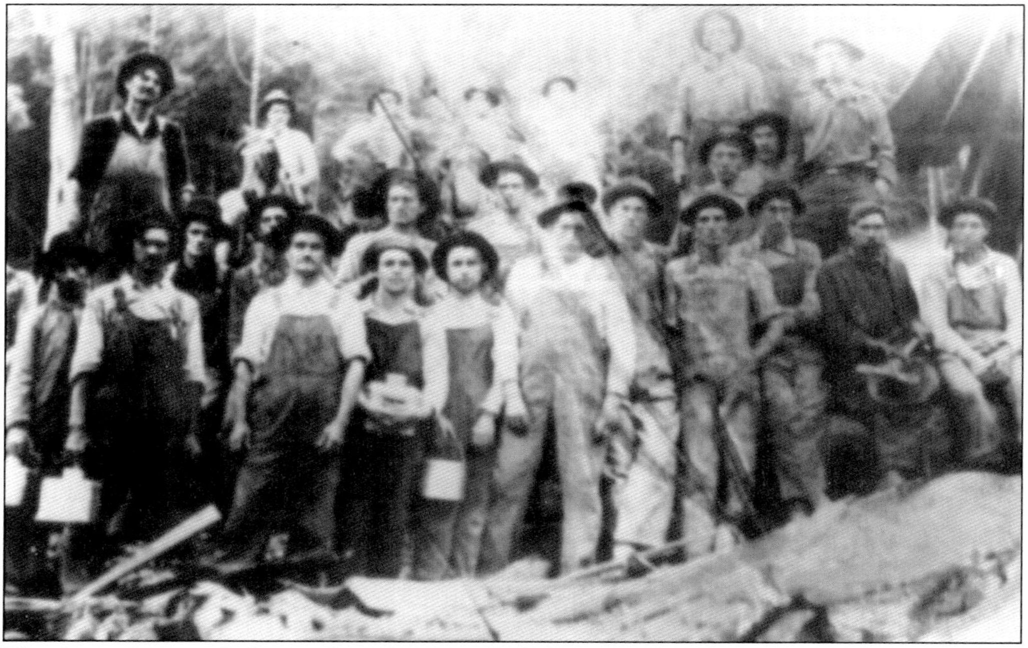

The above photograph from early 20th-century Buladean shows a crew of loggers. Several men hold the tools of the trade, including axes and the ever-present lunch bucket. In many North Carolina places, particularly after the Civil War, timber became a lucrative business. (L.G. Sheets.)

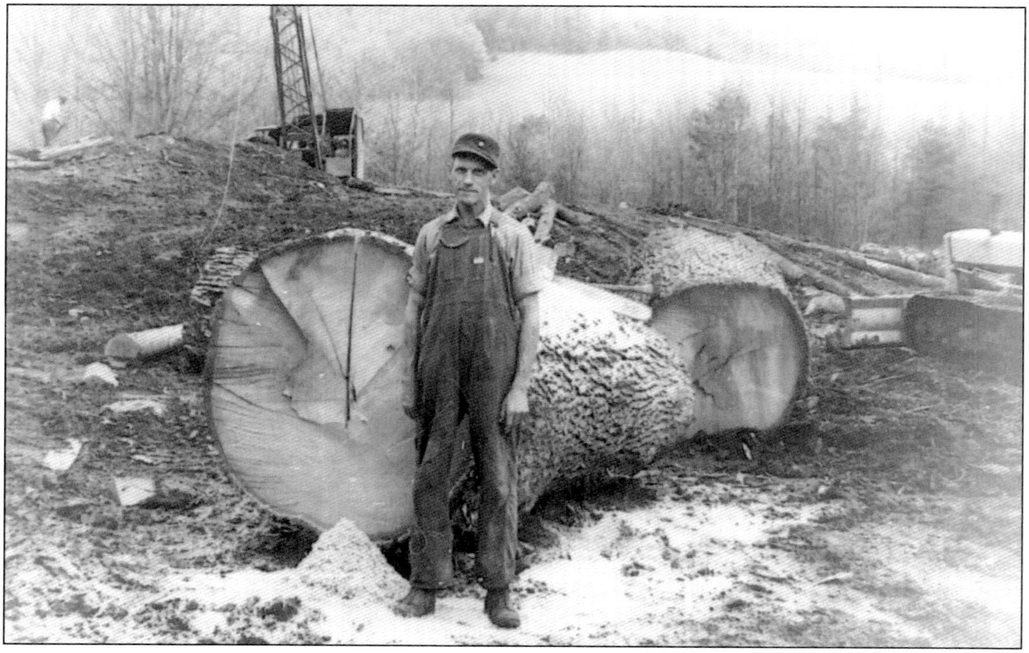

In this photograph, the industrial age has hit the area. Large pieces of machinery were used to clear and cut greater numbers of trees. While construction was a good customer, the furniture industry in North Carolina was also an extensive business, fueled by easily accessible wood. (Thelma Hughes Cumbie.)

Wearing glasses to protect his eyes, Frank A. Hughes, a sawyer, watches as trees and logs become boards to make homes and furniture. Lumber was a labor-intensive industry. Logging and sawmills provided employment to many of the residents of towns around Bakersville and often provided the materials for them to make their own homes. (Thelma Hughes Cumbie.)

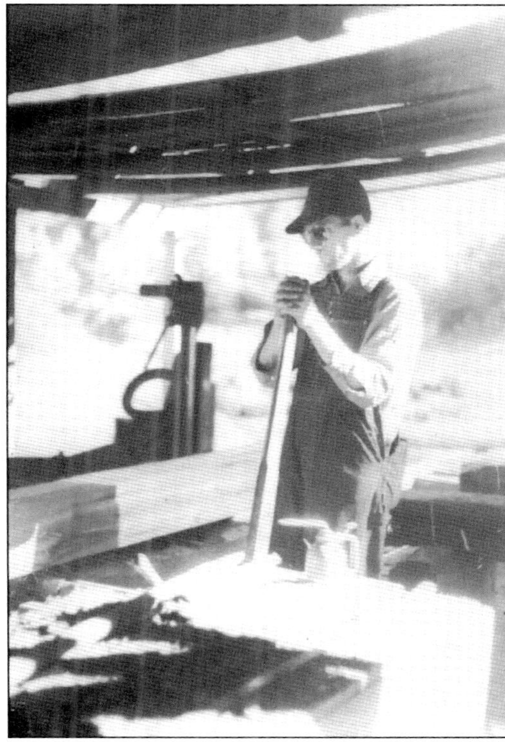

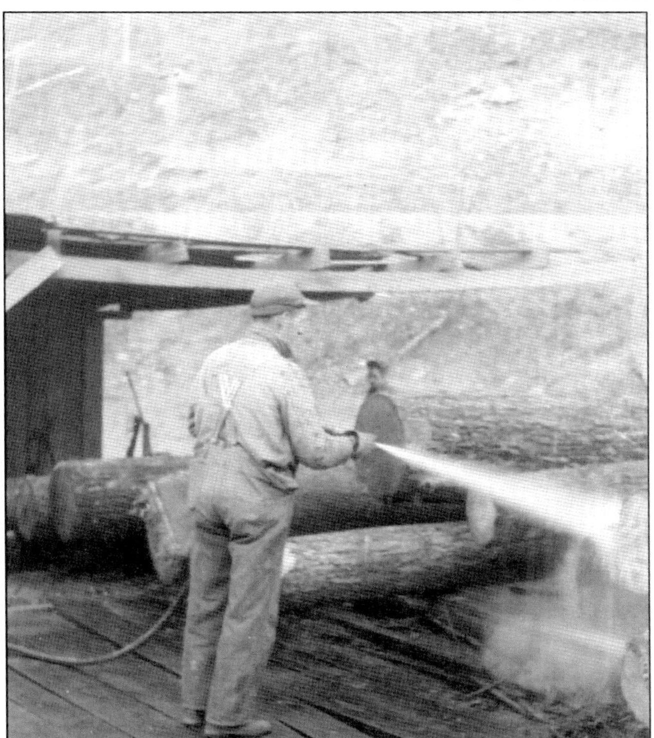

Frank A. Hughes sprays the newly cut trees with water, helping to remove the bark before cutting the pieces into board lengths. High-pressure sprays of water made it easier to accomplish the debarking process. Lumbering and sawmilling have been occupations for many centuries, but now the processes are highly mechanized. (Thelma Hughes Cumbie.)

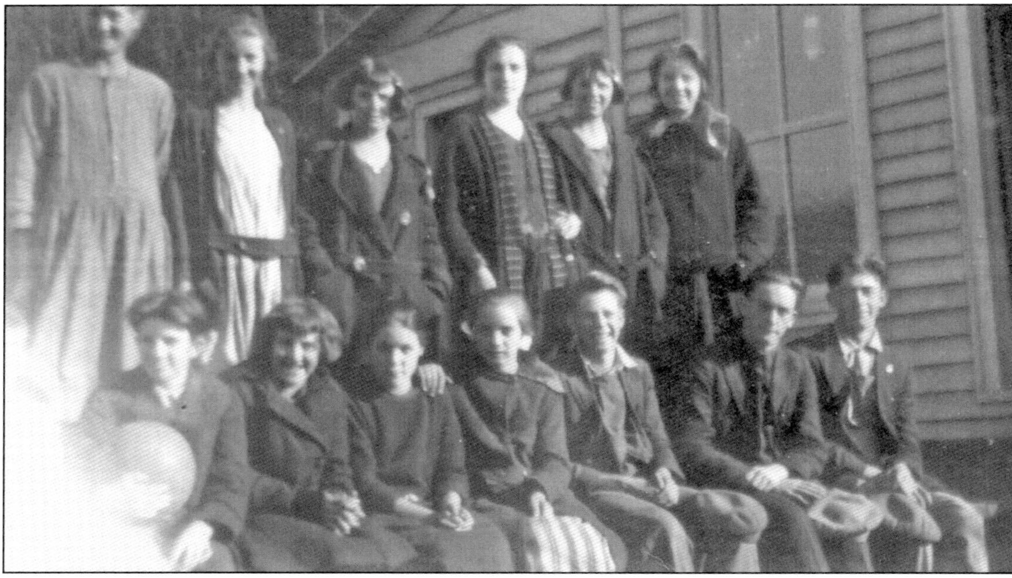

The Holston Presbyterian Church home mission sponsored the first school in Buladean. Seen here in the 1920s, the students pictured above were a mix of locals who went back home after their classes and students who were able to board at the school. (Thelma Hughes Cumbie.)

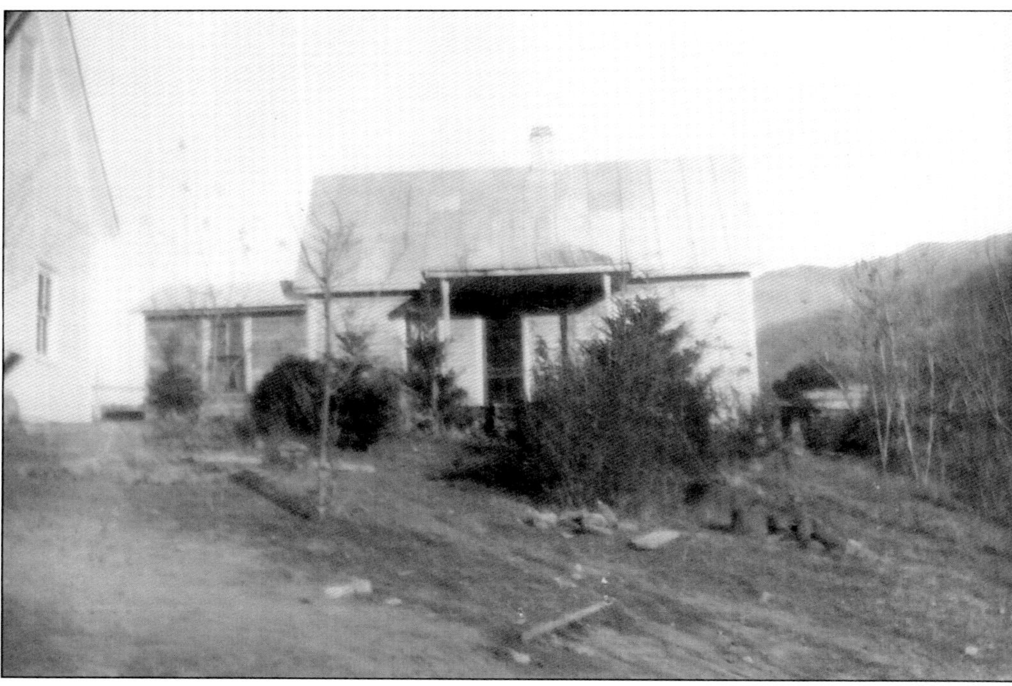

School was held in the church building, as were community meetings. Two missionary women were the teachers, supported by the Holston Presbyterian Church's home mission. These women lived in a tiny yellow cottage and were paid $30 a month to teach from whatever books the friends of the mission sent. (Shelby Street.)

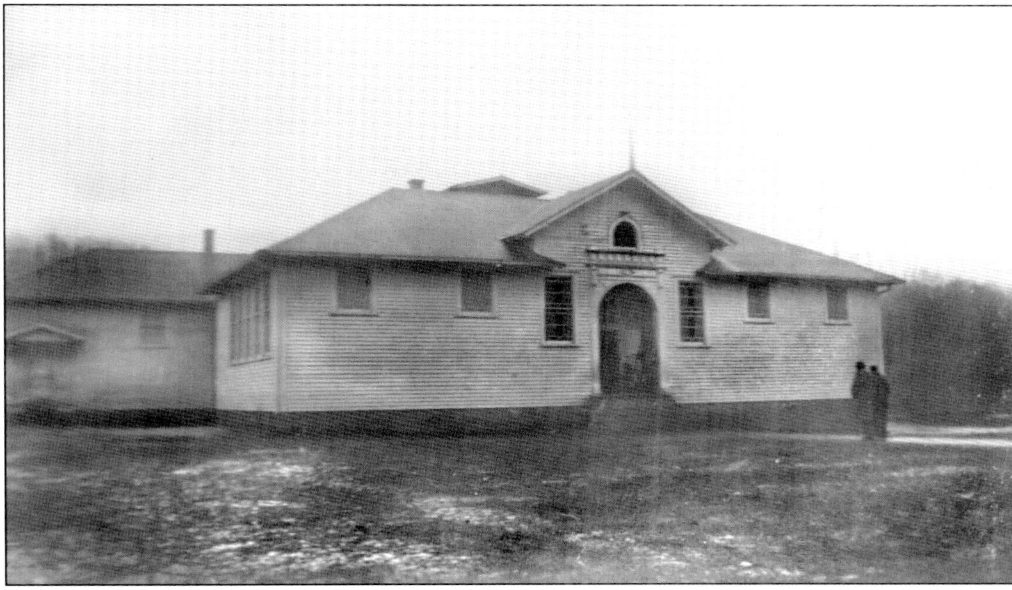

In the early 1920s, the state began to provide education for the children of Buladean and all of Mitchell County. The building pictured above is the school in 1938. Because the state took over the education process, taxes were imposed on the citizens to pay the salaries of the teachers. (Longleaf Media.)

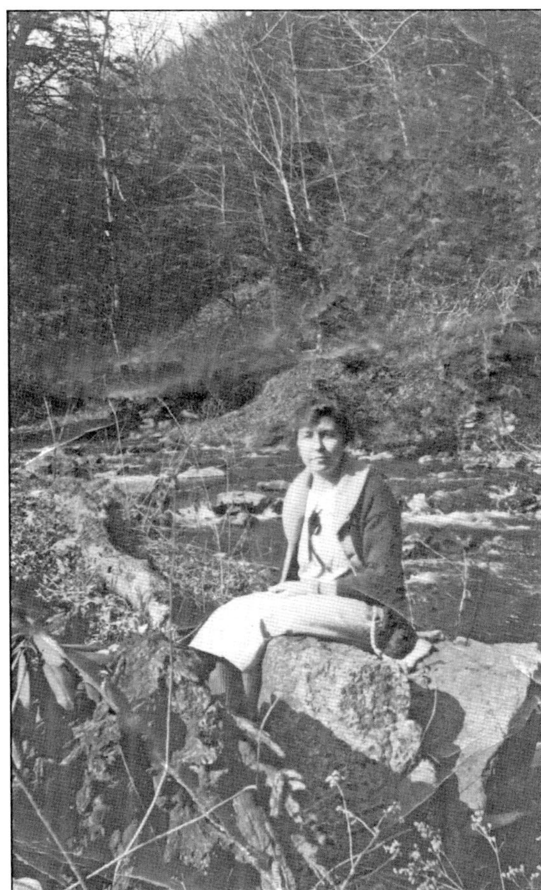

Once the school became a part of the public system, teachers were recruited from colleges to teach in rural areas. Seen here around 1930 is a favorite of the Buladean School, Mildred Clark. Teachers were often given apples, potatoes, onions, and slaughtered livestock to supplement their salaries. (L.G. Sheets.)

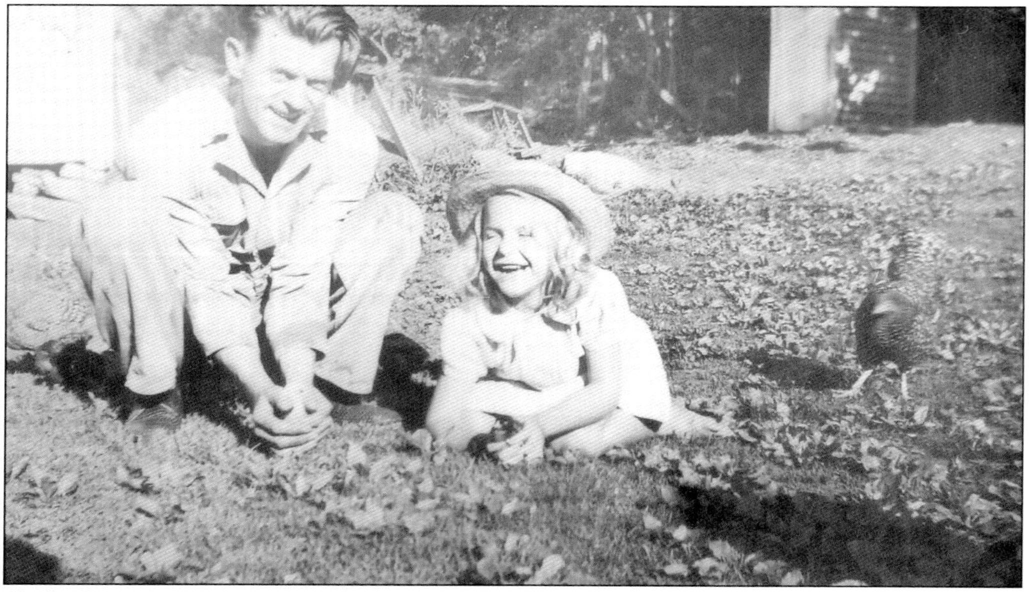

Shelby Bennett Street is seen here in 1945 with her foster brother Cecil Bennett and their new chicks. Note the hovering mother hen lurking in the background as her babies are handled by humans. Most families had their own chickens that provided a continual supply of eggs—and perhaps, on Sunday, a fresh chicken dinner. (Shelby Bennett Street.)

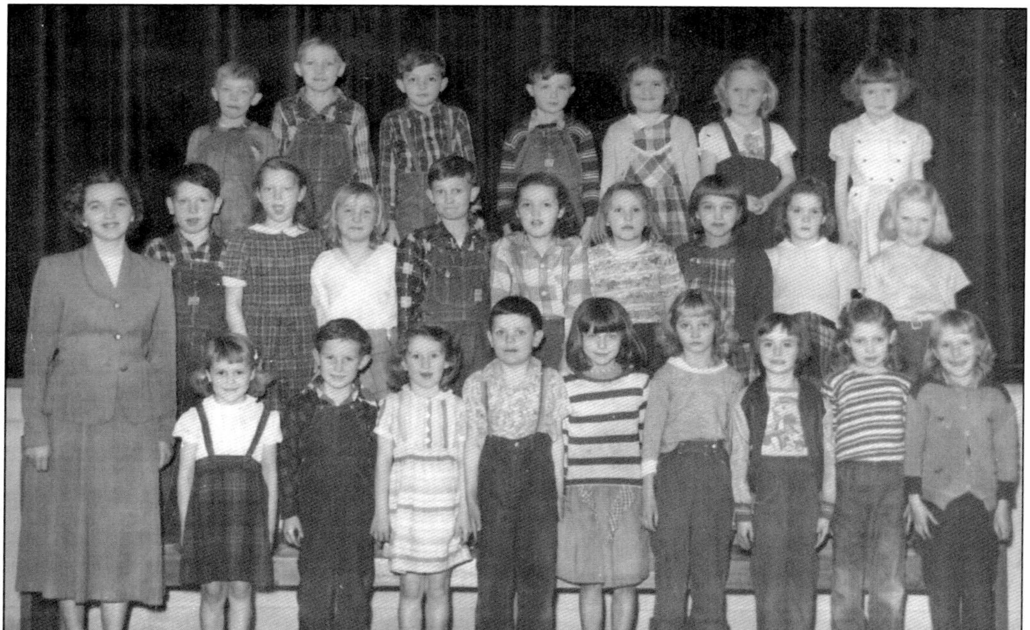

Graduating in 1947 from Tipton Hill High School, Mildred Bennett Masters returned to her hometown to teach the sixth-grade class at Buladean. She is seen here posing with her 1950 class. By this time, large families were going out of fashion, and the populations in schools had began to decline. (Mildred and Kay Masters.)

Jesse Bennett (bottom left), Hattie Campbell bottom right), and friends strike a pose on the rocks of the mountain and proudly declare, "We are in love," on the border of the photograph. Jess holds Hattie's hand, though she is not smiling, like her friend is. (Mildred and Kay Masters.)

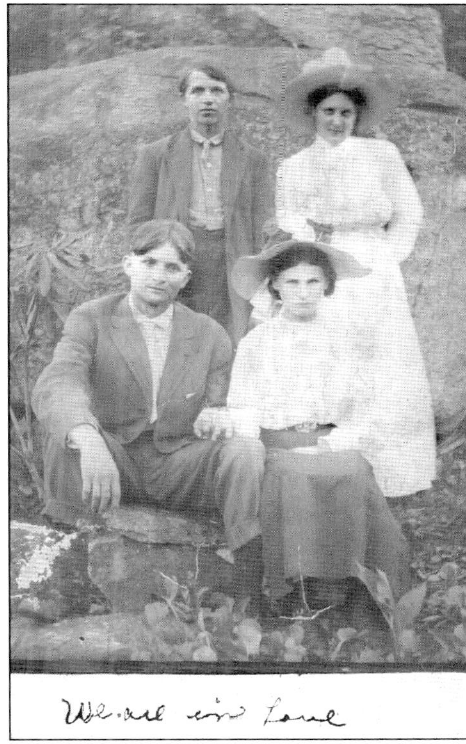

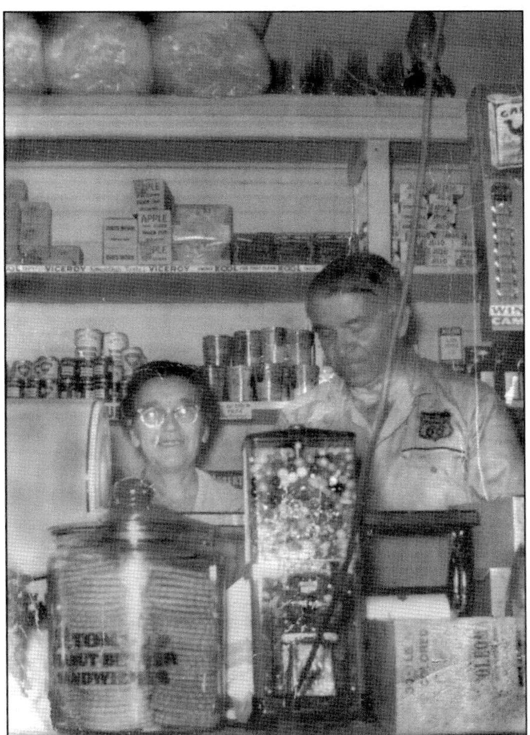

Jesse and Hattie Campbell Bennett ran the local store and service station in Buladean (1940–1961), which provided many of the staples for families. Note the variety of items for sale in this photograph: canned goods, a variety of tobacco products, and a Tom's Peanut Butter Sandwich jar full of something good for the kids for only 1¢ each. (Shelby Street.)

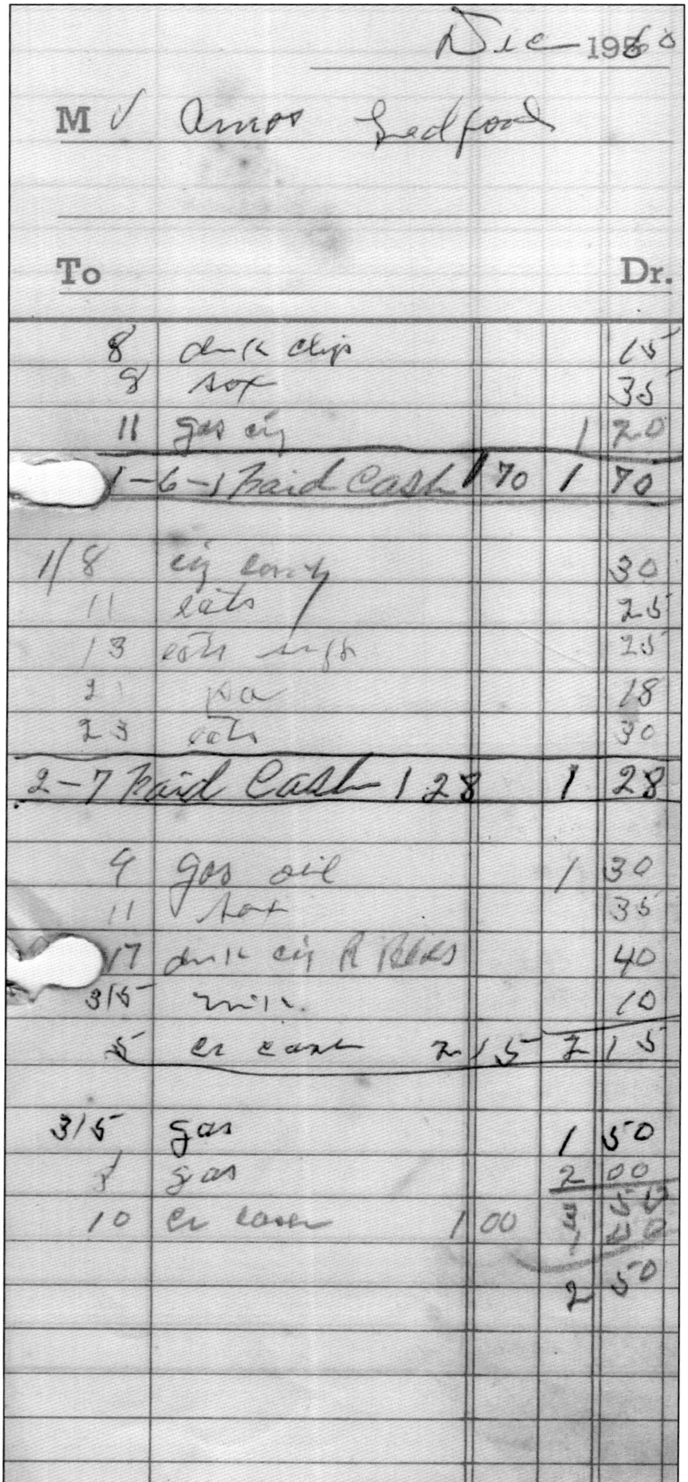

Here is a 1960 ledger from the Three Way station owned by the Bennetts. Note the prices: eight socks for 35¢; drink and chips for 15¢, and gasoline $1.50 for a fill-up. Payment was noted as “hard cash.” Note that the last entry shows that the buyer, a Mr. Ledford, paid $1, leaving the other $2.50 for a later date. (Shelby Bennett Street.)

Nine

Glen Ayre

Glen Ayre was settled in the 1830s by the Ayres family, whose ancestor, Jacob Ayres, got a government grant, paid 25¢ an acre, and owned all of Roan Valley and Grassy Ridge. The first name of the post office there was Brighton, but it was changed to Glen Ayre in 1916 when rural mail delivery was initiated.

The town had its share of the elements previously discussed: mines, farms, country stores, churches, schools, illicit alcohol production (locally called Roan Mountain Dew), and murders, but it had one advantage over most of the other places studied here—it was on the road to the Cloudland Hotel.

Built first as a log inn with 20 rooms, the Cloudland Hotel hosted the many business associates of its creator, Gen. J.T. Wilder. The general had come to the area to mine mica and feldspar after the Civil War and soon expanded into the hospitality business. The inn soon grew too small to house these guests, and he replaced it with a 268-room hotel (estimates range from 160 to 365 rooms, depending on whose ancestor tells the story). Sitting on the top of Roan Mountain, the hotel rested half in Tennessee and half in North Carolina. Because Mitchell County was dry, one could go to the Tennessee part of the dining room, have a drink, and then go to the North Carolina side to sleep. Guests could also hike, picnic among the rhododendrons, enjoy the extraordinary view, read a good book, or listen to the string band music of local musicians.

Years later, local musician "Fiddlin'" Steve Ledford, an exceptional fiddle player and an occasional distiller of white lightning, took his string band music as far away as New York City, and he even cut a record called *Roan Mountain Dew*.

The weather in Glen Ayre is likely the most extreme of all the places in this book. In 1960, a snowstorm dumped four feet of the fluffy white stuff on the area. The roads were blocked for six weeks, and residents pulled sleighs to go to Carver's Gap, near the peak of the Roan.

The history and residents of Glen Ayre have much to teach about living in an alpine environment in western North Carolina.

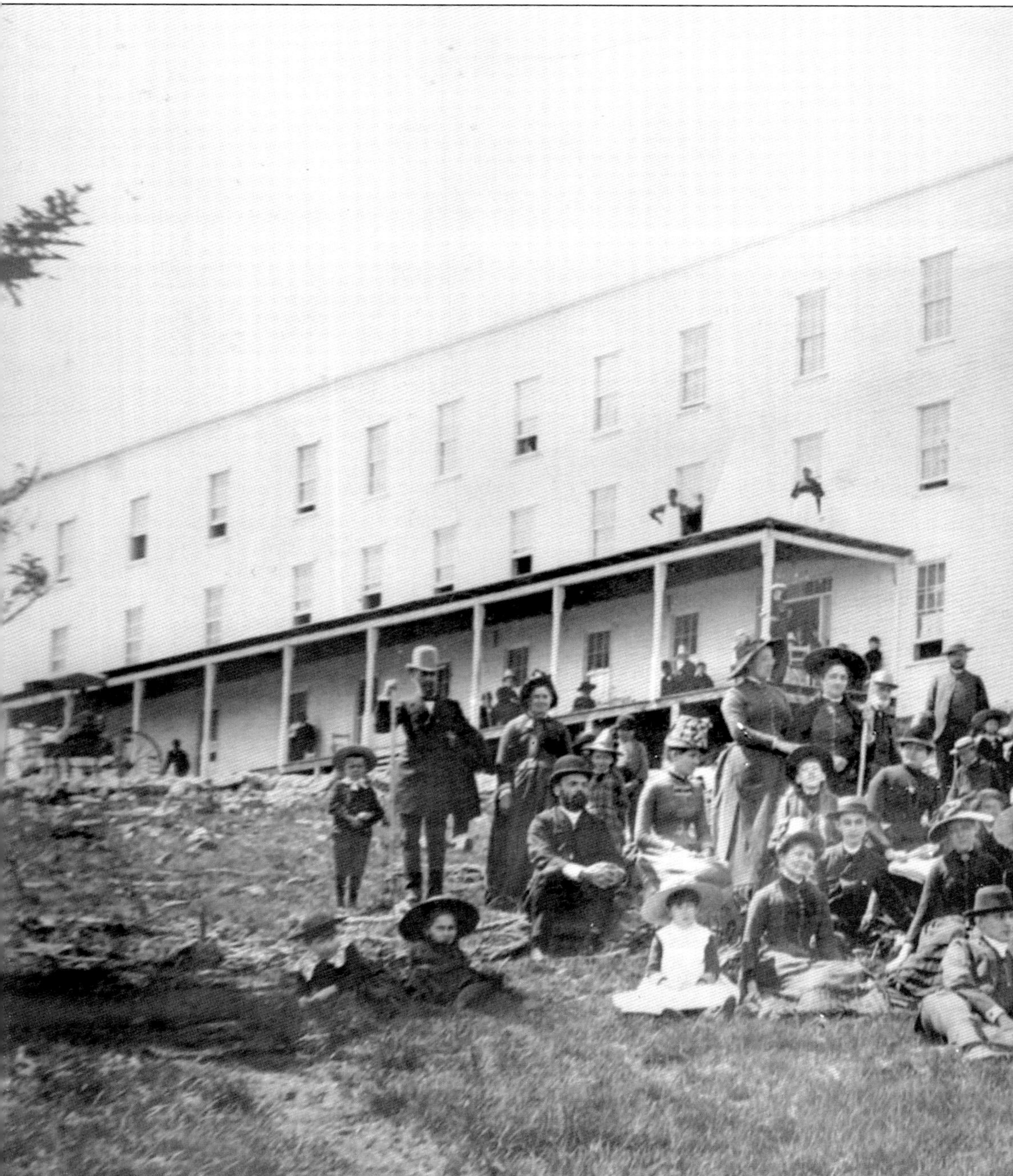

This photograph was taken at the Cloudland Hotel as it was close to completion. At least half of the hotel appears open for business. Gen. J.T. Wilder is in the back, center left, with the hat and gray beard. It appears that most of the people are his guests for a grand-opening celebration. His idea for a hotel on the top of Roan Mountain brought many city folks to western North

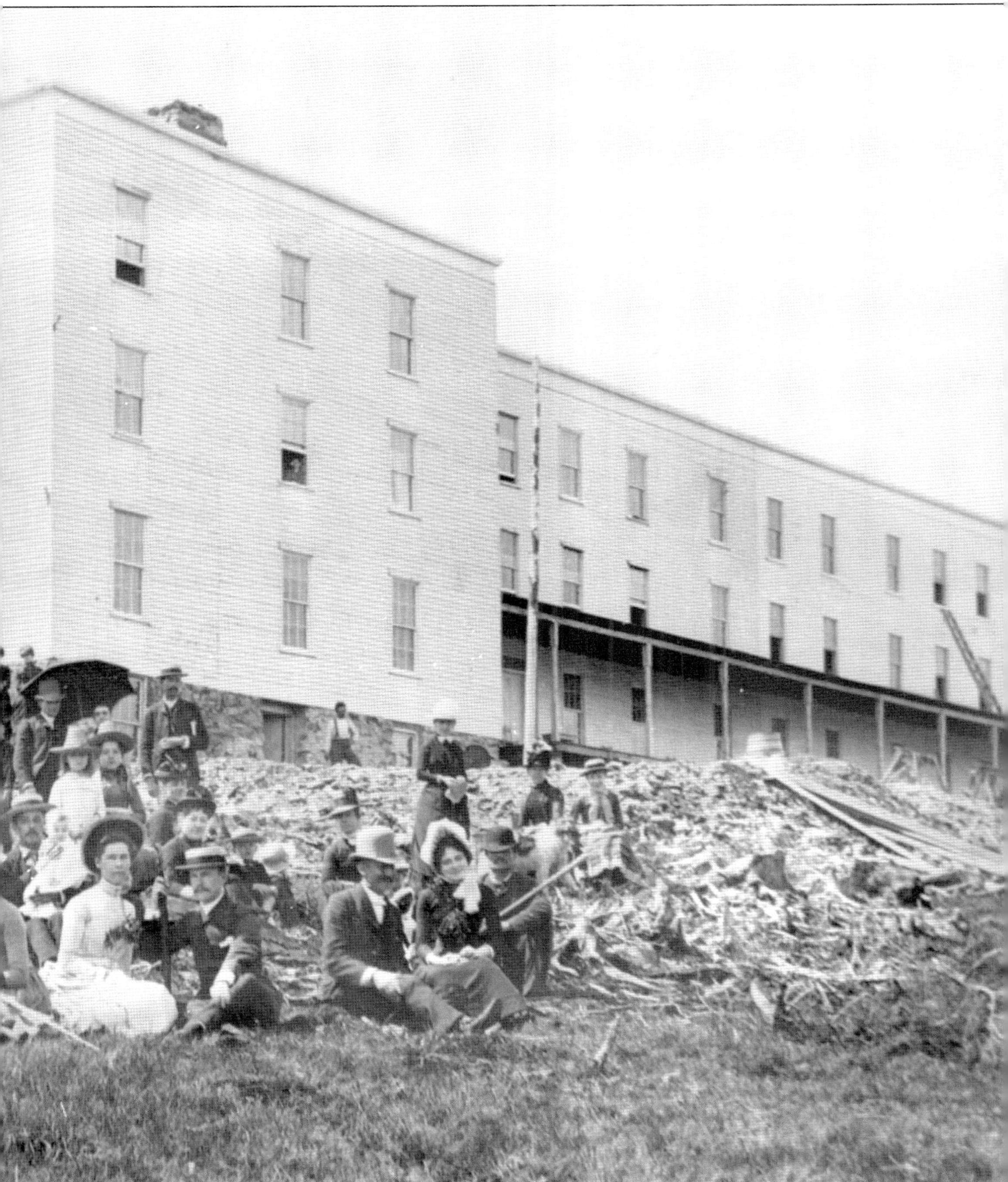

Carolina. African Americans, though few in number, were said to work there. Consider those on the roof—perhaps a maid and a carpenter? Unfortunately, their names are lost to history. The Cloudland stayed in business for 25 years, and its history remains a fascination for many people to this very day. (Appalachia Archives, ETSU, Murrell Collection.)

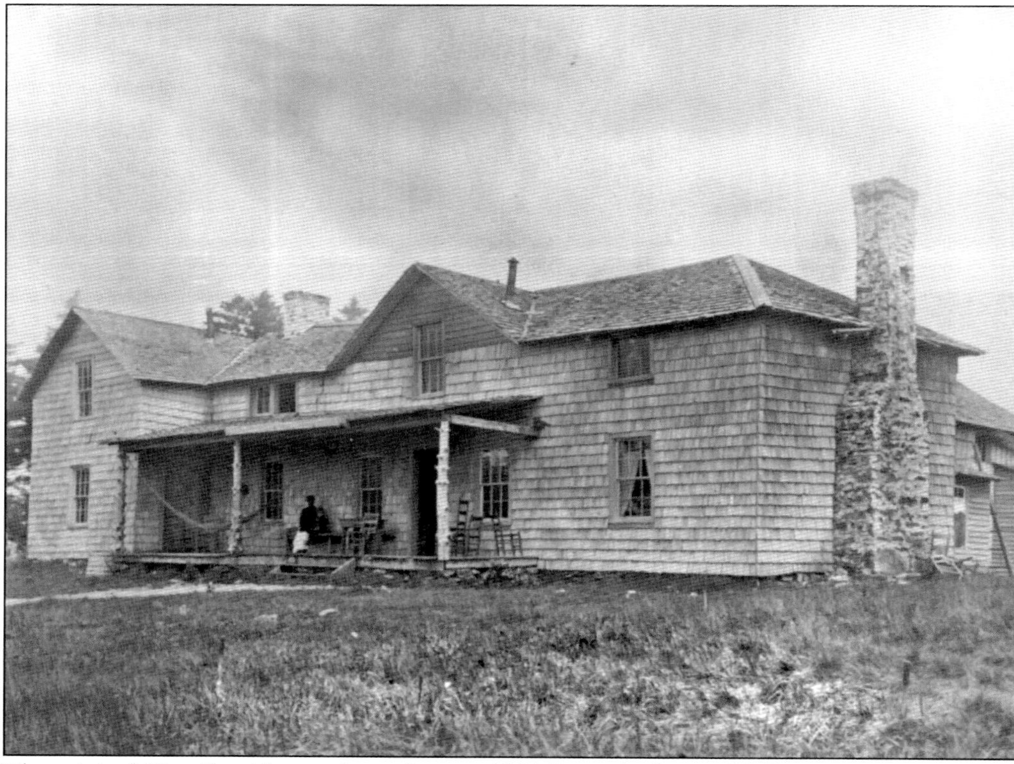

The original Cloudland Inn is shown here in 1884. It was built in 1877. Featuring just 20 rooms, the inn was initially used to house Gen. J.T. Wilder's business guests as they dealt in the products of local mining. Wilder quickly surmised that he needed a bigger place and began construction of the Cloudland Hotel in the 1880s. Wiley Gouge was purported to have worked there as a carpenter. (North Carolina Collection, UNC Library at Chapel Hill.)

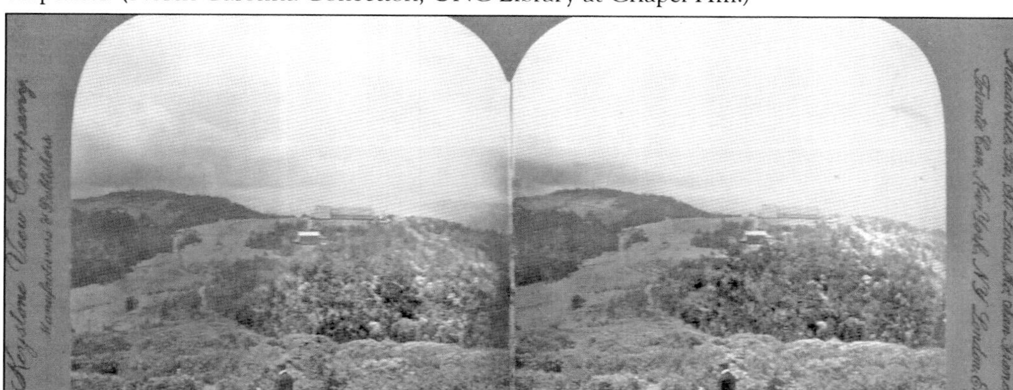

Stereopticons were a popular household item in the late 19th and early 20th century. Merging this double picture meant that parts of it became three-dimensional. Looking at the Cloudland from this distance gives the viewer an idea of the incredible sights that must have been available to those who vacationed there. (Appalachia Archives, ETSU, Murrell Collection.)

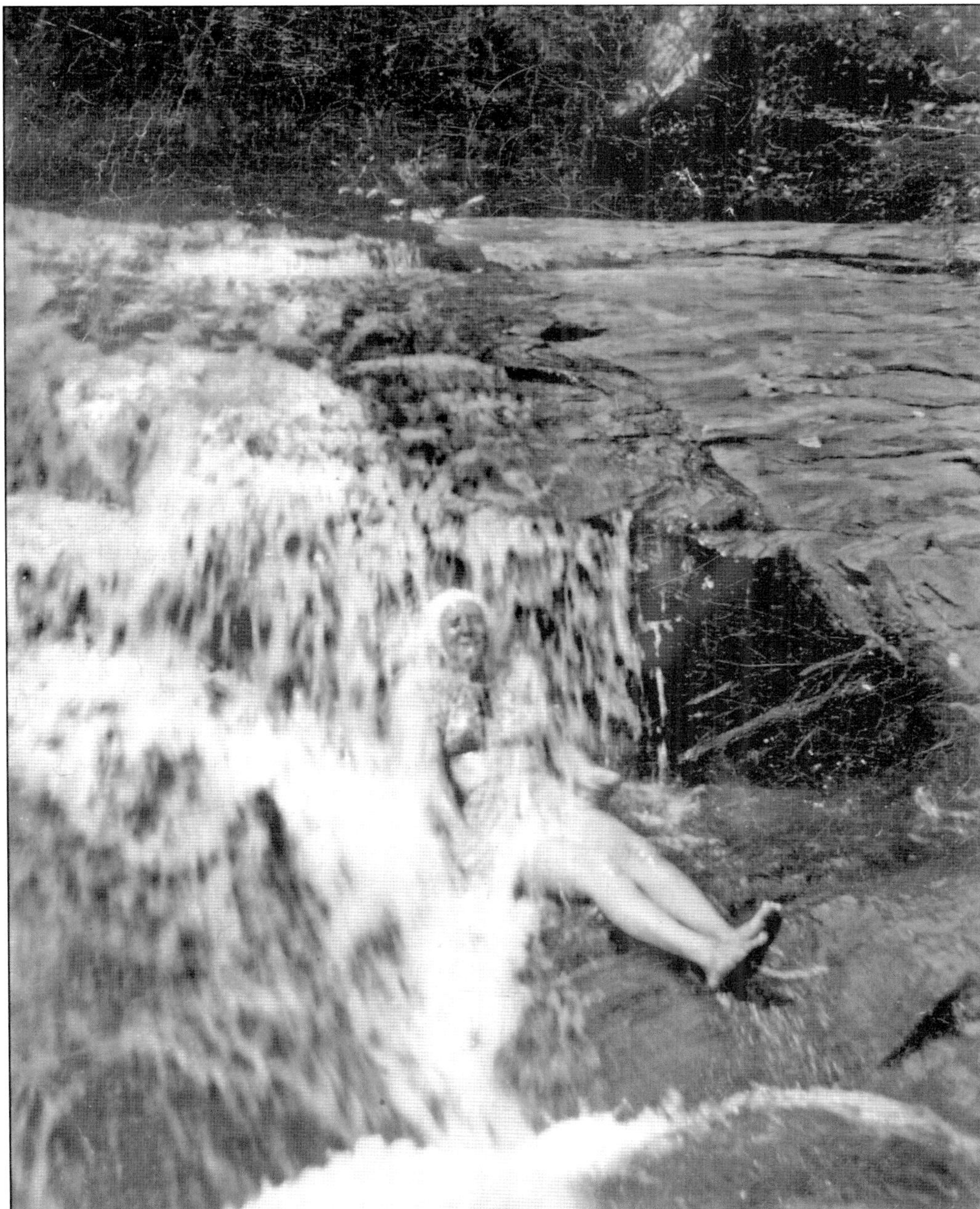

Once termed "the place rivers are born," cold alpine steams race through the mountains near many area towns, including Glen Ayre. Here, Reba Gouge is clearly enjoying just sitting in the path of the water on a large rock in Falls Creek. It was a tradition with many of the families that lived in the area. On any given day, dad might come home and say, "Get the picnic basket ready. Let's go up the Roan." Growing up in the mountains meant that one was usually comfortable with all the beauties and challenges of nature, and picnicking on the Roan drew young adults, like Reba, to eat, wander through the woods and rhododendron thickets, and play in the water. (Maxie Gouge Buchanan.)

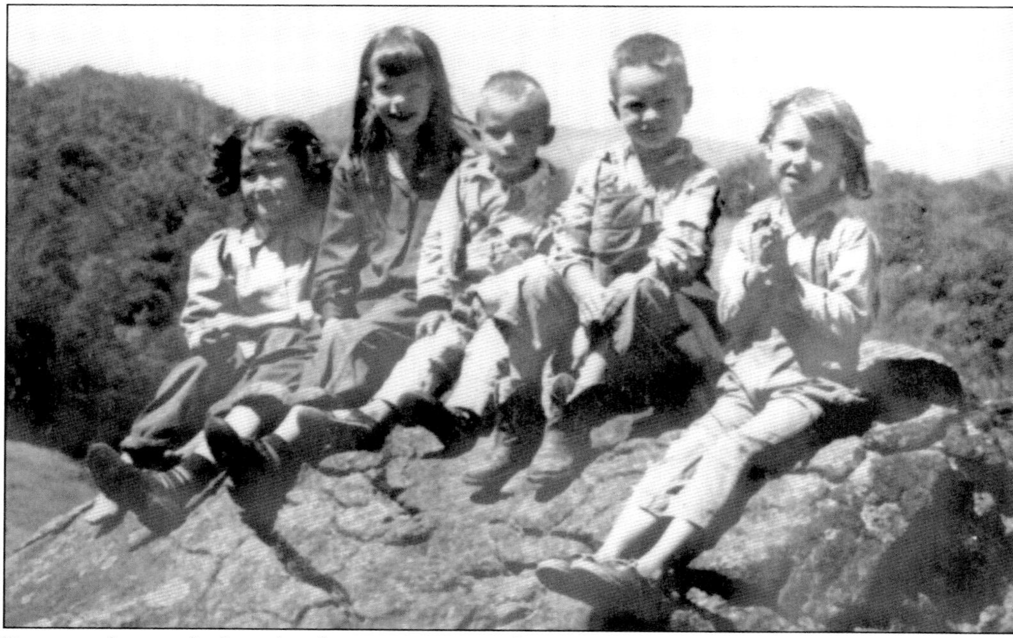

Parents often took their families to picnic on the Roan, especially in the summer as a special treat. Sometimes they cooked the fish they caught in the streams, and sometimes they simply ate sandwiches prepared at home. Children especially enjoyed these picnics: climbing on rocks, playing with their toys and dolls, swimming in a small spring pond when it was warm. Clothing was optional, up to a certain age. Family picnics were an important part of mountain culture. Pictured in the 1940 photograph above are, from left to right, Crystal Kuhne Bradshaw, Jerrie Sullins, Keith Kuhne, Phillip Castro, and June Kuhne. Pictured in the 1940 photograph below are, from left to right, Jean Gouge Burleson, June Kuhne, Crystal Kuhne Bradshaw, Verla Gouge Kuhne, and Phillip Castro. (Phil Castro.)

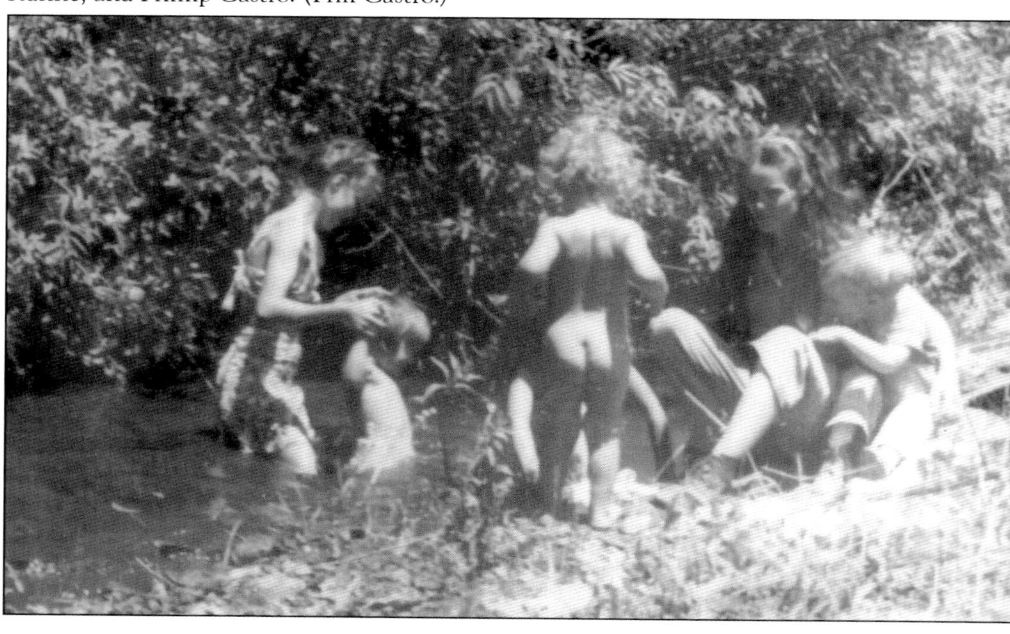

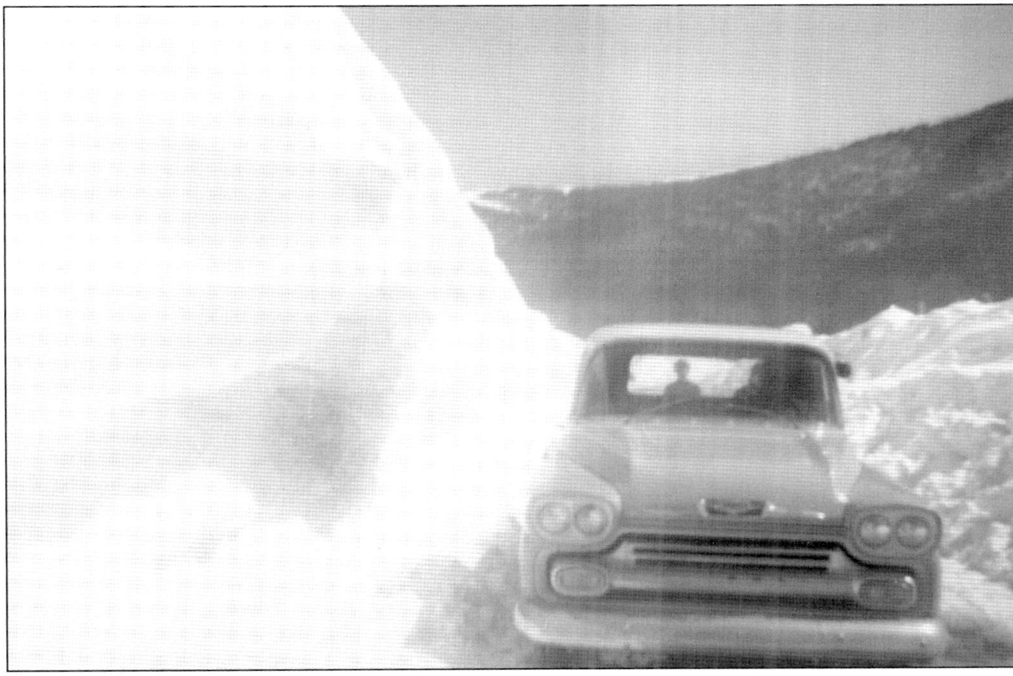

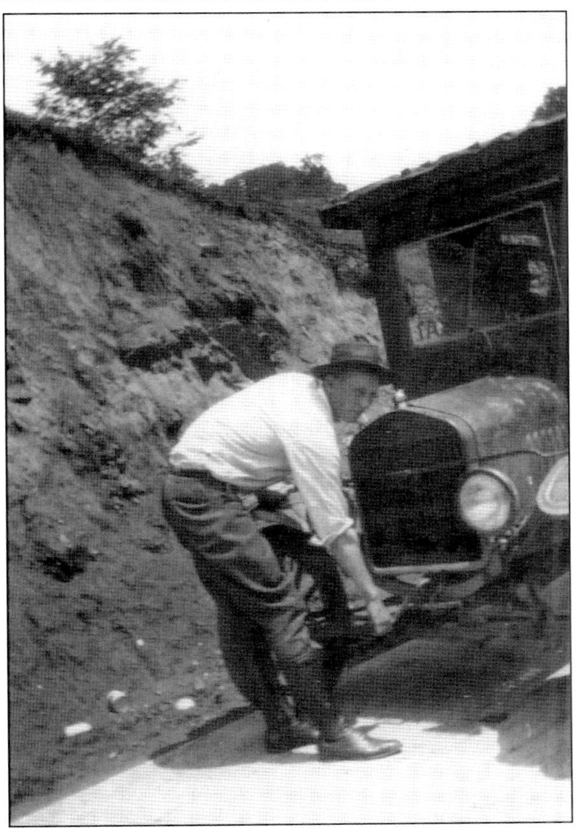

Living in an alpine environment means sometimes suffering with extreme winter weather. The year 1960 brought record-breaking snowfalls to folks who lived there, as evidenced by this photograph in which drifts tower over a vehicle. People were isolated for quite some time and had to use wagons to get to Carver's Gap. (Wayne Ayres.)

Getting to the top of the Roan with an automobile was not an easy task, as the roads were not yet all paved. In addition, Charles Kettering had not yet invented the electric starter. Here is Coy Holder, trying to crank his Model T. On sunny days, it was not a problem; in rain and snow, it was not fun. (Wayne Ledford.)

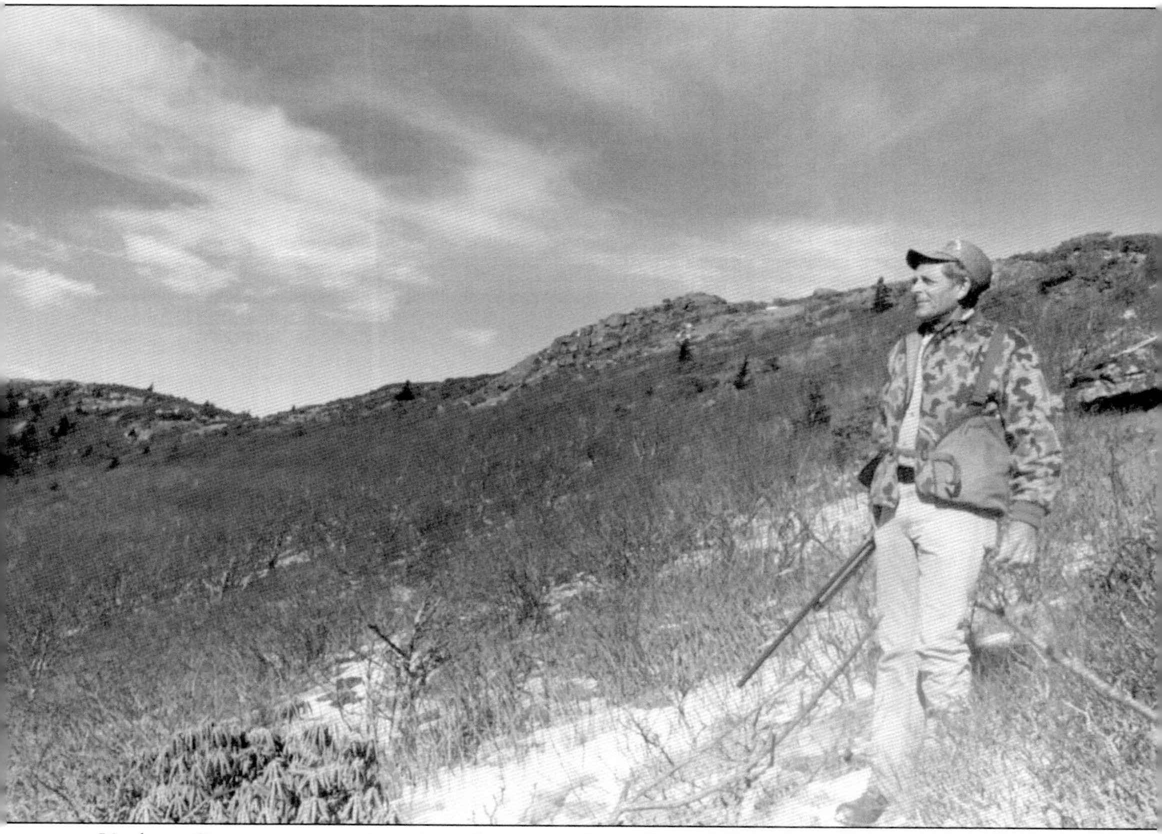

Herbert Gouge seems to be a lone hunter seeking the wildlife that often sustained the family's diet. These hunting skills, honed from childhood, also protected people from wild animals that might look on them as prey. Most of the farmers and residents of area hunted during the year to provide both food and other materials such as leather for knife sheaths. Guns were a necessity on the mountain as bears roamed the area and threatened residents. Smaller animals like squirrels, coons, and rabbits often provided extra food. Gouge is standing in what is known as a "bald," a place in the mountains that is void of tall trees and often provides an open range for hunting small prey. One of these balds is visible at Carver's Gap near the top of the Roan. (Gary Gouge.)

One of America's most original forms of music, bluegrass, characterizes the Appalachian Mountain culture, and these places had their share of it. Descended from the music of the Scottish, Irish, Welsh, and English, it employed string instruments including the mandolin, acoustic guitar, banjo, fiddle, bass, and others. Steve Ledford organized this group, the Carolina Ramblers, which consisted of his family and neighbors in Glen Ayre. They often sat on the front porch, playing and singing. In 1929, they performed at home as well as in New York City, and while there, they made records for the ARC label. Pictured at right, the Ledfords are, from left to right, (first row) Taft, Rittie, and Jane; (second row) Smith, Waits, and Steve. In the 1972 photograph below, shown keeping the musical tradition alive are, from left to right, Wayne and Byrl Ledford and James Gardner. (Wayne Ledford.)

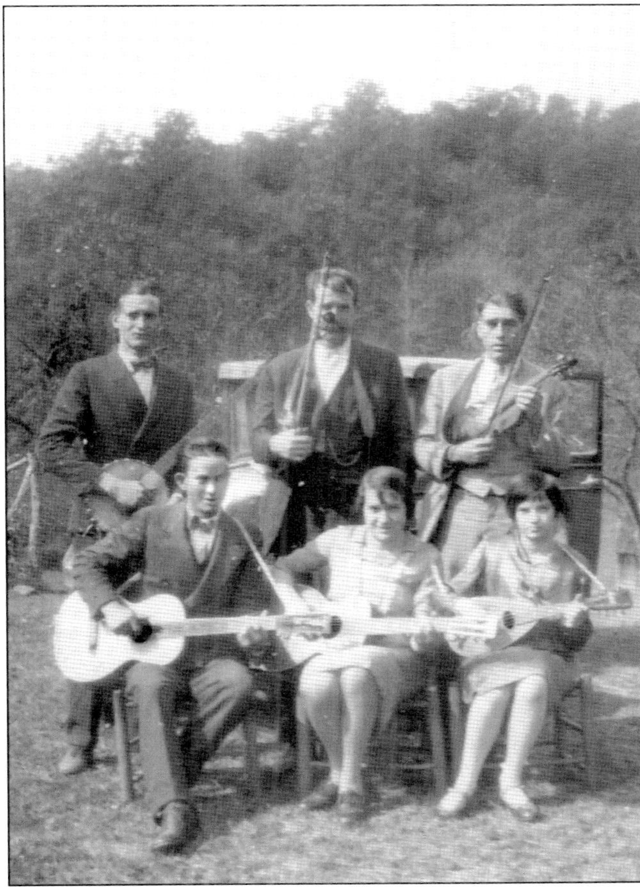

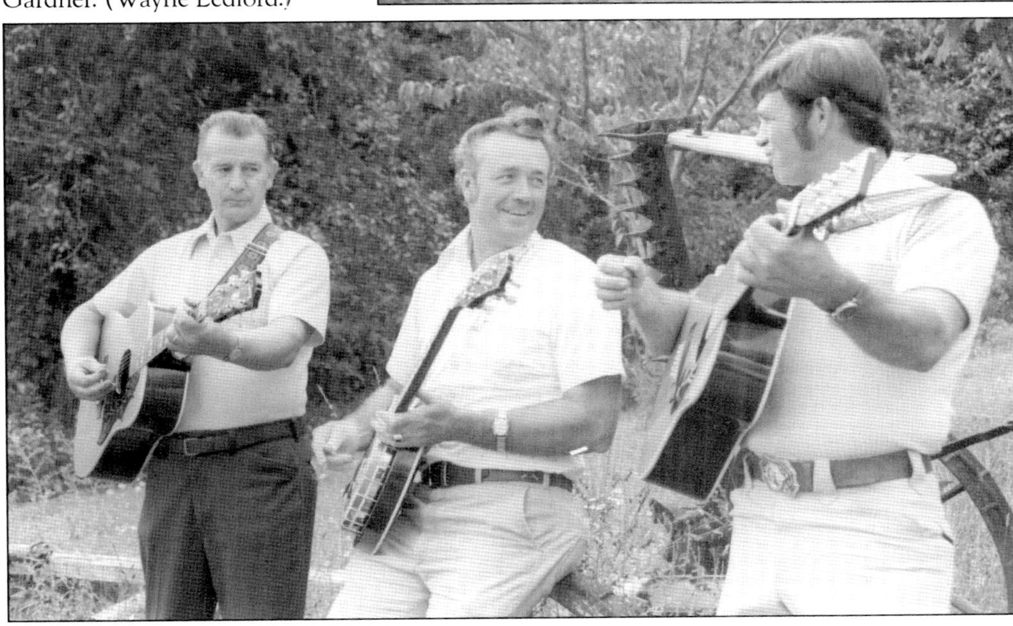

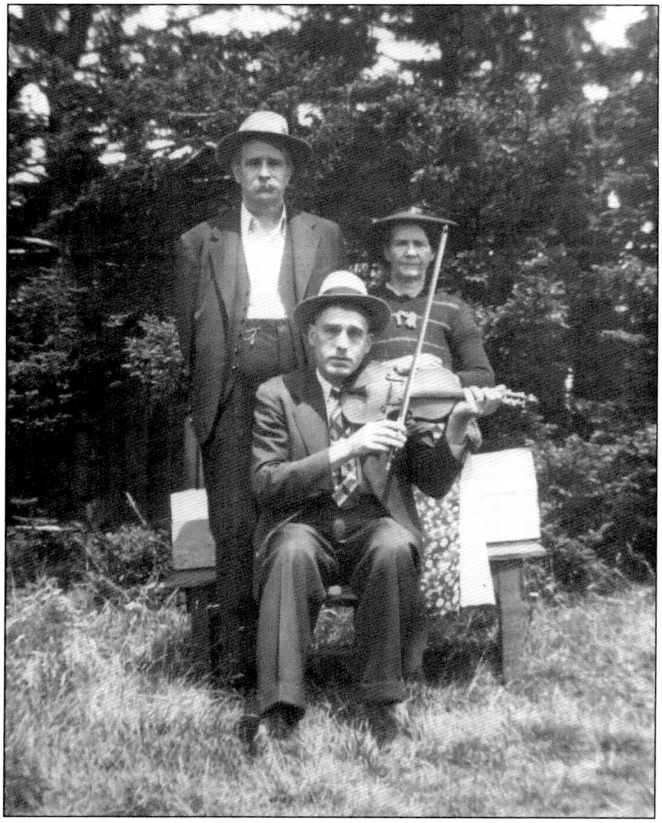

Though the Cloudland Hotel was long gone by 1941, memories of its grand days included recognizing the importance of music as a part of the guests' enjoyment. Years later, local musicians sought out the site to pose for pictures with their instruments. Seen here are Waits, Melissa, and Steve Ledford. (Wayne Ledford.)

Frank Griffith's grandfather is pictured here at his home in Glen Ayre. The house at the left is typical of the late 1920s and early 1930s. The bridge is the type that most people used to straddle the area's many streams. Floods often took these wooden structures away with ease. (Frank Griffith.)

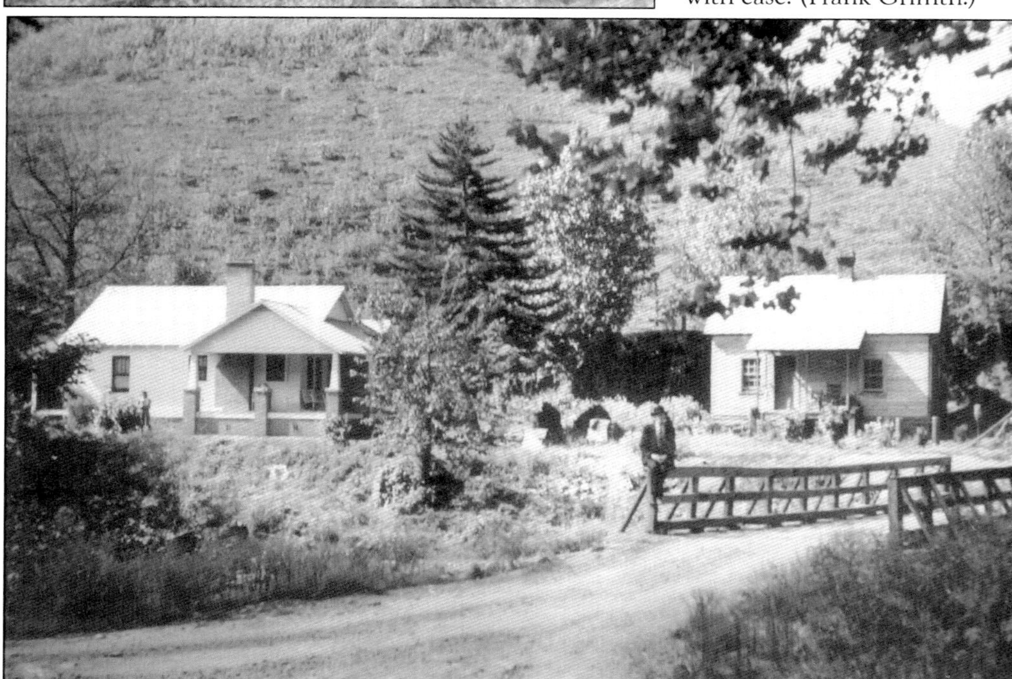

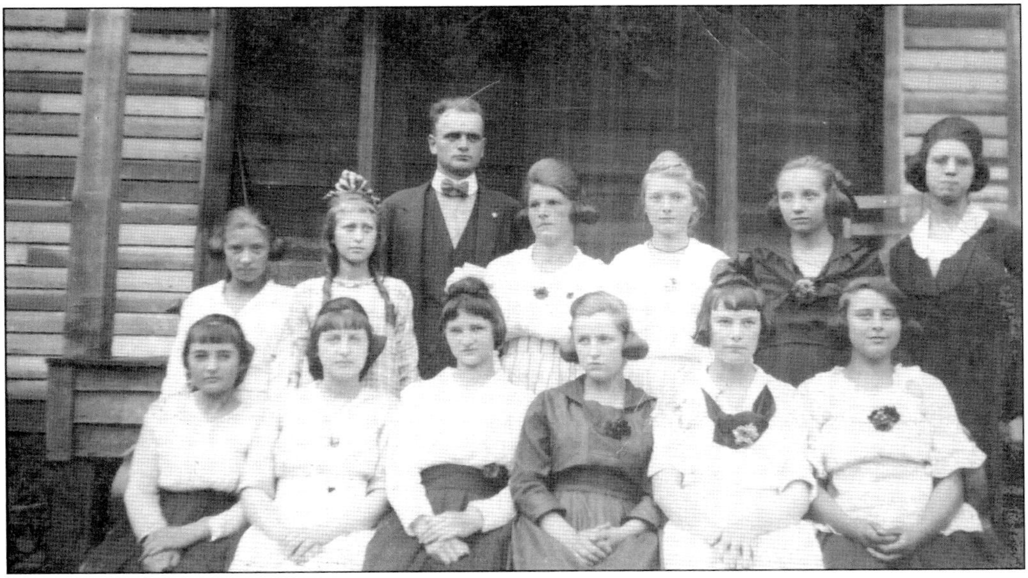

All over the mountains, small schools dotted the countryside with many different-aged students in each one. Four local schools served the Glen Ayre area until they were consolidated in 1922. In the above photograph from around 1924, the girls in Glen Ayre School, with teacher Jeter Burleson, were quite dressed up for the picture but probably did not attend school dressed like that on a daily basis. Below, a separate picture of graduates of Glen Ayre School, around 1923, shows men and women. Education was important to the citizens of this area. In 1901, there were 124 students in the Glen Ayre School alone. (Above, Maxie Gouge Buchanan; below, Wayne Ledford.)

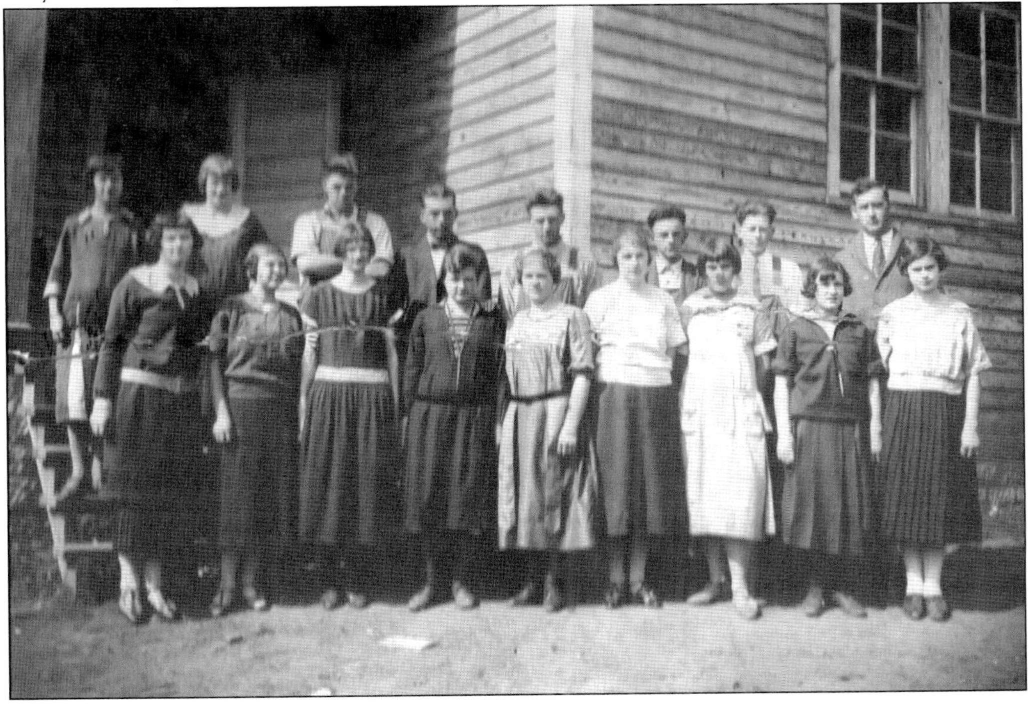

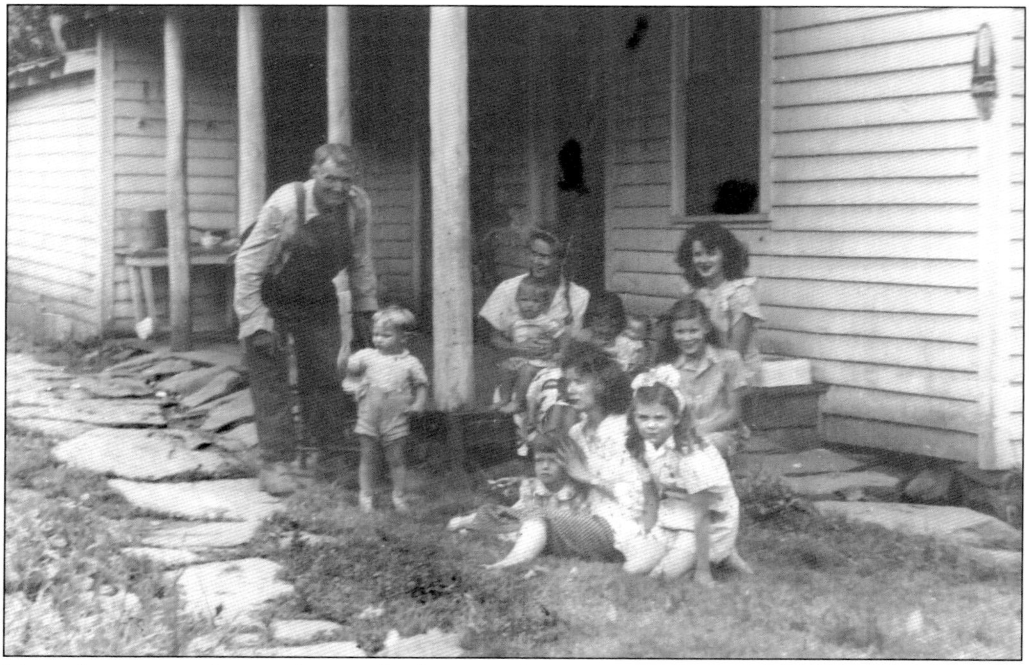

Here, three generations gather on the front porch on a warm summer day in 1947. Herb Gouge stoops to the left to admonish his grandson while other family members are distracted in a variety of ways. (Gary Gouge, Phil Castro.)

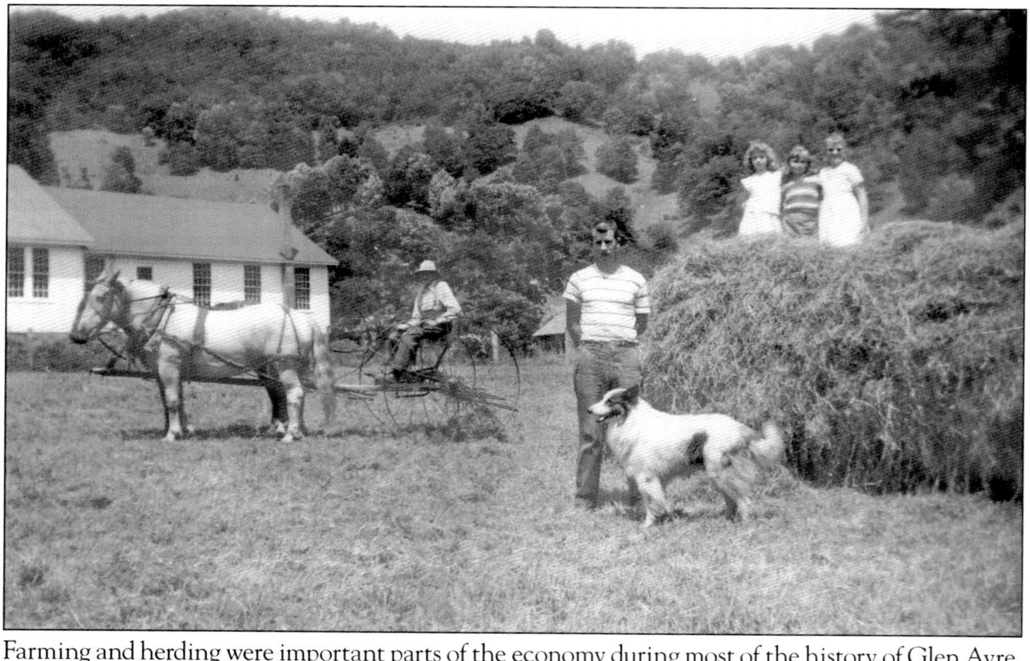

Farming and herding were important parts of the economy during most of the history of Glen Ayre. This is a typical scene of gathering hay during the summer for winter feed for the animals. Pictured in this 1959 photograph is A.F. Buchanan with the horses, Wayne Ledford in the center, and, from left to right, Kay Ledford, Mary Frances Buchanan, and Carolyn Harold. (Wayne Ledford.)

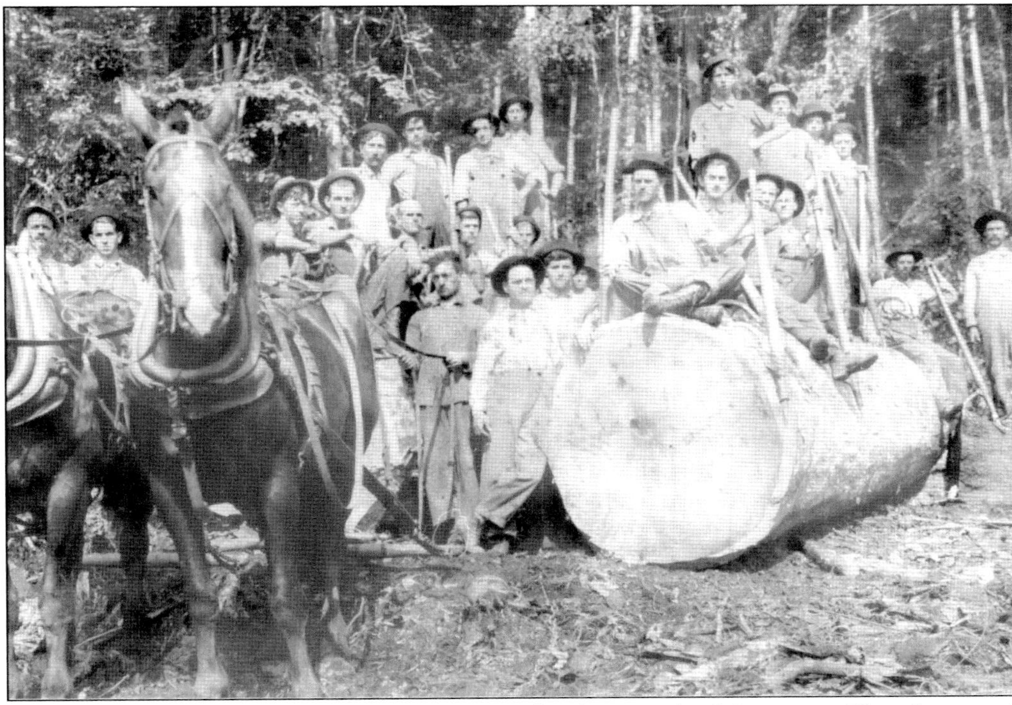

Logging was a popular means of supporting one's family in much of the region. This photograph is likely from around 1910. The horses had to work as hard as the men did to get the towering "crop" off the mountain and to the markets. While it is unlikely that these are virgin forests, this log had been growing in the Appalachian Mountains for a long time. (Anne Castro.)

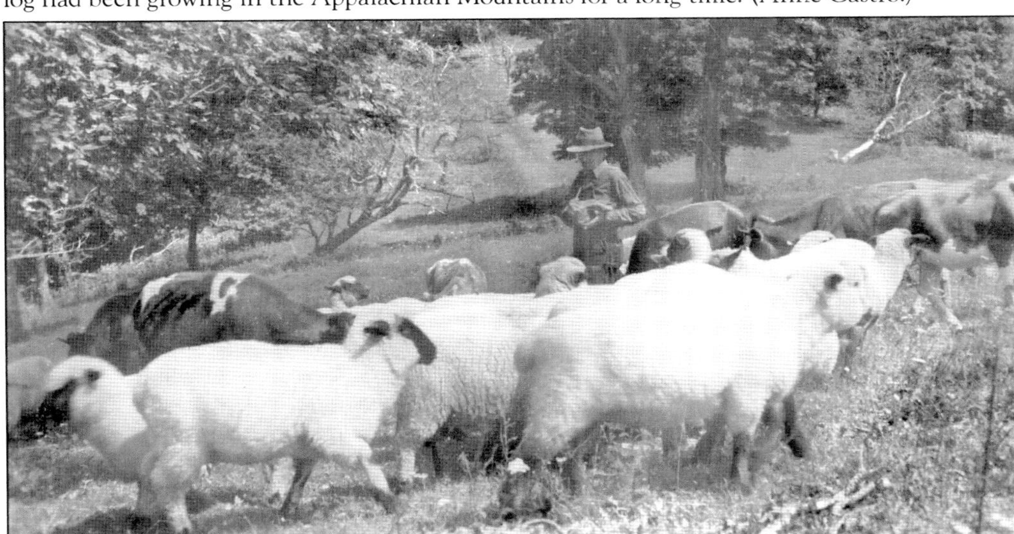

The alpine nature of this terrain lent itself to sheepherding. This picture from the 1950s shows the herding of animals from one pasture to another. During the summer, different flocks would graze together, and in the fall, they would separate according to their owners. Often, a family would have up to 250 in their flock. Herbert Gouge is pictured guiding these animals across the road. (Phil Castro.)

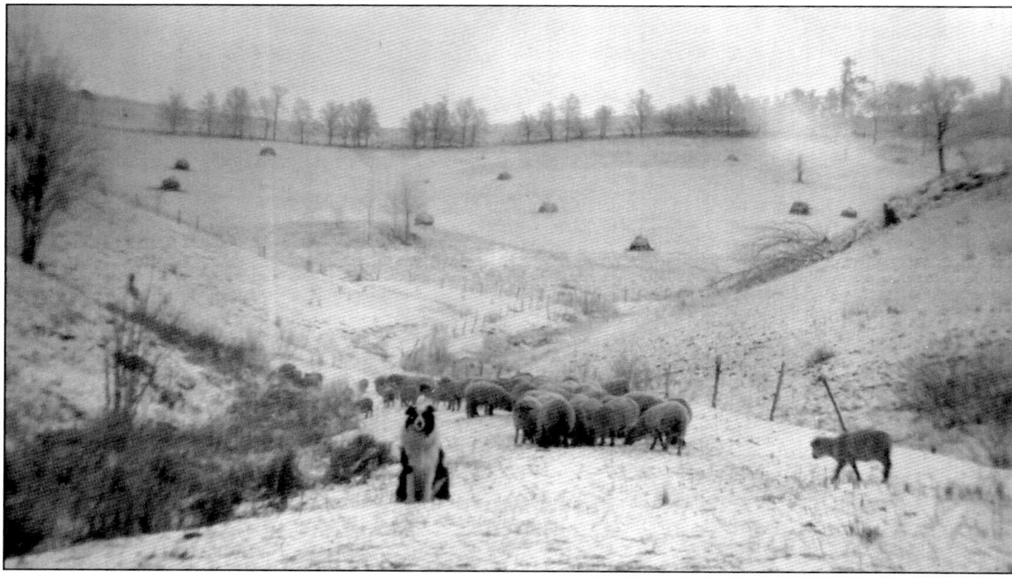

This border collie takes his job seriously as he watches sheep on the mountain during the winter in this 1952 photograph. Note the haystacks in the background for feeding the stock as the weather cooled. The mountain was cleared of undergrowth and trees. Life in the mountains meant hard labor, inclement weather, and possible floods and other disasters that could limit families' incomes every year. (Anne Castro.)

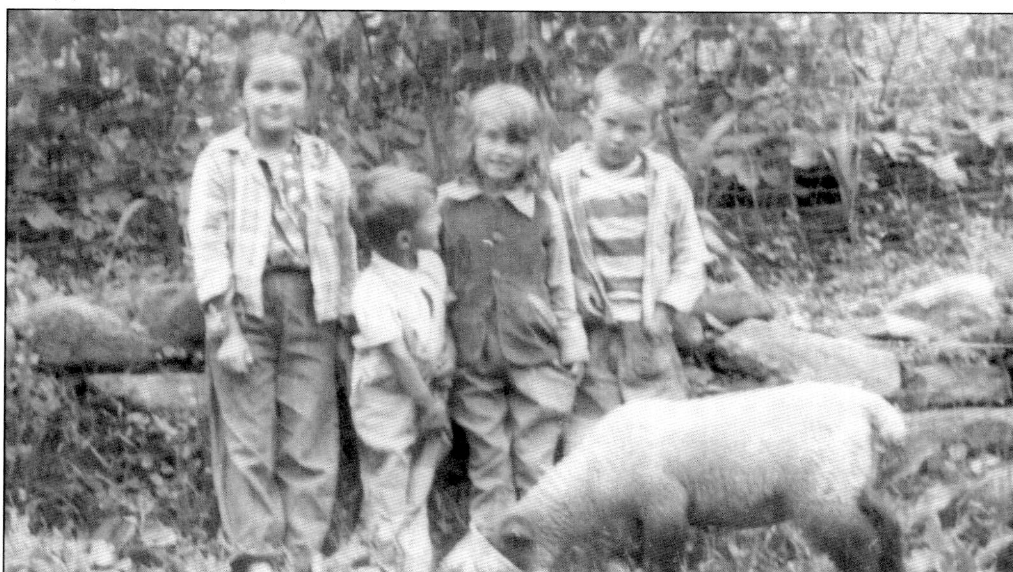

As this 1949 photograph demonstrates, children often had their own jobs to help make the farm run, such as feeding smaller animals. With parents doing the heavy work, it was common for the older children to take care of their younger siblings, as well as carry their own share of the load. (Phil Castro.)

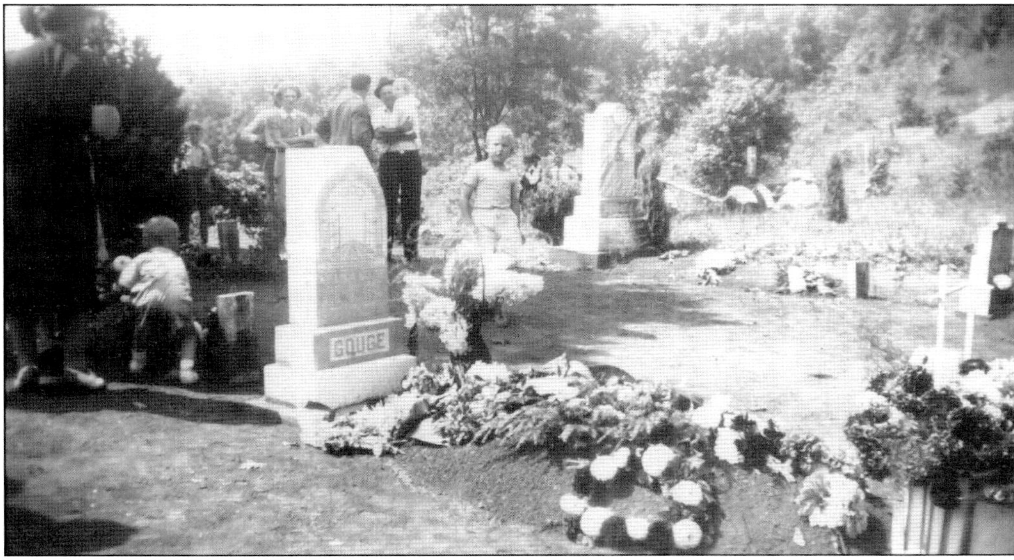

Decoration Day was an annual event. The custom of cleaning the cemeteries and decorating the graves with fresh flowers continues. Many local cemeteries are still family plots, and it was important that children learn of their ancestors, thus in most Decoration Day pictures, children are often present. The graves in front look fresh, yet others in the picture are also decorated. This photograph dates to 1939. (Maxie Gouge Buchanan.)

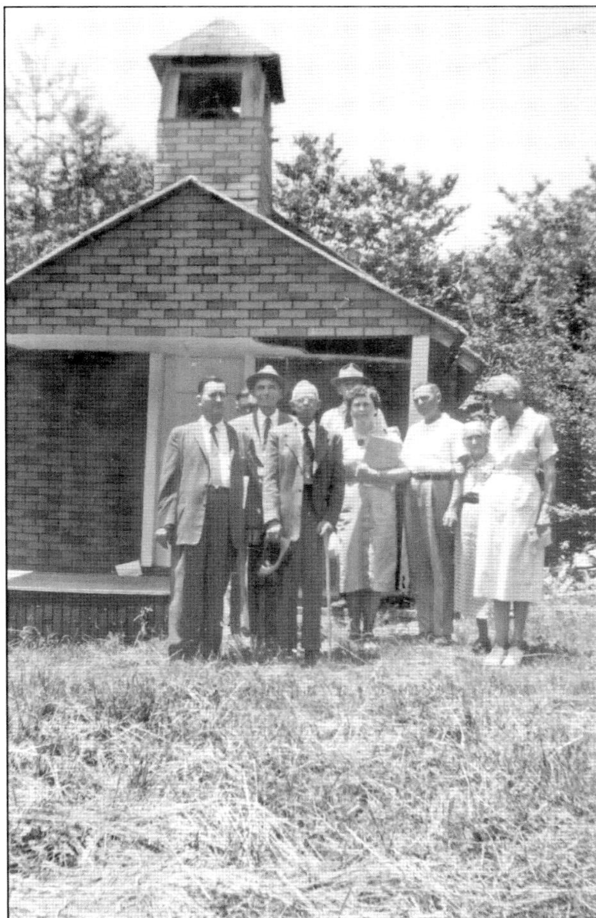

Probably taken on a Sunday sometime around 1950, these people gathered around the Roan Valley Baptist Church have obviously just come out of the church service. They are dressed in their best, with ties and good dresses. Even though the size of the building is small, and it is unimposing, there is still a steeple—a "tower to heaven," which is a traditional part of Christian church design. (Wayne Ayer.)

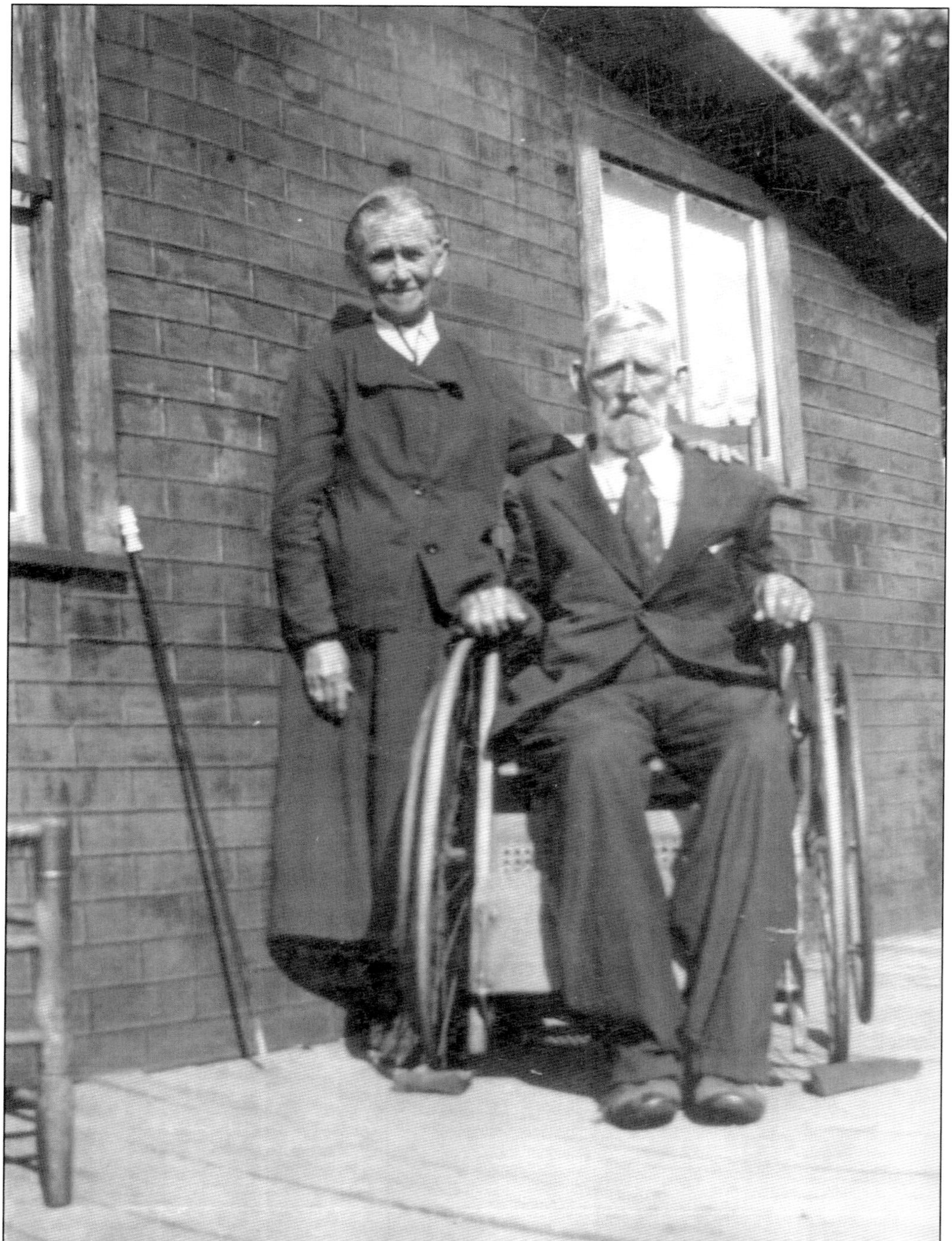

Jacob Ayers was 21 years old when the Civil War started. He fought for the Confederacy, and at Chickamauga, he was wounded in the hip. Barely able to get back home, he carried the "pumpkin ball" (the bullet) in his side for the rest of his life and was wheelchair-bound for most of his days. Born in 1840, he died in his 90s. (Wayne Ayres.)

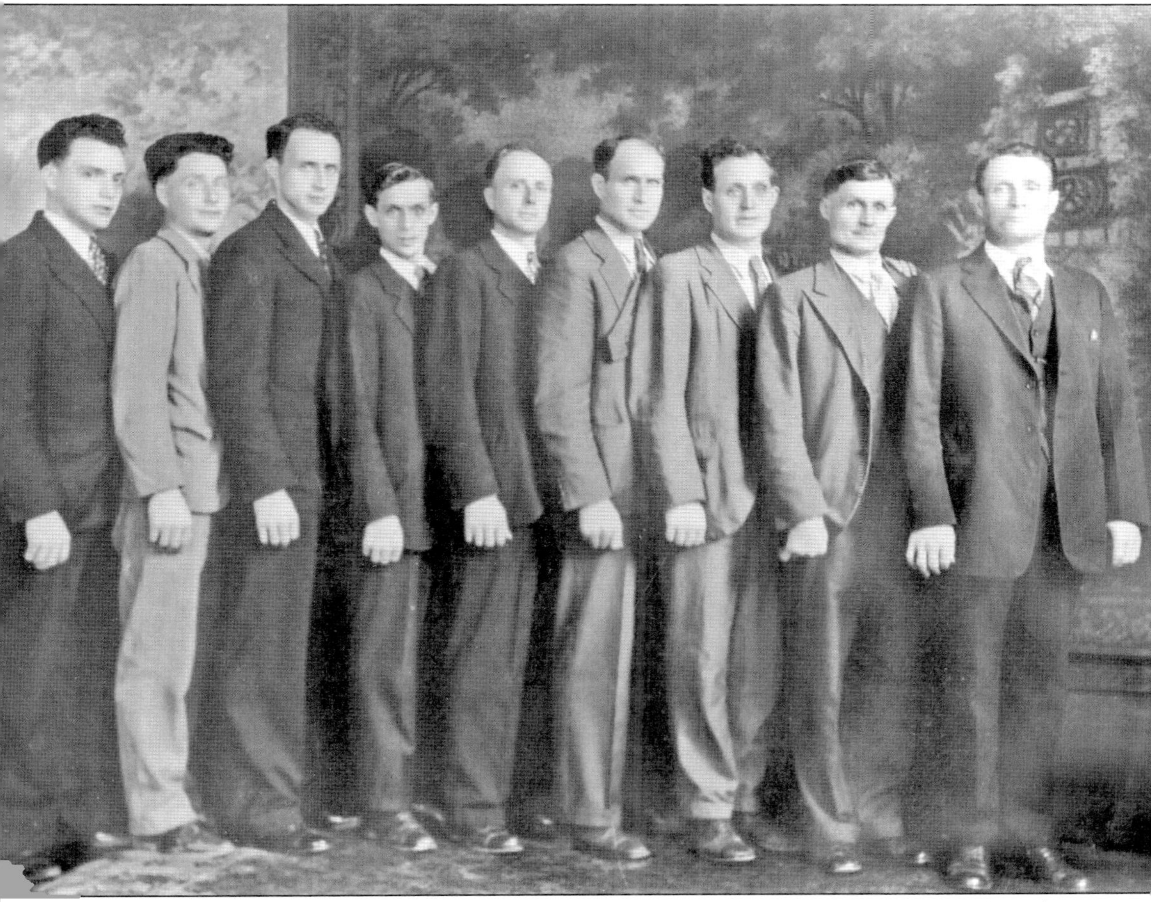

The Gouge family included nine sons and one daughter. Pictured here in 1930 are sons Joseph Orlando, Kary, Essie, Jim, Bill, Wiley, Avery, Herby, and Rathy. The only girl, Tempie, is not pictured. Large families were the norm and were often the result of a widower's remarriage. (Gary Gouge, Phil Castro.)

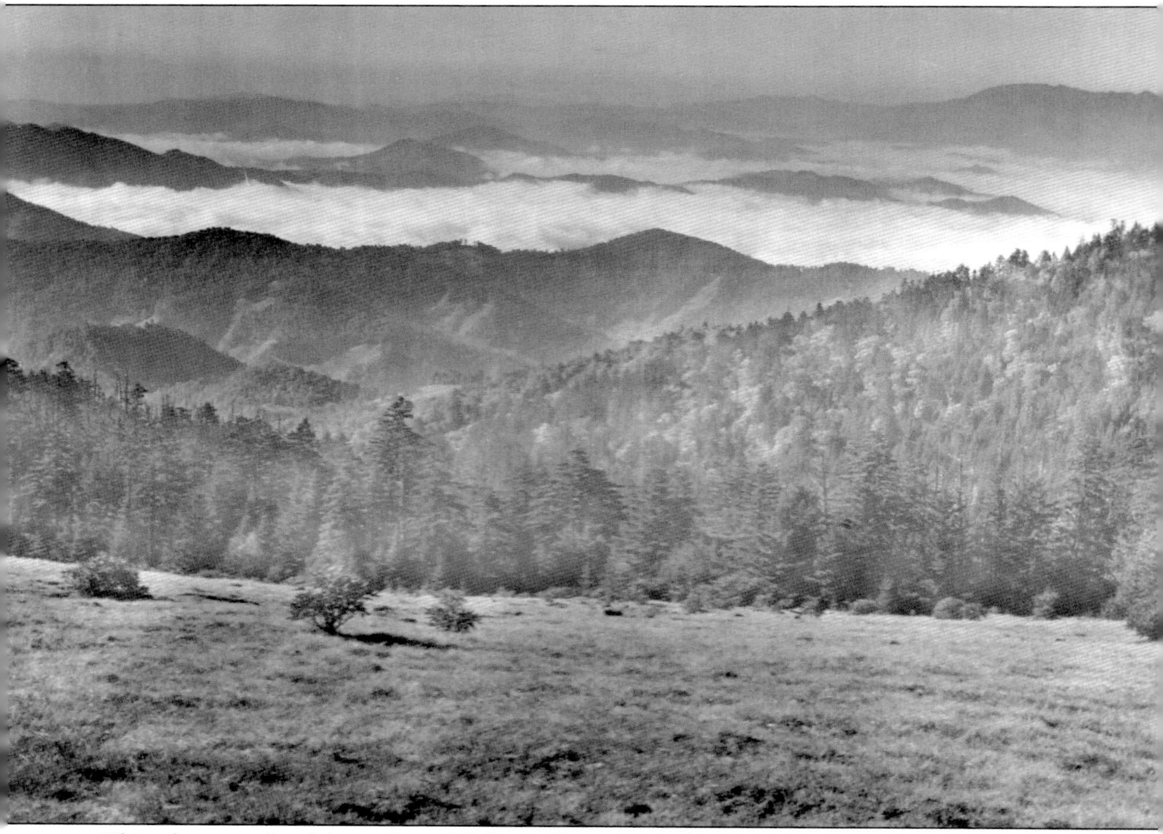

This photograph of the valley of Bakersville is reputed to have been taken at sunrise from the front porch of the Cloudland Hotel in the early 1900s. It is easy to see why the name "Cloudland" was given to the hotel. The beauty of the mountains on display in this image can still be seen in the 21st century. (Appalachia Archives, ETSU, James Goforth Collection.)

BIBLIOGRAPHY

Ayer, N.W. and Sons. *American Newspaper Annual and Directory, 1918*. Philadelphia, PA: Ayers and Son Publishers.

Bailey, Lloyd. *The Heritage of the Toe River Valley*, Vol I (1994); Vol II (1997); Vol. III (2001); Vol. IV (2004); Vol. V (2006); Vol. VII (2008); Vol. VIII (2009); Vol. IX (2010). Missouri: Walsworth Press.

Baker, Elmo W. *The Rugged Trail*, 1973. Texas (self-published).

Cook, Thomas Allen and Jane Ledford. *In The Shadow of the Roan*. North Carolina: self-published.

Dellinger, Jack David. *Dellinger Grist Mill On Cane Creek*. 2004. North Carolina: Folk Heritage Books.

Goforth, James A. *Building the Clinchfield*. 1989. Ervin, TN: GEM Publisher.

Griffith, Frank W. *The Life and Times of Frank W. Griffith*. North Carolina (self-published).

Hardy, Michael C. *Images of Mitchell County*. 2009. Charleston, SC: Arcadia Publishing.

Parris, John. *Mountain Bred Tales*. 1967. Asheville, NC: *Citizen Times* Publishing Company.

Presnell, Lowell. *Mines, Miners, and Minerals*. 1999. Alexander, NC: Parkway Publishers, Inc.

Proceedings of the American Academy of Arts and Sciences, Vol. 51, 1916. Boston: American Academy of Arts and Sciences.

Whitson, K.B. and S.R. *Red Hill: The Untold Story of the Whitson Brothers and the Murder of Kit Byrd*. 2007. Clinton, TN: self-published.

various uncited newspapers from the Murrell Collection, East Tennessee State University Archives, Johnson City, TN.